Absolutely Everything** You Need to Know about Teaching and Performing Improv

** Fast Acting! Super Absorbent! Low in Fat!
(and it works, too!)

Absolutely Everything** You Need to Know about Teaching and Performing Improv

** Fast Acting! Super Absorbent! Low in Fat!
(and it works, too!)

TRACE CRAWFORD

Electric Whirligig Press
2015

First Printing: 2015

Electric Whirligig Press
Columbus, OH

www.tracecrawford.com

to

my wife, Veronica

for her help and encouragement

TABLE OF CONTENTS

INTRODUCTION, OR SO WHY WRITE THIS BOOK?

There has never been a better time to be doing improv. No longer is improv merely the guiding beacon at the forefront of innovative comedy, but it has also become a primary staple of both film and television. Even scripted shows are often developed as if to appear that they are being improvised. Whether you are an educator, a theatre professional, or just an avid fan, there are so many reasons to get busy cranking out a healthy dose of improv.

For teachers, there are almost limitless benefits from including improv in your theatre curriculum. From the practical financial realities plaguing virtually all of education, to the concern that students are graduating without enough creative problem solving ability, to the basic artistic truth that great improvisers by and large make great actors, improv is simply, in my opinion, a must have.

Did you know that according to a poll mentioned in Backstage Magazine, one of the primary skills that casting directors look for on a performer's resume is experience in improv? Why? It's not simply because they will be quick-witted enough to deal with a disaster should it occur during a performance. Performers of improv understand how to GIVE to their fellow performers in a way that other actors simply don't. As we will discuss later, one of the basic rules of improv is to understand when to give focus to other players. In what is arguably the most narcissistic profession possible, this is a very valuable skill.

TEACHING AND PERFORMING IMPROV

Improv can trace its roots all the way back to the ancients, yet it remains completely relevant today. It offers the potential to tap into a performer's creativity, build teamworking ability, gain confidence, and all for a virtually nonexistent price tag. While I would never suggest that improv alone can provide a full and complete arts education (or even a complete theatre education, for that matter), it offers an exciting way-in for reluctant performers, it allows even the most cash-strapped of school districts a means to provide some level of performance opportunity, and it can improve the quality of even the most established theatre program around. Educational justification aside, it's also a heck of a lot of fun – for the performers, the instructor, and the audience.

This book is not a regimented program. It is designed, rather, to be used as a guide to help you discover what components will enable you to reach your group's personal improv goals. To that end I have gathered together in one spot the most successful materials that I have used in my career teaching improv. Here you will not find just a mere listing of games, but also the reasons why to choose or to avoid them. You will find the principles that performers must follow and pitfalls that they must learn to avoid in order to be successful. You will find sample workshops applicable for almost any purpose, a complete guide to producing your own improv performances, and more lists of beta-tested materials than you'll know what to do with – as well as a detailed improv glossary and indexes not just organized by page number, but by skill set. Cherry pick the best of what works for you.

In an age where educational arts programs are becoming more and more endangered yet future employers virtually unanimously state that creativity through arts education is the number one aspect lacking in schools, improv can be a powerful tool to ensure the survival of a program. Let's face it – comedy is an even more powerful drug than theatre. Once a performer gets that first laugh from an audience, they're hooked for life. But enough proselytizing.

So, why write this book, anyway? As a theatre student, some of my best experiences centered around improv. When I became a theatre teacher, I knew that I wanted to pass on those same experiences to my own students. As the years went on, I discovered that not only had improv provided some of the most fun experiences that I had with my performers, but also many of the moments of my students' greatest personal growth were rooted there as well. I do not by any means make myself out to be the next Del Close, or even Drew Carey for that matter, but I hope that this book contains information that makes your job working with improv performers a little easier and hopefully a bit more secure.

Trace Crawford

NOTE: With very few exceptions, the improv challenges, warm-ups, and games contained within this book are not my original creation, nor do I make any claims that they are. These activities are staples of the greater improv community that I have found to be remarkably successful in dealing with fledgling performers.

Whether being used in state-wide competitions or classroom lessons or intimate workshops, the material that I've selected has been remarkably effective in developing students that understand the nature of improv and have become stronger performers in all areas because of it.

However every situation is different and every student is different.

Please take these ideas and adapt them, amend them, retrofit and mutilate them – do whatever you have to do to make them work for you in your own unique situation.

And, for Pete's sake, have fun!

Improv Fortune Cookie

The actor who can think on their feet
need not worry that they'll fall on their butt

CHAPTER ONE:
ALRIGHT, HERE COME THE RULES

What?! Improv has rules? Of course it does! How else could a performance without a script ever be successful? People who have never done improv before often have a tendency to think that improv is simply a group of a few high energy actors jumping around and telling fart jokes. As any experienced performer will tell you, however – IMPROV ISN'T ABOUT BEING FUNNY, IT'S ABOUT TELLING A STORY.

Some of the funniest movies ever filmed have relied heavily upon improv. In fact, many directors choose to shoot a project entirely from an outline rather than a completed script. In this method, actors with a strong improv background are given lots of freedom to explore a scene and come up with their own bits while they work their way through the story. By experiencing the material in this fashion, the comic sensibilities of several artists (rather than just two – the writer and director) are free to come out and play, often producing a level of hilarity one could never achieve without the give and take of improv.

However, that does NOT mean that the funniest material is guaranteed a spot in the movie. When it comes to editing, the bottom line of a successful project is always whether or not the material advances the story. If one takes too many detours on route from point A to point B the audience ends up lost, and so those (often side-splitting) detours end up on the cutting room floor, waiting for their turn to become DVD extras.

Now go watch *Spinal Tap, Waiting for Guffman, Best in Show,* and *A Mighty Wind.* I'll wait. See how it's done? Good.

This same principle holds true for a live improv performance as well, but players don't get the luxury of having an editor to fix their mistakes. An audience absolutely cannot follow a bunch of hyper improvisers bouncing around like excited atoms, screaming and hitting each other. Unfortunately, this is what the typical inexperienced (in my background, this means teenage) improv performer will launch into almost universally. However, with a little nudging and some practice with the following principles, that same spastic energy and willingness to take risks can transform into their greatest asset.

So, I guess the point is that it's all about STORY. An audience needs a story for the jokes to be funny. Think of the scene's story as performing the same function that rhythm does for a piece of music. Without the structure that the rhythm provides a song, all you are left with is noise. Without the structure that the story provides a scene, all you are left with is a bunch of spasmodic ninnyhammers blazing a trail to nowhere.

So without further delay, I give you...

THE FIVE RULES OF IMPROV

Rule One:
*Always **Agree** and **Embellish** - "Yes, and..."*

Ok, so you've just been given your variables: The mall, a ball of yarn, and a plumber. The emcee has gotten the audience focused and begins your scene. You begin by asking your teammate if they want to go to the big knitting competition at the mall. Your friend's response? "No thanks, I'd rather fish."

Every improv performer has had something like this happen to them at some point, and let me tell you it is a real scene killer.

So what went wrong? The first performer gave a possible direction for the scene to head toward – in improv terminology, they "made an offer." The second performer, in turn, "blocked" their offer. If there is any more grievous a sin in the church of improv, I don't know what it would be.

If you take anything away from this book, I hope it is that in improv, the performer must always *agree and embellish* – AGREE with their acting partners and EMBELLISH upon the offers provided (in formal improv training this is sometimes referred to as to "accept and advance" or to "explore and heighten"). While this can be done in many ways, the gist is always to agree with the <u>context</u> and then take it <u>a step further</u>. That could mean any response from "Yes, I love the mall, especially the new smoothie store" to "I hear that last year the Knitting Grannies started a riot" all the way to "No way man, I'm terrified of malls. One time at Christmas, an old guy made me sit on his lap." In all three – even the last one that began with a "no" – the second performer agreed with the context provided and then added something new.

One of the best exercises that you can use with your students to emphasize this point is the tried and true "Yes, and..." As we'll cover throughout the book, the "Yes, and" principle is the backbone of all improv theory, so the exercise is a good first step in a solid improv education. I go over it in detail in the Tune-up portion of the book, but the basic idea is that each performer must literally agree with an offer and then continue the idea further, by saying "Yes, and ..."

For example, a "Yes and ..." scene based on the initial offer above, could go like this:

Player 1: Let's go to the big knitting competition at the mall.

Player 2: **Yes**, let's! **And** the signup table is over there. You should enter!

Player 1: **Yes**, I will! **And** the judges will love this set of waffle iron cozies I got to bribe them.

Player 2: **Yes. And** when you win first prize, I'll take you to get some smoothies.

Player 1: **Yes, and** make sure you stay away from the old bearded guy surrounded by all the short people dressed in green. He smells like cheese and failure.

Player 2: **Yes**, let's go!

Rule Two:
Stay in the Present

There is nothing more boring (outside of watching competitive ice fishing) than watching a performer simply talk about what it is that they are eventually going to do. I hate to quote any corporate entity, but, for the love of God, "Just do it!"

Inexperienced improv performers have a tendency to hold (at times lengthy) discussions about what they will do later in a scene, or worse still, discuss with all the other performers what they should do in the their present situation, instead of just doing it in the first place. My assumption is that this comes from the natural insecurity that accompanies any unscripted performance. "Without a plan, how will we all know what to do, right?"

Put yourself in the audience's position for a moment. If you have just watched a scene in which the performers verbally gave the details of what will happen next, where is the surprise that should delight you when it actually does happen? Instead of the joy that comes with witnessing an exceptional improv, you have watched a scene that is dull and tired, because the performers "expositioned" themselves to death.

As a general rule, it is imperative that improv performers remain in the present in their scene. So, instead of discussing the course of action that must be taken on sometime in the future, just go ahead and do it. As long as their fellow performers are all **AGREEING and EMBELLISHING (Rule #1)**, no one will have any difficulty going along with the scene's dramatic action.

While there are many good activities to help train actors to remain in the present, the best tool for many students is simply continued experience with a consistent group of improvisers. Once there are bonds of trust established between performers, the "lack of a plan" insecurity slowly begins to fade. This is also an aspect of their training that as an instructor, one has the power to facilitate.

One really good challenge to try with performers that are stubbornly having trouble fending off "discussionaire's disease" is Scene Beyond Words. Give the group a specific task that they must accomplish as a variable, and then have them go at it. Since the basic requirements of the challenge state that they can't speak, the performers are consistently forced to remain in the present moment. You are also afforded an opportunity to see who emerges as a leader and see how well the others follow.

Speaking of leaders and followers, this bring me to...

Rule Three:
Give or *Take* **Focus** *as needed*

Designating focus is easily the most challenging aspect of improv for virtually every performer - even seasoned veterans. It is a fairly easy task for a talented actor to merely come up with a premise for a scene or to do some piece of comic shtick for a quick laugh. It is a much harder skill, however, to know how to be a good listener to your teammates and when to follow their lead.

On a typical high school improv team (if there is such a thing), a natural dynamic often develops for many groups of kids. If you've ever facilitated improv before, you probably know exactly what I'm about to mention. One of the kids seems to have an attitude of "I'm going to always be the leader because I'm just so freaking funny, and the rest of you are going to follow along wherever I go whether you like it or not" - so to speak. And usually, the rest of them will do just that with no protest at all, partly because they genuinely find the individual funny as well, and partly because they frankly don't know any different. This isn't surprising. Most schools have their students that are considered the "funny ones" - those blessed with some sort of a natural charisma - and they frankly tend to get idolized to a certain degree in a "big fish-small pond" sort of way.

A successful improv team, however, does not adhere to this leader-follower model. On a good <u>team</u>, one member might lead this moment, another might lead the next – it all simply depends on who came up with the idea on that particular occasion. And despite the fact that I might have thought of something absolutely brilliant, if it doesn't fit in well with the scene that was already established, I'm gonna keep it to my darn self. Now there's the hard part – in good improv there is no single driver.

Let me backpedal a bit and qualify my use of the word "lead" here. Why I say "lead," what I am really referring to is simply the act of making an offer, nothing more. I doubt that anyone would ever advocate for a model in which a single team member would make every decision for how a scene progresses – in fact "driving" a scene is actually one of what I consider to be the seven deadly sins of improv. If a scene is little more than a verbal "follow the leader," the audience (and eventually the performers, as well) will get extremely bored. A huge part of both the fun and value of improv is in the fact that every member of a team has the power to shape every single moment a scene. An improv team that works well together will produce scene work that is significantly more engaging than that of any single performer.

Much like **Staying in the Present (Rule #2)**, probably the best thing to help develop the skill of knowing when to give focus is simply practice. An improv team is essentially the acting equivalent of a jazz combo, and the more a team works together, the more they get in tune to the natural rhythms that ebb and flow between its members. A sixth sense of sorts begins to develop amongst teammates that allows them the freedom to trust in one another, relinquish their need for control and put the collective fate of their performance into the other players' hands. They instinctively begin to "feel" where their other players are headed creatively.

Exercises that are useful in helping to develop this skill would be those that are designed to have players tell a story – those exercises in which everything must be based on the statement that immediately preceded it. This forces the performer to remain completely in the moment and to really listen to their teammates. If they can strengthen their ability to listen completely to one another in performance, knowing when to give or take focus becomes a much simpler task.

Really, this can't be that hard, can it? All of us already do this every single day within every good conversation that we have, right? But are all of our conversations good ones? Pause for a moment and think about some of your less-than-stellar dialogues. I'm sure all of us can recall a conversation or two in which the other person was obviously just waiting for their turn to speak again and had effectively stopped listening. How frustrating was that? Now imagine that as an outside observer, you had to watch that same conversation take place as a means of entertainment. A conversation with only one active participant isn't very fun to watch.

Try a few rounds of Story Ball, but don't allow players to make it funny. Give them a variable of some sort as a platform for their story, start it off for them, and then pass the ball to someone else in the group. One of the nice things about Story Ball is that since the ball can be passed to any player at any time, everyone really has to stay on their toes. You can control when the ball is passed by ringing a bell or you can let the players choose when to pass it off. Note however, that a problem does tend to arise with inexperienced improvisers when you allow them complete control of the exercise. Just like on any green sports team, you will have players that are complete ball hogs. In improv, these individuals will ramble on and on and on until the only person that they are amusing is themselves. Conversely, you will also have those that don't want the ball at all and will only say three words before they pass it as far away for themselves as physically possible. Equal contributions from everyone are essential to the success of the game.

Rule Four:
Be Physical

Virtually all inexperienced improvisers will fall into two categories when it comes to physicalization – those that just stand there talking without moving and those that are, frankly, a complete and total spazz. Both groups of performers are likely compensating for their nervousness to a certain degree, but our task is to try to get them to the happy medium, one in which a scene has plenty of dialogue, but is also very physical.

Some of the least engaging improvs that I see are those that consist of nothing more than a group of "talking heads." For beginning performers, this almost universally occurs when the team is given a challenge that forces them to really concentrate in order to successfully follow the rules. An example of this type of challenge is Alphabet Scene. This game forces participants to use their brain actively – in some cases <u>much</u> more actively than they are used to – just by having to remember the alphabet, and in the process it can make them forget that they have bodies that they can use as well.

So, why is this a problem? Because this isn't <u>radio</u>, people - it's <u>theatre</u>! An audience <u>needs</u> to see the action played out in front of them. IT'S IMPORTANT! The root of the word "theatre" means "a place for <u>seeing</u>" and you know as well as I do that much of an audience's response to any given performance – be it improv, music, dance, or even your run-of-the-mill box-set straight play – will be based on visuals.

One of the most fundamental skills that an improv performer needs is an ability to pantomime – to be able to create what are referred to as space objects, literally any item that is not actually there. Improvisers are being asked to create a scene with absolutely nothing physical except for themselves and a few chairs (and really the only reason that we get the chairs is because as a species, humans cannot as yet levitate) so it is primarily through this mime that players are able to communicate setting. Unfortunately, mime is an area in which most teenage performers are extremely uncomfortable. As soon as the word is mentioned, many of them have visions of walking against the wind, being trapped inside a box, and being ridiculed by tourists. Is it any wonder that they might be a little reticent at first to try it?

If improv is all about telling a story, and there is no scenery around to give that story context, it then becomes a primary responsibility of the performer to provide that context for the audience. Remember that an audience can't follow a scene that they don't understand! Therefore, defining invisible objects, landmarks, locations, and such is of the utmost importance. Fortunately for us, there are many good exercises around that can help a new performer cozy up to their inner mime.

If you can handle the inevitable snickers that are destined to emanate from actors the first time you say its name, then Magic Stick is a great activity to try. This game involves taking an invisible "stick" (a space-object of your creation) and turning it into a variety of different items. (The "stick," by the way, is considered "magic" because it can change into absolutely anything.) Begin by demonstrating the act of transforming it into something elaborate with an extremely detailed mime - remember that DEFINING the DETAILS of the object is the most important skill of mime for them to learn at this point – then transform it back to a stick to pass off to the next person in the group. You can vary the activity a bit by making the stick a Magic Ball (also snicker-worthy) that can be passed to absolutely anyone, instead of following a particular order. A neat twist is to pass (and catch) the ball as if it is the last object that it was transformed into – always fun when it's a piano or tiger, or something.

Scene Beyond Words (mentioned earlier with **Rule #2**) is obviously ALL about mime. The performers must tell a complete story, use audience supplied variables, and successfully work together, all without being able to speak. After a few successful rounds, being allowed to actually talk during a scene can feel positively luxurious.

Even if a scene does not require a great deal of mime, being physical is extremely important. What would a round of Freeze Tag be like in which the players just stood there? There would be nothing for anyone to react to. What about an endowment scene like Party Quirks in which the actors simply said, "Glad to meet you. I'm Elvis," instead of doing some of his signature moves? Where's the fun in that?

A good improviser strives to be like a talented writer. Just as all good writers <u>show</u> their subject to their reader instead of simply <u>talking</u> about it, a successful improviser shows the audience the action, instead of discussing it. To quote the maxim, "Show – don't tell".

Rule Five:
<u>*Always*</u> *Agree* and *Embellish!!!!!*

The rule so nice, I included it twice. Agreeing and embellishing is the foundation of absolutely all improv. There is no such thing as successful improv that does not follow this rule. More than anything else in this book, it is absolutely ***<u>imperative</u>*** that performers understand this concept.

That's it for the rules.

No seriously, that's it.

Next, let's talk about a few of the things not to do.

THE FIVE RULES OF IMPROV

1

Always **Agree** and **Embellish**
"Yes, and..."

2

Stay in the **Present**

3

Give or Take **Focus** as needed

4

Be **Physical**

5

<u>Always</u> **Agree** and **Embellish**!!!!

CHAPTER ONE, PART TWO:
THE SEVEN DEADLY SINS OF IMPROV

Since most of this book is devoted to covering the skills that a performer needs to perfect to achieve success with improv, it seems appropriate to also include a section detailing the most common scene-killing mistakes that improvisers should work to avoid. Purely for the sake of sensationalism, I have dubbed these mistakes *The Seven Deadly Sins of Improv.*

So what exactly are the behaviors that players should never ever engage in?

All of the *Sins* do something that interferes with the primary directive of improv – telling an excellent story. Some of the *Sins* negate offers, some monopolize offers, some involve players not responding naturally to offers, but every single one of them is a simple mistake that will compromise a player's ability to effectively tell a story. Oh, and since improv is an activity that is all about teamwork, pulling any of these *Sins* on a fellow player is just plain rude.

I recommend posting the complete list of *Sins* found at the end of the chapter in a conspicuous location (along with the Five Rules of Improv list) as a reminder to your troupes of both what TO do and what NOT to do.

So, without further ado… let the Sin begin!

Sin Number One:
Blocking or *Canceling*

Both blocking and cancelling are actions that negate an offer. Since to tell a story, players should always do everything in their power to accept offers and advance the scene, negating an offer goes against all of the fundamental principles of improv.

Blocking is literally saying "no" to something.

> Player 1: We should all go to the woods and camp!

> Player 2: No, I hate camping.

Player 2 *blocked* the offer that was made by Player 1. Now thanks to that Player 2 jerk, the scene has nowhere to develop. Remember that all of improv is based on the simple concept of "Yes, and..." In order for the story to advance, offers – and that means ALL offers – need to be accepted. Players can then embellish the offer to take the scene in any direction that they wish, and they can do so without the danger of smashing headfirst into a metaphorical storytelling brick wall. Blocking is one of the most frequent mistakes made by improv novices.

Cancelling differs from blocking in that blocking stops an action immediately, whereas *cancelling* stops it down the road by rendering a previously established offer as irrelevant.

For example, Team A has been developing a scene in which they just discovered that the magical key to the secret chest that has been the focus of the entire story is located deep within the Amazon Rainforest. Just as they are about to leave and go on their adventure (where the plot for the rest of the scene will be headed) a team member finds the key in their pocket. While, yes, the offending team member probably will be able to milk that moment for a quick laugh, the scene now has no place to develop. Instead of a strong adventure story in the jungle, primed with interesting possibilities, we're left with a forgetful numbnuts and a scene with a premature conclusion – and we all know how unsatisfying <u>that</u> is.

Possibly the biggest struggle for new improv performers is discovering where the good scene lies – what is typically referred to as finding a sense of "The Game." Well, here's a great place to begin that discovery. Good drama, no matter the art form, always stems from a good conflict, not the resolution.

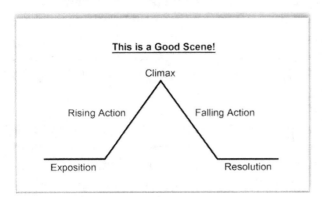

Remember that "plot peak" thing you probably learned about in middle school English?

Like all good stories, a good improv must also follow the basic structure of setup, conflict, build to a climax, and wrap it up.

A scene that jumps right from exposition to resolution without going through all of the conflict in the middle is just a flat line – D.O.A.

That's a pretty darn uninteresting experience for an audience.

The conflict IS the scene!

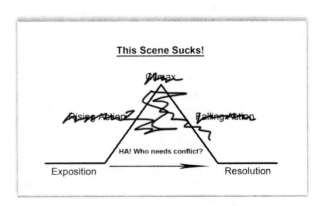

Sin Number Two:
Driving

Not so much a problem for first time performers, but a frequent abscess on an otherwise exceptional intermediate team, Driving refers to any time a single player monopolizes the direction of a scene.

A well-oiled improv team wants to remain open to the many possible options that can present themselves from *all* of the performers during the course of a scene. Just as a committee will likely see far more ways to fix a problem than an individual member ever could, an improv <u>team</u> will likely see many more options for telling a story than a single player would.

All too often I see teams that are experienced enough to have just gotten the improv bug fall victim to the trap of letting the "funny" team member – the one with the established reputation of being a comedian – drive the scene while the others just go along for the ride. The team member will often produce something amusing, but just being amusing isn't enough. So much of the enjoyment that the audience derives from watching improv (whether they know it consciously or not) is in the give and take between team members as the scene moves ahead. Watching a scene that is being driven is just like watching a kid taking part in imaginative play. It might be amusing, but really we're just watching one person's fantasy – we're not watching a team. We're not watching a story. We're not watching improv.

This Sin is also (and more violently) known as *bulldozing*. I actually think this word describes the behavior better than "driving," because instead of implying that one member has simply taken control of the reins, calling it out as bulldozing goes right to the heart of why it's a problem – it DESTROYS the creative impulses of the rest of the team members. Successful improv is all about a group of people working <u>together</u> to explore <u>all</u> of the possibilities of a scene – not to be told by one player what they will be.

It is really, REALLY annoying to perform with someone that tries to drive a scene.

So, don't do it!

Sin Number Three :
Gossiping or Becoming *Talking Heads*

In any context in life, being a gossip is an undesirable trait to possess, but in improv it has been upgraded from personality annoyance to full-fledged Deadly Sin.

Gossiping refers to any time that players talk about what they will eventually do instead of actually doing it (remember **Rule #2 - Staying in the Present?**). This is a really common mistake for new performers who may very well be uncomfortable becoming physical during their scenes. As a result of this trepidation, instead of creating a scene in which the team goes on a vacation and has an exciting adventure, they treat the audience to a scene of watching them plan their trip. I can see the brochure now – "Skip the beach this year – Come hang out at AAA!" There is very little as boring for an audience to have to sit through as a performance in which the team plans out what the scene will be like as a substitute for actually performing their scene. I think the problem's pretty obvious here.

So, what are *talking heads*? (Insert David Byrne joke.) Much like gossiping, this is a frequent problem for new performers, often occurring when a player is trying to process several bits of new information at the same time. Taking its name from newscasters of old, performers become talking heads anytime that they are standing around talking instead of actually doing something.

Alphabet Game poses a particular risk for this to happen. Players can become so focused on remembering that K comes after J that even though their conversation is quite active, their bodies don't go along for the ride. So although gossiping is one way for performers to become talking heads, it certainly isn't the only one. Players can technically be following all the requirements of a challenge and still fall into its nasty clutches.

You can help your players avoid becoming a team full of gossiping talking heads, by looking to the even-numbered Rules of Improv – **"Stay in the Present"** and **"Be Physical."** Remember – even though this is improv, it's still ACTING – and therefore all about ACTION.

Sin Number Four:
Ignoring Offers

Pop quiz: How does a performer alienate themselves from the rest of their team, become an instant pariah, and bring shame on their family's very name for even their children's children's children? (And that's an understatement.) By *ignoring* the offers made by their fellow improvisers. This fault is extremely easy for a player to remedy once it has been recognized, but when left untreated can only lead to a <u>lifetime</u> of pain and loneliness.

In a nutshell, the *Sin* of ignoring occurs whenever a player doesn't acknowledge an offer that was made by another player.

> Player 1: Oh my gosh! I just found this message! What could it mean?
>
> Player 2: Alright team, the first thing to do is to search for clues.

~ OR ~

> Player 1: Look out! The twister is about to hit!
>
> Player 2: You know what, I really like ice cream.

~ OR ~

Player 1: I'm so glad you could drop in, Mr. Bond (evil laugh!)

Player 2: "My bologna has a first name…"

~ OR EVEN ~

Player 1: This is a great place to have a picnic.

Player 2: One time when I was bored, I went to the carnival and stabbed a clown.

These are all pretty obvious examples of ignoring a player's offer. In the context of a complete scene ignoring might not happen quite so blatantly, but no matter how it presents itself, it is always detrimental to the spirit of a team.

Blocking or cancelling an offer are bad enough, but at least with those *Sins* the offending player has acknowledged the offer's existence. Apart from stealing their girlfriend, ignoring an offer is about the worst thing that a player can do to a fellow team member. It completely devalues that person's contributions to the scene and effectively sends the message that what they have to say is completely meaningless. They just might as well have been locked out of the building.

The art of successful improv is all about awesome teamwork and, as such, players have to do everything in their power to help each out other during a performance.

It's sports metaphor time! A strong improv scene is actually very similar to a game of volleyball – one player sets the ball into position and the other player scores the point. One moment Player 1 might set it up for Player 2 to score, but a few seconds later, Player 2 will set it right back up for Player 1. It's a delicate give and take that must be nurtured at every turn.

Don't EVER ignore the offers made by a fellow player. Accept the offer and use your creative genius to embellish it in a wonderful new direction. I'm sure your teammate will return the favor.

Sin Number Five:
Gagging/Mugging/Wanking

I know I've only written it about a dozen times so far, but in case you somehow missed it, the most important skill in all of improv is for players to *agree and embellish* in order to tell a coherent story – the "Yes, and..." principle. Well, a big part of being able to tell that story is for all players to consistently act and react <u>naturally</u> to the offers that their teammates are making.

However, be forewarned. Do not succumb to the tempting... enticing... dare I say... *alluring* paths that one can choose to take that, while they might elicit a brief audience response, will ultimately destroy the power of a team's scene. It's just like The Force – it may be really tempting to go over to the dark side to get what you want, but ultimately you will lose what's most important to you – your improvisational soul.

When it comes to reacting naturally, there are several potential traps that can befall young and experienced players alike. In my experience however, the big three temptations to steer clear of are *gagging, mugging,* and *wanking.* (Have I mentioned how much I love the names of improv terms?)

First, let's deal with *gagging.* While the term can refer to any attempt by a player to do something during the course of a scene that doesn't flow naturally from the offers being made, more often than not it involves the inclusion of ready-made stock jokes or, as the name implies, "gags." In the process, any degree of dramatic illusion that players have created for the audience is destroyed only to be replaced with a cheap, unsustainable laugh – one that eventually trickles down to a mild chuckle then ultimately peters out into an awkward silence. For the sake of everyone involved in the process it is very important that players DON'T BREAK OUT OF THE CONTEXT OF THE SCENE TO GAG!

As shameful as I now know the disgraceful act of gagging to be, for the sake of my credibility and to prove that I do know whereof I speak, I will now relate my own very negative personal experience with it. At the ripe old age of twelve, after having done what I felt was surely enough improv to qualify me as an expert in my eighth grade drama class (during which my teacher had never mentioned any of the "rules" of formal improv – likely because she just wanted us to have fun and learn to enjoy performing), a few friends and I decided to enter a local middle school improv tournament. Since I didn't know any better, I decided to bring a few funny props with me for us to incorporate into our scenes.

I will never forget the feeling I got when the audience reacted in horror – or at least what I felt in my warped middle school perception was horror – to the moment when I pulled a bunch of magic flowers out of my sleeve during the scene. It was awful. There were boos. Actual boos! At kids! We ended the scene almost immediately and made a very abrupt exit. Personally, I couldn't get away fast enough. I remember feeling really ashamed, like I'd completely let my team down in the worst possible way. No doubt the filter of traditional middle school angst has aggrandized my experience of that awful moment, but regardless, it left enough of an impression that now several decades later I can use the story as a "learn from my mistakes" cautionary tale. Remember... do as I say <u>now</u>, not as I did <u>then</u>. I wouldn't recommend a repeat of that experience to anyone.

Sidebar: Some readers may notice what seems to be a similarity between the use of stage gags in improv and the stock jokes integral to commedia dell'arte. It's not a bad comparison (and congratulations on staying awake in Theatre History, by the way!) Commedia does have improv at its roots, after all. However, unlike commedia dell'arte, improv as we know it is all about creating the performance from scratch right there in the moment. As such, the use of gags in performance really amounts to a crutch. So, despite this similarity, we're really talking apples and oranges – or at least inedible crabapples – so stay away!

Time to move on to the second trap – *mugging*.

Mugging is simply when a player chooses to make silly faces instead of genuinely reacting to the offers that are being made by their teammates.

It's Rodney Dangerfield pulling on his collar while he twists up his face. It's Phil Silvers delivering his reactions directly into the camera. It's young Jim Carrey… all of the time.

But it's not honest. It's not accepting other player's offers. And it's certainly not good teamwork.

This is not to say that players shouldn't be extremely expressive. Performers should, in fact, be encouraged to have very animated reactions to what happens within the context of the scene – but that isn't mugging. Mugging is a purely gratuitous act. It removes the audience from the world of the performance and, like gagging, goes against the basic fundamental principles of good improv. It places one player into a starring role instead of everyone on the team working together. It goes for a quick laugh instead of trying to create a coherent and interesting story. But mostly, it goes against the founding idea that all actions in a scene must agree and embellish the offers that players are making.

Finally, any time that a player does something purely to get an audience response, they have committed the grievous *Sin* of improvisational *wanking*.

Let's pause for a moment to reflect. Remember that "other" definition of "wanking?" You know the one I mean. The one I'm not actually writing because I want to maintain the book's PG rating? Well, in improv terms, that's exactly what a player is doing here. Instead of creating a satisfying real experience, they are simply getting their jollies via a quick and cheap audience reaction.

First off, wanking is a bad idea because it takes away from the sense of unity that is essential for a team's success. It's showboating, pure and simple. No one wants to be working on a team with someone like that. More importantly, though, as I've mentioned with a ridiculous amount of repetition in this section, all acts of wanking go against the basic idea in improv that players must be advancing the story with their offers. In its best possible context, when a player has been wanking, the scene will become stagnant. In its worst, however, the fabric of the scene becomes completely unraveled.

Because wanking refers to ANY time a player goes for the audience reaction instead of working with their teammates to naturally advance a scene, both gagging and mugging are examples of wanking. (I love that sentence!)

So, the upshot of all of this is that players must always remain focused on the context of their scene. They need to react to each other naturally and let the embellished offers do their joke-telling for them, not the other way around.

In improv, everything – and I do mean EVERYTHING – always comes back to "Yes, and…"

Sin Number Six:
Postponing/Waffling/Wimping

Sin #1 showed how destructive it can be to a scene to negate an offer by either blocking or cancelling it. **Sin # 4** illustrated how demoralizing to a team ignoring an offer can be. However, there is also a third way that players can incorrectly respond to an offer and thus fail to advance a scene appropriately. (Bad things always come in three's don't they?)

Postponing refers to any time that a player stalls (either consciously or unconsciously) the flow of a scene through some form of inaction. In other words, the offer is accepted, but instead of embellishing it to advance the scene, the players talk in circles or keep the story at the same stage of development or simply don't do enough to fulfill its requirements. When players postpone the flow of a scene they bring the action to a *plateau*, or a place of stagnation. Talk about boring an audience.

There are two primary methods that players may inadvertently use to postpone a scene.

<u>Method One</u>: *Waffling*

When someone is waffling during their daily life, they fail to make a clear cut decision about something.

> "Well, blue is nice, but I also like red. But brown matches your eyes. That's it, brown. Brown is the perfect color for this room. Of course, green is pretty, too…"

It's no different in the world of improv. When players begin to waffle, they stop making the definitive choices necessary for a clear story and the scene hits a plateau. This can be a huge issue for all beginning players, but those that are really taking the process of learning improv seriously are the ones that are guilty of waffling more often than not. Young performers that just want to have fun often have no trouble shouting out whatever idea pops into their heads to advance the scene. This is both their best asset and their Achilles heel.

However, newbies that really, really want to succeed at improv and are focused on becoming good team players are often afraid of doubling down on their own ideas out of, for lack of a better word, politeness. In the effort to be respectful of their teammate's ideas they sometimes fail to commit to their own; they fail to make bold choices. Other times, players are simply afraid that the "funny scene" will have only existed down the path of whatever option they don't choose and consequently don't pick anything.

While it is definitely a good thing to be able to see all of the myriad story options available to one as a performer, players have to be willing to eventually choose a single path for their scene. The "funny scene" is <u>always</u> the one that moves briskly, keeping the audience's enraptured attention through the use of an easy-to-follow story.

Method Two: *Wimping*

The easiest of the *Sins* to define – being a wuss.

A performer is guilty of wimping when they acknowledge an offer's existence, but they fail to act on it appropriately – usually through a lack of dramatic commitment to the context of the scene. Players can't set up an expectation in their audience that they then fail to deliver on. That's just getting their hopes up only to leave them feeling disappointed and cheated in the end. It's like being promised a puppy for your birthday and instead opening a box full of new socks. Talk about unsatisfying.

I often see first-year improv students that are guilty of blatant wimping when performing a challenge like The Die Game. A player could get an awesome, action-packed method of death like "death by a swarm of bees" and instead of performing an exciting chase scene or receiving a series of stings at an ever-increasing tempo, followed by a graphic collapse to the floor, they simply give a half-hearted "Ahh" and claim to be finished. Now, that that's a pretty glaring example of wimping!

However, wimping doesn't have to be quite so obvious. Players can be guilty of wimping by simply gossiping about what they should eventually do in the scene because acting it out has the potential to be embarrassing. Players could also be wimping by waffling because if they never commit to a concrete choice, then they won't have to actually do anything.

While players of any experience level could be guilty of wimping, like the rest of the *Sins* it is most commonly a problem among brand new improvisers. Players that are just starting out are likely to have far greater performance insecurities and inhibitions than their more seasoned counterparts. Consequently, it is not surprising that many will let their fears get the better of them and wimp out on a scene. Given time and a lot of practice, however, even the biggest wimp can toughen up.

Sin Number Seven:
A Split Scene

A *split scene* occurs any time that more than one focus is allowed to develop simultaneously during a single scene. Basically, it's two conversations going on at the same time.

Typically this takes the form of two players becoming engrossed in a part of the scene that for some reason excludes the other team members. The other players then end up starting their own bit of dialogue that is usually related to the subject of the overall challenge, but is not related to the scene between the other two players. This dialogue could be taking place in the same location as the other scene or even somewhere brand new. In either case, the end result is two different conversations taking place simultaneously – and a thoroughly annoyed audience.

I don't think that I've ever (and I do actually mean EVER) had a new team that hasn't been guilty of creating a split scene at least once within their first five challenges. It's kinda like a rite of passage in that way. Despite being such a common mistake, during a performance it is absolute DEATH for a scene. An audience can only focus on one thing at a time and as soon as that dreaded second conversation starts, you can literally see folks shifting in their seats out there.

The key to avoiding a split scene lays in **Rule of Improv #3 - "Give and Take Focus as Needed."** Once a team has had enough experience (because this is a skill that really only develops through experience) to gain a feel for the natural flow of scene development, they will automatically make sure that this doesn't happen without even having to think about it. When a team gets a feel for "the game" and can intrinsically sense a scene's focus, they will innately avoid sending the scene in two directions at the same time.

But never fear - there is plenty of hope out there for new players who fall into the trap of a split scene. Although they might not fully understand why it is so undesirable when first explained to them, usually after a group has experienced the phenomenon first hand, they tend to be able to recognize it when it starts to happen again and will quickly switch gears – on their own. Personally, I think this is one of the biggest steps in a team's development, so I guess some good does come out of causing a split scene.

Also, it should be noted that split scenes are most common with teams that have four members. They almost never occur with teams of three (one player would have to be engaged in a split monologue) and in teams of five, the urge to break off into a splinter conversation seems not to crop up very often. However in a group of four, it is really - REALLY - easy to develop.

This is a *Sin* that you want to address as quickly as possible.

So there you have it – seven easily correctable behaviors that interfere with storytelling. That wasn't so bad, was it?

Remember – don't try to address all of these issues at once, but rather deal with them one at a time – most likely as they crop up in performance.

So, let's talk about warm-ups.

THE SEVEN DEADLY SINS OF IMPROV

1

Blocking or **Cancelling** an offer

Driving the direction of a scene

Gossiping or becoming **Talking Heads**

Ignoring the offers from other players

Not Natural**! Gagging/Mugging/Wanking**

Not Acting! **Postponing/Waffling/ Wimping**

Allowing a **Split Scene**

CHAPTER TWO:
WARM-UPS FOR IMPROV

Acting teachers have been espousing the benefits of a good warm-up routine for performers since before Stanislavski put a word of theory down on paper. Consequently, I'm not going to waste a bunch of your time and mine trying to sell you on an idea that you've already bought into. What I <u>will</u> do, however, is attempt to define what constitutes a effective warm-up, provide an explanation of a variety of warm-up exercises that have been very successful in my personal experience, and hopefully provide a little advice that will help you to design your own productive warm-up routines.

If you aren't already, both you and your performers need to become familiar with a wide assortment of quick warm-up activities that target a range of different performance areas. Just as you wouldn't exclusively work a single individual muscle set in the gym over and over, you don't want to work on only one skill set for the stage. In addition to teaching your performers a variety of different activities, I feel that it is also important that they feel welcome, even encouraged, to bring in their own purposeful ideas to add to the collective shelf of possibilities. Indeed, some of the best warm-ups that I use were originally taught to me by my students. Having a large grab-bag of ideas to pull from when planning your routines helps to ensure this required diversity.

So, what *are* the characteristics of a good improv warm-up routine?

TEACHING AND PERFORMING IMPROV

A good improv warm-up (just like a good acting warm-up) <u>must</u> be three things: Vocal, Interpersonal, and Physical – VIP.

- **Vocal** – Warm-ups that target this characteristic can involve anything from tongue twisters to muscle isolations to volume and breath control exercises. Since an actor's two basic tools are body and voice, strong vocal control is essential to a successful performance. Volume, diction, inflection, and safe vocal manipulation are all aspects to target in a vocal warm-up.

- **Interpersonal** – While a tongue twister or breath exercise is invaluable, it is an activity with exclusively individual benefits. Successful improv, however, is all about teamwork, so a warm-up cannot be allowed to exist solely within a personal vacuum. It is absolutely essential that all warm-up routines include group activities that require members to work together. The more interpersonal work that a group does, the easier telling a story as a team will become for them.

- **Physical** – Every performer must <u>always</u> be in complete physical control of themselves. This does not mean that every actor needs to have the physique of a professional athlete, but rather that they must have developed a mastery of the use of their own body as well as a certain degree of physical stamina. There are plenty of overweight performers that can dance rings around their skinny counterparts because they have developed endurance and are comfortable moving within their own skins. Plus, all of the physical fitness in the world doesn't automatically give a person the ability to effectively use their body as a communication tool. Just like any other skill, it must be practiced to be mastered.

Is it OK to Double Dip?

You've probably already noticed that most warm-up activities potentially hit at least two of the three areas at the same time (some will even get all three). But don't shy away from a particular idea simply because it only hits one area. Just like in dance, sometimes working a skill (or muscle group) in isolation can be extremely valuable as well.

Does Size Matter?

A complete warm-up routine should last approximately five minutes or less and should be both high energy and high focus. There might very well be an area or skill set that you particularly want to target or maybe the group is collectively feeling a bit sluggish on a particular day, so make sure that your warm-up is tailored to each specific group and task. No matter what your goal of the warm-up might be, it is very important that your performers get a thorough opportunity to "sweat before they stretch."

It's All About Control

After the natural rhythm of a daily (or however often your group meets) warm-up routine has been established (after four or five sessions, probably), control of it should then be handed over to the performers who will then take turns leading. This is important not only so players take ownership of their individual progress, but it also enhances the interpersonal aspect of the warm-up. The simple act of peers guiding peers also re-emphasizes at a gut level the idea that as improvisers, we are all in a network where we will spend equal time as both leaders and followers. However, it is also extremely important that you are personally an active participant in the warm-up yourself and are available to help guide or support the leader when necessary.

Review: The Key Points of a Solid Warm-up Routine

- Wide variety of activities
- Open door policy on new exercises
- Must be vocal
- Must be interpersonal
- Must be physical
- Approx five minutes – NO LONGER
- Tailored to the specific group or task needs
- Shared responsibility for leading warm-up routines

TEACHING AND PERFORMING IMPROV

The improv warm-up activities that I have included are, of course, a mere starting point for you and your actors. Just about anything – and I literally mean anything – can be potential warm-up fodder. (I'm amazed at how often students bring in great ideas from Girl Scout camp.) As long as you never forget to ensure that a routine is VIP, you will always be helping your students' progress.

Now let's turn up the heat…

MY FAVORITE WARM-UP ACTIVITIES

(In <u>Reverse</u> Alphabetical Order!)

Section One:
Group Action Warm-ups

PLEASE NOTE: Unless otherwise specified, all of the included the activities are intended to be done in a large group circle.

Zip, Zap, Zop (aka Zing!)

How to: One of the granddaddies. Form your group into a large circle. The basic task in Zip, Zap, Zop is to send an impulse from member to member within the group. As the impulse is exchanged, the sending player needs to make laser-sharp eye contact with the receiver while they also clap and point in their direction. Begin by having players simply say "Zing" as the impulse is sent. Make sure that participants are committing vocally with a strong, strident voice and maintaining a steady pace. Once they are capable of maintaining this task quickly and with confidence, switch to the words "Zip," "Zap," and "Zop." The words must be said in that order and the pattern simply repeats itself as it continues around the circle.

NOTE: When I originally learned this warm- up, it was taught as an elimination round. When a mistake was made or the pace was lost, the offending player had to sit down. This can make it an excellent motivator – or detract from its purpose if you have a particularly inexperienced group. More often than not I try to keep the chain going at all costs, but there's nothing wrong with a little friendly elimination – provided there isn't always a consistent loser in the group.

Variations: There are almost limitless variations possible with Zip, Zap, Zop. Here are a few of my favorites.

#1 – Change the category. Instead of simply repeating the name of the game, you could instead ask for players to provide an example of a particular category. Some of my favorite categories include:

- The player's name
- The receiver's name
- The name of the player to the right of the receiver
- Bands
- Foods
- Types of clothing
- Colors

- Countries
- Places to go on a bad date
- Things you can't eat
- Words that sound dirty, but aren't
- Etc. – obviously, the sky's the limit, here

#2 – Have a ball. Once a round of Zip, Zap, Zop gets into a comfortable rhythm, start tossing a medium sized ball around the circle in a different pattern. Having to concentrate on two tasks at the same time will get your actors focused like you wouldn't believe. Seriously, I usually go brain numb.

#3 – Get emotional. Have each individual come up with a particular phrase said in a particular emotional state (i.e. "I love you!" said with anger.) The phrase can be an indicator of a character or mood, or it can be completely random. After a while, reverse it – have the sender state the receiver's original phrase as they said it.

#4 – Hush up! Try a round of Zip, Zap, Zop with no sound - or even better, while standing completely still, too. Play the entire game with nothing more than the eye contact between players. This one can get REALLY intense!

VIP:

Vocal	Interpersonal	Physical
Yes!	Boy, Howdy!	Kinda.

Skills:
- Eye Contact
- Focus
- Inflection
- Listening
- Stage Presence/Confidence
- Team Building
- Timing/Pace
- Vocal Manipulation
- Volume

Yes, Let's

How to: Everyone in the group begins by walking around the room. Eventually one member of the group will shout out "Hey! Let's (perform some action)!" The rest of the group responds by shouting "Yes, Let's!" and then begins to perform the suggested activity. Once the action has gone on for a moment everyone stops and begins to wander around the room again until the next player shouts out.

For example: The group is walking around the room when one player shouts out "Hey! Let's climb a tree!" The group responds, "Yes, Let's!" and all begin to mime climbing a tree. They stop and wander again when a group member shouts "Hey! Let's build a canoe!" The group responds, "Yes, Let's!" and all begin to mime hollowing out a canoe. They stop and begin walking again when a group member shouts, "Hey! Let's all impersonate Elvis!" and so on, and so on, and so on.

You guessed it – this one can be a lot of fun. Plus, since players suggest the activities on impulse, it has the benefit of giving every player the opportunity to lead the action at some point.

Variations: Each suggestion could also require a particular vocalization. Or to focus on space-object work, it could be done entirely in mime!

VIP:

Vocal	Interpersonal	Physical
Yes!	Group Chanting!	And a half!

Skills:
- Flexibility
- Focus
- Mime
- Listening

- Stage Presence/Confidence
- Stamina
- Team Building
- Vocal Manipulation
- Volume

Stretching

How to: To be honest, since I'm paranoid a student will overextend, get hurt and subsequently blame me, I don't usually do much in the line of stretching (or backrubs – which can be a good choice, too). Practicality, professionalism, and conventional wisdom (even my own limited brand) dictates that one should stretch before becoming physical, however, and that's why I've included here.

If improv is going to be physical (and **Rule #4** says that it had <u>better</u> be) then it is important for an actor to be limber in order to be able to free themselves physically without risk of injury.

Anything from arm crosses, to lunges, to butterfly stretches, to neck and shoulder rolls can be a positive addition to a warm-up routine. In general, breathe in and hold the stretch for a 10 count then exhale. NEVER force it. And if you include head rolls, for the love of God, don't ever allow players to roll their head all the way back.

Variations: Not really applicable.

VIP:

Vocal	Interpersonal	Physical
Not really.	That's pushing it.	In spades.

Skills:
- Flexibility
- Stamina

Slap, Slap, Animal

How to: Another game of passing the energy from player to player, this time with a focus on visual listening.

Players sit in a circle. Each player decides on both an animal and a physical gesture to represent that animal (i.e. flapping arms for an eagle, miming a trunk for an elephant, or a quick wiggle back and forth for a penguin). Players should first go around the circle once quickly to demonstrate their gestures for all of the players. Now the game begins.

The energy is passed around the circle by a player first slapping their lap twice, then demonstrating their own animal gesture, then again slapping their lap twice and performing the gesture of another player.

For example, a pattern could be:

    Player 1 (Elephant): Slap slap <u>elephant</u> – slap, slap <u>penguin</u>
    Player 7 (Penguin): Slap slap <u>penguin</u> – slap, slap <u>eagle</u>
    Player 3 (Eagle): Slap slap <u>eagle</u> – slap, slap <u>elephant</u>
    Player 1 (Elephant): Slap slap <u>elephant</u> – slap, slap <u>gerbil</u>

And so forth and so on around the circle…

This is a fun game that is just as good on day one as it is on day one hundred. Because it can get really fast and intense, it is a great way to get a group focused – when done silently.

Variations: It's always fun to add animal noises to the gestures, although please note that this makes the game more about vocal manipulation and performer confidence than about group focus – which, of course, is perfectly fine, depending on which skills you would like to target.

And, of course, you could easily change the category from animals to just about anything else.

VIP:

Vocal	Interpersonal	Physical
Only in a variation.	One of the best!	Yes. A bit.

Skills:
- Eye Contact
- Focus
- Listening
- Mime
- Stage Presence/Confidence
- Team Building
- Timing/Pace
- Vocal Manipulation (Variation)

Slap Circle (aka Slappy Hands)

How to: The players form a circle on their hands and knees on the floor, intertwining their hands with those of the players to their left and right. Beginning with the leader, an impulse is sent around the circle by each member slapping the floor in succession. As the player's arms are linked (and thus their hands are alternating) this can be challenge enough, but let's not stop there. The impulse can also reverse directions around the circle if any player slaps the floor twice. If at any time a player flinches or slaps at an inappropriate time, the offending hand is removed. The game continues either until there are only two hands left, or it gets annoying.

Variations: I don't know of any, but if you get a particularly adept group, it would be fairly easy to add other possible slapping commands.

VIP:

Vocal	Interpersonal	Physical
Sadly, no.	Uncomfortably so.	Some.

Skills:

- Focus
- Listening
- Team Building
- Timing/Pace

Shakes!

How to: Another game of passing the energy around the group in a circle, but with a very physical twist!

One player begins to shake a part of their body vigorously. Slowly they move the shake to a different part of their body (i.e. beginning at their hand and ending at their foot). The shake is then passed across the circle to another player who "catches" the shake by beginning to shake the part of the body it was sent from (in the example, the foot). This player would then move the shake to a different part of their body and the process continues indefinitely.

Remember that the shake can be in any part of the body from a hand to a leg, to a finger, to the left ear, to a piece of hair – literally anywhere.

Variations: Try adding creative gibberish sounds to accompany the shake.

VIP:

Vocal	Interpersonal	Physical
Potentially.	Definitely.	Indubitably!

Skills:

- Eye Contact
- Flexibility
- Stage Presence/Confidence
- Stamina
- Team Building

Shakedown (from 8)

How to: A great way to wake up a Saturday morning rehearsal! Start by raising one hand high above your head and counting off in a full voice as you shake it – "1! 2! 3! 4! 5! 6! 7! 8!" Switch the other hand and repeat. "1! 2! 3! 4! 5! 6! 7! 8!" Next shake one of your feet. "1! 2! 3! 4! 5! 6! 7! 8!" Then the other foot. "1! 2! 3! 4! 5! 6! 7! 8!" Start the cycle again with the first hand, this time only going to seven. Then six. Then five. And so forth all the way down to one. As the count gets shorter and the pace gets faster, the exercise also gets more and more frenetic.

A true trifecta of VIP!

Variations: I've tried altering the numbers and adding other steps, but they only served to mess up the pacing. I recommend keeping it simple.

VIP:

Vocal	Interpersonal	Physical
Absolutely!	You Betcha!	Hot Diggity!

Skills:

- Stage Presence/Confidence
- Stamina
- Team Building
- Volume

Schwing! (plus Bong, Bounce & Opa!)

How to: A fun, fast-paced, team activity. The group should be seated in a circle when they begin. Like so many of the other warm-ups that I recommend, the basic task in Schwing! is to send an impulse around the circle, however there are several different ways that players can manipulate the direction in which the impulse flows. The basic moves/phrases in the game are:

Vocal:	*Physical Action:*
Schwing!	The player pumps his/her arm in front of them in the direction of the impulse.
	The impulse will now be referred to as the "Schwing!"
Bong!	The player raises their hand as if to block the Schwing!, forcing it to switch directions.
Bounce!	Using two hands the player can pass the Schwing! like a basketball to any other player in the circle.
Ker-Plunk!	When the Schwing! is "caught" after a bounce, all members of the circle mimic the act of catching it, and say this in unison.
Opa!	When sending the Schwing! around the circle, a player can raise their arm in a diagonal manner over the head of the next player. The Schwing! then skips over that player and is continued with the next person in order.

Notice the exclamation marks. These are not gratuitous. The key words for this game (once the basics are learned by the group, of course) are FAST and LOUD. Keep it high energy!

Variations: Can also be done standing. All members of the group should put their arms around each other's shoulders for support. The moves are slightly altered here, as everyone's hands are busy buttressing the other players.

Additionally, as your students get more adept at Schwing!, you can add any other moves and phrases you want.

VIP:

Vocal	Interpersonal	Physical
Yes!	And then some!	Especially if standing!

Skills:
- Diction
- Eye Contact
- Focus
- Listening
- Team Building
- Timing/Pace
- Volume

Ride That Pony!

How to: A fun call and response game – I've even seen huge groupings of theatre kids doing this game in marathon sessions for hours and hours straight at state-wide events (I swear I'm not exaggerating). Split the members into two groups, one large and one small. The large group will make an outer circle; the small group will make an inner circle. (With a group of twenty, I would keep sixteen in the outer circle, and only four in the inner one.)

The outer circle begins to clap in rhythm and the inner circle begins to run around the inner edge of the circle in… well… sort of a gallop.

The chant then begins as such:

> Inner Circle: Come on, Baby!
>> Outer Circle: Ride that pony!
> Inner Circle: Come on, Baby!
>> Outer Circle: Ride that pony!
> Inner Circle: Come on, Baby!
>> Outer Circle: Ride that pony!
> ALL: This is how we do it!

At this point, the inner circle stops running and each member now turns to face an opposing member of the outer circle. As the chant continues, the inner and selected outer members dance freestyle in the positions described as they all chant.

Vocal:	*Physical Action:*
Front to front to front, my Baby!	Both flip around
Back to back to back, my Baby!	Both flip back around
Side to side to side, my Baby!	They more or less do-si-do to exchange places
This is how we do it!	The groups have now reset for the next round

The selected outer circle members have now become the new inner circle. The process can continue indefinitely, but, personally, I'd stop before the grinding headache sets in.

An extremely fun game for the players – it's all about team building and confidence, plus it lets them be productive while just acting like kids.

Variations: None that I know of, but it would be pretty easy to personalize the chants.

VIP:

Vocal	Interpersonal	Physical
Yep. Yelling!	Yep. Dancing!	Yep. Galloping!

Skills:
- Eye Contact
- Stage Presence/Confidence
- Stamina
- Team Building
- Volume

Rainstorm

How to: This simple activity is a great way to get a high energy group focused and calm enough to productively work together. I save it for the days when everyone is bouncing off the walls. As a group, players will mimic the sounds of a rainstorm by going through a series of simple actions.

The leader will begin each individual action and one by one, the rest of the group members will duplicate the same action going around the circle. The next action does not begin until the previous one has worked its way around the entire circle, and each player must continue doing their action until it is replaced by the next one.

The actions are:
1. Rub your palms together in a circle
2. Snap in an irregular pattern
3. Gently slap your chest and arms, also in an irregular pattern
4. Speeding up, slap your lap
5. Quickly stomp back and forth – once everybody is on this step, raise and lower the speed and intensity to both mimic the sounds of a storm and to get a little physical.

6. Go back to slapping your lap
7. Go back to slapping your chest and arms in an irregular pattern
8. Go back to irregular snapping
9. Rub your palms in a circle
10. Dramatically stop the action. This should also go one by one around the circle as the storm fades away.

This must ALL BE DONE SILENTLY – absolutely no talking! On those days when the performers are really scattered, this is a wonderful activity to get them focused and working together.

Variations: None.

VIP:

Vocal	Interpersonal	Physical
Nada.	Fantastic!	Only Slightly.

Skills:
- Eye Contact
- Focus
- Stage Presence/Confidence
- Stamina
- Team Building

Pterodactyl

How to: This is easily one of the silliest (and most fun) warm-ups that I use.

Pterodactyl is an elimination challenge. How does one get eliminated you ask? Simple. By accidentally allowing their teeth to be seen.

Every player in the circle covers their teeth with their lips. They then pass an impulse from person to person around the circle by making direct eye contact and saying either the word "Pterodactyl" while making large wings with their arms (which makes the impulse move forward) OR crowing/growling/howling like a Dinosaur while making little T-Rex arms (which makes the impulse reverse directions).

The goal is to go fast and furious while somehow not bursting into laughter or letting your teeth become visible. If even the slightest glimmer of enamel peeks through, that player is out and the game continues without them.

Especially valuable for young performers, this game presents an opportunity to fight distraction and maintain focus in a very fun environment.

Variations: I have never used any, but like "Schwing!" it would be easy to personalize this game with all sorts of dinosaur-themed commands.

VIP:

Vocal	Interpersonal	Physical
Yes!	And Silly!	Not so much.

Skills:
- Diction
- Eye Contact
- Focus
- Inflection
- Stage Presence/Confidence
- Team Building
- Timing/Pace
- Vocal Manipulation
- Volume

Martha

How to: I have absolutely no idea who came up with this warm-up (or why in the heck it's named "Martha"), but it is without question one of the best. Begin in your standard group circle. One player will step into the circle and proclaim that they are an object, then physically become that object (i.e. "I'm a tree!" then assume the standard "tree" pose.) The next player steps in and builds onto the context of the first player's object ("I'm a squirrel!" and attaches themselves to the first player's leg.) The third follows suit ("I'm a lamppost!") and so forth until everyone has joined the scene.

Actual objects should be used, not concepts ("I'm happiness!" doesn't give players anything concrete to work with) and the pace should be fast. Really fast. Lightning fast. Players should even overlap each other a bit if possible. Martha is a great exercise for agreeing and embellishing that really gets performers focused and thinking.

Variations: I have tried a few variations here – "Silent Martha" immediately comes to mind – with much less success than I would have liked. As of yet, I have not found any variations that I would recommend over than the basic activity.

VIP:

Vocal	Interpersonal	Physical
Some.	Could there be more?	Good God, Yes!

Skills:
- Flexibility
- Mime
- Stage Presence/Confidence
- Team Building
- Timing/Pace
- Volume

Machines

How to: Another of the blue chip warm-ups. Every member of the group will work together to create a machine with interrelated parts that are controlled by the group leader.

Begin with all of the players on one side of the room. The first group member goes to the other side and begins repeating a simple action accompanied by a related sound. Once their movement has been established, the next member joins in by also performing a simple action and sound, however they MUST relate to the first member in some way, either directly or indirectly. This pattern continues until everyone in the group is involved. Don't forget that a machine can be built in all directions, not just on the two ends.

Once the machine is complete, the leader becomes the machine operator. They have the ability to speed the machine up, slow it down, reverse it, even make it blow up (a great way to conclude the activity.) Everyone must continue to work together and relate to each other in an appropriate rhythm as they are manipulated.

Variations: I've never tried any, but knock yourself out!

VIP:

Vocal	Interpersonal	Physical
Yes!	Yes!	Yes! Yes! Yes!

Skills:
- Flexibility
- Mime
- Stage Presence/Confidence
- Stamina
- Team Building
- Timing/Pace
- Vocal Manipulation

Kwah!

How to: One of my favorites! Similar to Zip, Zap, Zop in that the players will send an impulse around the circle, however there is only one word to remember and the physical component is much more significant.

The player sending the impulse will raise their hands above their head, forming a triangle. As they bring their triangle down to point towards another group member, they also will yell "Kwah!" using some sort of interesting inflection – vocal variety! The other player receives the Kwah by yelling "Kwah!" as they raise their hands into the triangle shape. Simultaneously, the players to the left and right of the receiver will also yell "Kwah!" while moving their hands into a diagonal slash in front of the receiver.

To clarify, <u>three</u> players simultaneously yell "Kwah!" when the impulse is received. The process continues around the circle indefinitely.

The pace for this game is fast and furious – and personally, I think it's a heck of a lot of fun. When a group has mastered it, this becomes a wonderful way to get them focused quickly.

Variations: None that I have personally used, although it would be rather easy to switch up the gestures or sounds. The most important aspect of this activity is the multi-player interaction in response to the impulse. As long as that remains intact or is embellished upon, then really, the sky's the limit.

VIP:

Vocal	Interpersonal	Physical
And then some!	Very much so!	Almost full-contact!

Skills:

- Eye Contact
- Flexibility
- Focus
- Inflection
- Stage Presence/Confidence
- Team Building
- Timing/Pace
- Vocal Manipulation
- Volume

Jumping Jacks

How to: Do I really have to explain jumping jacks? This is a great one to use on a day when everyone is feeling sluggish to get the blood pumping.

Be sure to do at least ten and count off as you go in a full, strident voice.

Variations: Start at a whisper and make each number a little louder than the last.

VIP:

Vocal	Interpersonal	Physical
Yes!	Suffering brings us closer!	What it's all about!

Skills:

- Stamina
- Team Building
- Volume

Human Knot

How to: More of a "getting-to-know-each-other-through-really-uncomfortable-physical-contact" activity than a true warm-up, but it's a great choice to use as an icebreaker with a new group. Due to the amount of time that it eats up, it is not a choice that I would make often.

Have every player reach across the circle and join one hand with another player. Then do the same for the other hand, making sure that no one is holding both of another player's hands. Through twisting, turning, and assorted awkward manipulation it is the group's responsibility to work together to untangle themselves.

Variations: Add a time limit.

VIP:

Vocal	Interpersonal	Physical
Nope!	And how!	Painfully so.

Skills:
- Flexibility
- Team Building

Half-Sheet

How to: Like Human Knot, this is more of a getting comfortable with each other activity, but it's a great choice for a new group to use to get acquainted.

Lay a large sheet, tarp, or blanket on the floor. Everyone in the group must situate themselves in a manner that they all are able to fit on top of it. Pretty easy. Now fold the sheet in half and repeat. Again, this is usually not too much of a challenge. Fold the sheet in half again and repeat. Now, it's starting to get interesting. Keep going until you have a ridiculously small sheet that they should never be able to all get on top of. Once they manage to succeed you should feel a fantastic sense of camaraderie developing.

Students tend to get very creative with this one. Groups often end up with members on each other's shoulders, interlocking arms for balance. They tend to get pretty comfortable with each other quite quickly. Just be sure to keep it safe. You don't want to start the team building process off with an injury.

Variations: None that I know of.

VIP:

Vocal	Interpersonal	Physical
Not at all.	YEEEEEESS!	Quite a bit.

Skills:
- Flexibility
- Team Building

Ha, Ha!

How to: Not a great daily warm-up activity, but a really good "getting comfortable with the other people in the room" one – especially if those people are giggly teenagers (or act like them.)

All of the players will lie down on the floor in a chain with their head on the diaphragm (or keeping it simple, the stomach) of the person behind them, essentially making the shape of a staircase. Beginning at one end of the group and moving to the other end, each players must, in a full and strident voice, say "Ha, ha!" This phrase will make the head of the person on top of them bounce up and down in a manner that feels quite awkward. The task is to try to make it all the way to the end of the line without laughing. I usually make the rule that they get three attempts to try to "win," and to "win" they have to make it through the entire line three times.

If you are working with eleven year old girls, I'd avoid this game at all costs – unless you've got a lot of extra time on your hands.

Variations: None that I know of.

VIP:

Vocal	Interpersonal	Physical
Only slightly.	Uncomfortably close!	Not too much, no.

Skills:
- Inflection
- Team Building
- Vocal Manipulation

Groupstop
(aka F-stop, aka All Stop, aka For the Love of God, Stop!)

How to: Another game all about visual listening.

All of the players leave the circle and start to wander around the space either purposefully or purposelessly. Eventually one player will completely freeze in mid-walk. When this happens, all of the other players are to follow suit and freeze as well as soon as they notice that the first player has stopped. Once everyone has frozen, the group then begins to walk again until another player chooses to freeze.

Obviously this game is all about facilitating players' awareness of each other. The point isn't to scan the room as much as possible looking for other stopped group members, but rather to develop a conscious perception of what we are "hearing" through our peripheral vision and to hopefully allow that to translate into stronger connections with each other in performance.

Plus it's pretty fun.

Variations: See what happens when you add a bunch of other distractions to the environment. Maybe turn on some really loud heavy metal or a sound effects recording, maybe do it with a strobe light on – whatever you choose, the point is to provide the players with external stimuli that they must actively work through in order to be successful.

VIP:

Vocal	Interpersonal	Physical
Nada.	A lot.	Not the focus.

Skills:
- Eye Contact
- Focus
- Listening
- Stage Presence/Confidence
- Team Building
- Timing/Pace

Gigolo

How to: A fun call and response game that can be done in a class or on the move. I was once working with a group of students that were doing this activity while walking down the streets of Edinburgh passing out flyers for the show that we were performing. It can literally go anywhere.

TEACHING AND PERFORMING IMPROV

The game follows a Verse-Chorus-Verse-Chorus format. Because it follows a rhythmic structure, I have tried to notate that in transcribing. Hopefully, this will help it to make sense and not make it seem more complicated than it is.

The verse is <u>spoken</u> between a lead group member and a 2nd group member of their choice. For the sake of this example, we will call the leader Steve and the chosen member Murray. The chorus will be performed by all group members in unison and alternates with every verse.

Beat:	1	&	2	&	3	&	4	&
							Steve:	Hey
	Mur-	ray!	**Murray:**	Yeah?			**Steve:**	Hey
	Mur-	ray!	**Murray:**	Yeah?		**Steve:**	Are	you
	rea-	dy				To	Jig-	a-
	lo?	**Murray:**	Hell		yeah!	I've	got	my
	hands	up	high,	my	feet	down	low	and
	that's	the	way	I	Jig-	a-	lo! **All:**	His
	hands	up	high,	his	feet	down	low	and
	that's	the	way	he	Jig-	a-	los.	

All: Chorus (2x)

Beat:	1	&	2	&	3	&	4	&	1	&	2	&	3	&	4	&
Phrase:	Jig		a	lo			oh!	Jig	Jig		a	lo			oh!	
Pitch:	D		A	G			A	D	D		A	G			A	

The chosen member, in this case Murray, will then become the new leader and choose another member of the group to pass the song on to. The process continues indefinitely until everyone becomes sick of it.

Variations: None that I am aware of.

VIP:

Vocal	Interpersonal	Physical
And rhythm, too!	Teamwork!	Depends.

Skills:
- Diction
- Inflection
- Stage Presence/Confidence
- Stamina
- Team Building
- Timing/Pace
- Volume

Free Association

How to: The warm-up that lets us see a little into your soul.

Based on the famous psychological exercise, this activity asks players to simply state the first thing that comes into their mind. One person in the circle will say a word, while making direct eye contact with the next player. The next player in the circle then says the first thing that they think of when they hear that word, and so forth and so on around the circle over and over. For example, player one might say "chair" prompting player two to say "sit" prompting player three to say "down" prompting player four to say "under" prompting player five to say "cover", etc.

Occasionally, a player will say something that seems to make no sense, but these are really the best moments of the game. Remember that the point is not to create a list of synonyms here - diversity is the key. One thing to be on the lookout for, especially with the inexperienced – be sure to remind players to <u>only</u> respond to the last word said. It's really easy to get an idea for what someone said three turns ago, but saying it now could completely throw off the flow of ideas around the circle.

And don't forget to maintain the eye contact!

Variations: A lot of fun to combine with Zip, Zap, Zop! And a Free Association based entirely on Gibberish or physical maneuvers could be really interesting.

VIP:

Vocal	Interpersonal	Physical
A bit.	Oh, yea!	Only in the variation.

Skills:
- Eye Contact
- Flexibility (variation)
- Focus
- Listening
- Stage Presence/Confidence (variation)
- Team Building
- Timing/Pace
- Vocal Manipulation
- Volume

Focus Circle

How to: This game is usually done as an elimination round.

The group sits or stands in a circle. The leader will pick a category – bands, movies, actors, etc. The members of the group have to provide an example of the category while sending an impulse around the circle by making direct eye contact with the player next to them. There can be no repeats or pauses. When a player makes a mistake, that person is out.

Variations: Can be combined pretty easily with Zip, Zap, Zop. A great Tune-up is created by mixing Focus Circle with Clap Circle **(see Chapter Three)**.

VIP:

Vocal	Interpersonal	Physical
Yep.	Sure Shooting!	Not…as…such.

Skills:

- Eye Contact
- Focus
- Stage Presence/Confidence
- Team Building
- Timing/Pace
- Volume

Energy Ball

How to: One of the most basic of all warm-ups, this one can be used effectively with groups of seasoned professionals as well as with preschool kids.

The leader mimes holding a ball of energy. The ball is then passed from person to person around the group while players maintain precise eye contact with each other. Essentially, this is a game of invisible catch. It's really about as simple as a warm-up gets.

Variations: Change the weight of the ball, the size, or what it's made out of. A bowling ball throws much differently than a ping-pong ball, and a ball of lead throws much differently than a ball of slime. Or you could change it from a ball into something else – a Frisbee, a bag of money, a precious vase, a hot potato – you get the idea. In this variation, however, a facilitator needs to live outside of the game to announce what the object is – and don't change it on every throw.

VIP:

Vocal	Interpersonal	Physical
Nope.	Yep.	Here's the magic.

Skills:
- Eye Contact
- Listening
- Mime
- Stage Presence/Confidence
- Team Building

Duck, Duck, Animal

How to: A delightfully youthful warm-up for kids and the inner child in us all.

Players sit in a circle, exactly as they would for a game of Duck, Duck, Goose. The player that is "it" walks around the circle gently tapping the heads of its members, but instead of simply saying "duck," the player must name a different animal as they touch each person in the circle.

Eventually, when the player decides to select a member of the group, instead of saying "Goose!" he/she will shout the name of another different animal. Both the player that was "it" <u>and</u> the player chosen from the circle must run around the perimeter of the group as if they were that animal (i.e. gallop like a horse, or waddle like a penguin, or crawl like a worm) to get back to the vacant spot.

This is a very silly game that works out inhibitions for older players and engages young ones with a new variant on an old favorite.

Variations: Add animal noises! Or change the category completely – something like "Duck, Duck, Mode of Transportation" could be fun.

VIP:

Vocal	Interpersonal	Physical
Some.	Absolutely.	Work up a sweat.

Skills:

- Listening
- Mime
- Stage Presence/Confidence
- Stamina, Flexibility
- Team Building
- Volume

Czechoslovakia (Sha-Boom!)

How to: A great vocal warm-up that also adds strong physical and interpersonal elements.

The group forms a circle and begins a clapping pattern – alternating between clapping themselves, and then moving their hands to their side to clap simultaneously with the players to their left and right. Essentially the pattern is "in-out-in-out." Once the pattern is established, the vocal component begins, in rhythm and in a strong, strident voice.

Physical Action:	*Spoken Phrase:*
In-Out-In-Out-In-Out-In-Out	Czechoslovakia, Sha-Boom, Sha-Boom!
In-Out-In-Out-In-Out-In-Out	Yugoslavia, Sha-Boom, Sha-Boom!
In-Out-In-Out-In	Let's get the rhythm of the HANDS!
Clap, Clap, Clap	
Out-In-Out-In-Out	We got the rhythm of the HANDS!
Clap, Clap, Clap	
Out-In-Out-In-Out	Let's get the rhythm of the FEET!

Stomp, Stomp, Stomp	
In-Out-In-Out-In	We got the rhythm of the FEET!
Stomp, Stomp, Stomp	
In-Out-In-Out-In	Let's get the rhythm of the HIPS!
Hip pop on each number	A-one, a-two, a-three
In-Out-In-Out-In	We got the rhythm of the HIPS!
Hip pop on each number	A-one, a-two, a-three

After this has been completed once, the entire routine is repeated silently, with the players merely thinking the words while performing the actions.

Once that, too, has been completed, the entire sucker is repeated again – double time! By the end, not only are most of the player's voices warmed up, but they are feeling a pretty darn good burn in their triceps as well.

Variations: I don't know any, but the script could easily be altered.

VIP:

Vocal	Interpersonal	Physical
YES!	YES!	Feel the burn!

Skills:
- Diction
- Focus
- Inflection
- Stamina
- Team Building
- Timing/Pace
- Volume

Count-Up

How to: Not just for slumber parties anymore, Count-Up is great way to get a group focused, settled, and feeling connected – simply by counting.

Everyone in the group closes their eyes and breathes to relax. One group member will get the ball rolling by saying "one." Eventually, on impulse, another member will say "two," another "three," and so forth. The trick is that only one person can speak at a time and no patterns are allowed. If two or more people say a number simultaneously, the whole sucker resets back to one.

Usually after a few failures, the group starts to get much more deliberate and focused, establishing (as crazy as it sounds) some sort of group consciousness with one another. For improv performers, this ability to be able to genuinely connect with your fellow players is not just an asset, but absolutely essential to success.

See how high the group can get. Maybe it's ten, twenty, thirty - I actually had one group that hit fifty-six. Usually after ten tries or so, however, most groups will start to lose their focus, so don't go on for too long.

Variations: Mix up the physical environment - the group can be standing, holding hands, lying down, in the furthest corners of the room, etc. Each arrangement completely changes the feel of the activity.

VIP:

Vocal	Interpersonal	Physical
Slightly.	They're Psychic!	A bit of a stretch.

Skills:
- Focus
- Listening

- Stage Presence/Confidence
- Team Building
- Timing/Pace

Clap Circle

How to: An intense exercise in eye contact! As the name suggests, the group should begin by standing in a circle. The leader will turn and make direct eye contact with the player next to them. As their eyes are locked, the two players will both clap in perfect unison. The receiving player then turns to the next person in the circle, repeats (eye contact, clap in unison) and it continues. After the pace has been established, the clapping can slowly begin to pick up speed. Expert groups could eventually get all the way around a group of twenty in two or three seconds.

The most important thing in this warm-up is communication through eye contact. As communication is a two way street, it is equally important to be an active receiver as it is to be an active sender. A player should not clap until they have received the impulse and they should not send an impulse if they haven't locked eyes with the receiver. If there is active communication through eye contact between players, then it will be impossible for them to be out of sync with each other.

Variations: A fun variation on a standard clap circle is to allow players to send the impulse back to the person who sent it to them – in other words to reverse directions. Just be sure to emphasize the need to keep the impulse going effectively.

#2: One of my favorite Tune-Ups is called **"Clap Circle plus Focus"** which includes the addition of categories to the game. Although it can take awhile to work through, it is one that I highly recommend. It's awesome!

VIP:

Vocal	Interpersonal	Physical
Sorry.	Intensely so!	And your hands can go numb, too!

Skills:

- Eye Contact
- Focus
- Listening
- Stage Presence/Confidence
- Stamina
- Team Building
- Timing/Pace

Body Slap

How to: A great way to warm up the body for any sort of performance. Beginning at the head and working their way down, the leader will direct the other members of the group in lightly slapping various parts of the body to "wake that area up."

A body slap routine should include:

- Head
- Neck
- Cheeks
- Chest (with Vocalization – maybe like Tarzan!)
- Right Arm, Left Arm (starting at the shoulder and go all the way down and back. Don't forget the hands!)
- Chest Repeat (with Vocalization)
- Stomach (the Gut!)
- Right Leg, Left Leg (Starting at the waist and going all the way down and back. Really get the foot!)

Then repeat the entire process in reverse to end with the head again. A well-done body slap will leave the entire person tingling all over and feeling energetic.

Please note that despite the name, players should not try to impress the Marquis de Sade with their self-flagellation. No hitting harder than a slight sting!

Variations: Mix up the vocalizations, mix up the pattern. Nothing here is set in stone.

VIP:

Vocal	Interpersonal	Physical
Yes!	Suffering breeds solidarity!	Ouch!

Skills:
- Flexibility
- Stamina
- Team Building
- Vocal Manipulation
- Volume

Big Booty

How to: A call and response game that requires rhythm and extra focus. For this warm-up, the group leader is referred to as "Big Booty" and the remaining group members are all assigned a number going around the circle based on their proximity to Big Booty (i.e. the first person to the left is Number One, the next is Number Two, etc. all the way around the circle.). For both rhythmic and concentration issues, it's best to keep the circle to thirteen or fewer members (Big Booty and twelve "numbers"), so be sure to split up larger groups.

In this game, an impulse is sent around the circle through a pattern of first naming yourself then naming another member of the group.

For example:

Player:	What they Say:
BB	"Big Booty – Number One"
#1	"Number One – Number Five"
#5	"Number Five – Number Two"
#2	"Number Two – Big Booty"

And so on...

Whenever a player drops the rhythm or makes a mistake, the run has ended and must start again. In between runs, the entire group chants a chorus of "Oh, yeah! Big booty, big booty, big booty."

The sample run above might look like the following:

Beat:	1	&	2	&	3	&	4	&
All:	Oh	-	-	-	Yeah!	-	-	Big
	Booty	Big	Booty	Big	Booty.	-	-	**BB:** Big
	Booty	Number	One **#1:**	Number	One	Number	Five **#5:**	Number
	Five	Number	Two **#2:**	Number	Two	Big	Booty	**BB:** Big
	Booty	Number	Six **#6:**	(Number	Six	makes	a	mistake)
All:	Oh	-	-	-	Yeah!	-	-	Big
	Booty	Big	Booty	Big	Booty.	-	-	**BB:** Big
	Booty	Number	Ten		Etc., etc.			

It takes a round or two to catch on, but it usually becomes a group favorite.

Variations: How I prefer to play! The offending player becomes the next Big Booty, forcing everybody's numbers to shift each round. Really ups the amount of focus required!

VIP:

Vocal	Interpersonal	Physical
And funky, too!	Absolutely!	Not unless you start to dance.

Skills:
- Eye Contact
- Focus
- Inflection
- Listening
- Stage Presence/Confidence
- Team Building
- Timing/Pace
- Vocal Manipulation
- Volume

Bananas!

How to: A fun chanting game with physicalization to boot.

With the group in a circle, start the first pair of lines at almost a whisper. Each subsequent pair of lines should be said at a louder volume than the one that preceded it. Try to make the volume increments even.

Each phrase should last a total of four beats, each line should take eight, and an entire pair should take sixteen. Each vocal passage is also accompanied by a physical action. The physical action is matched up with the phrase until the very end when it becomes completely freestyle.

Spoken Phrase:	*Physical Action:*
(Said Softly) Pick bananas. Pick, pick bananas. Pick bananas. Pick, pick bananas.	Reach with both hands, alternating, as if picking bananas from a tall tree
(A Little Louder) Peel bananas. Peel, peel bananas. Peel bananas. Peel, peel bananas.	Mime peeling a banana in rhythm

(Louder) Mash bananas. Mash, mash bananas. Mash bananas. Mash, mash bananas.	Mime mashing a banana, alternating between both hands, on an invisible surface
(Louder!) Go bananas! Go, go Bananas! Go bananas! Go, go Bananas!	Do "The Monkey!" – Remember the 60's dance move? That's the one.
(Really Loud!) B – A – N – A – N – A – S! Whoo!	Fist pump with each hand, alternating, with each letter
Go Bananas!	Freestyle spazzing.

Variations: Although it doesn't really make any sense, my students love to switch "bananas" with "potatoes." It's also entertaining to see how many people can't spell "potatoes."

VIP:

Vocal	Interpersonal	Physical
Heck, yeah!	Definitely.	Purposeful mime + freestyle spaz = the best of both worlds!

Skills:
- Mime
- Stage Presence/Confidence
- Team Building
- Timing/Pace
- Vocal Manipulation
- Volume

2 Truths/1 Lie

How to: Not really a warm-up, but a great "getting-to-know-each-other" activity.

Each player in the group is asked to make three statements about themselves. Two of these statements are to be completely true. One of them should be a lie. Give the group about thirty seconds to come up with their statements, and then go around the room taking turns saying them. The other players in the group have to figure out which of the three statements is the lie.

Remember that a lie like "I'm ten feet tall" or "I live under the sea" is a dead giveaway. Remind participants that this should be an exercise in creative, but believable, deception.

Variations: Alter the information asked for. "Three things that you've said to your teachers/boss." "Three ways that you've gotten a date." Etc.

VIP:

Vocal	Interpersonal	Physical
A tad!	A lot!	Not in the slightest.

Skills:
- Listening
- Team Building

Section Two:
Vocal Warm-ups

Wu, Wo, War, WOW!

How to: The best lip stretcher I know of. When doing this exercise, players attempt to keep their chins from moving and their lips in a square.

Each player sticks their lips out <u>as far as they can</u> in a square shape. Using *only* their lips, the group SLOWLY says the progression "Wu, Wo, War, WOW" five or six times. Remember to focus on keeping the chin still and doing all the work with the lips.

If done correctly, performers should really feel the burn for a few minutes after working.

Variations: Words could be altered, but they must start with W!

VIP:

Vocal	Interpersonal	Physical
Exclusively!	n/a	n/a

Skills:
- Diction
- Inflection
- Vocal Manipulation

Tongue Twisters

How to: The most popular type of vocal warm-up for a very simple reason – tongue twisters manage to be highly effective at working muscles that aren't always used to getting worked while simultaneously being a lot of fun!

Remember that since tongue twisters tend work a specific sound group, it is important to use several different ones together to ensure a solid warm-up routine. Also, to make tongue twisters an effective warm-up for performers, it is important that one exaggerates the movements of the lips, tongue, and mouth to reap maximum benefits.

Longer Phrases:

Repeat several times. Begin slowly at first and get faster with each repetition.

Whether the Weather (I think this one was the first vocal warm-up I learned as a child!)

Whether the weather be cold, or whether the weather be hot, we'll be together whatever the weather, whether we like it or not.

~ or ~

Whether the weather be cold, or whether the weather be hot, we'll whether the weather whatever the weather, whether we like it or not.

Thomas Tattamus

Thomas Tattamus took two T's to tie two tots to two tall trees.

Smothers Brothers

The Smothers Brother's mother's brother's father's other brother

Shut up the Shutters ** (Potential profanity warning!)

Shut up the shutters and sit in the shop

Proper Coffee

A proper cup of coffee from a copper coffee pot

Mother Plucker ** (Potential profanity warning!)

I'm not a pheasant plucker, I'm the pheasant plucker's son

Kantie Can

Kantie can't untie a tie so tie a tie like Kantie can.

I Slit a Sheet ** (Potential profanity warning!)
I slit a sheet, a sheet I slit, and on that slitted sheet I sit.

Betty Botta
Betty Botta bought some butter. "But," she said, "this butter's bitter.
"If I put it in my batter, it will make my batter bitter.
"But a bit of better butter, that will make my batter better"
So, she bought a bit of butter, better than her bitter butter.
And she baked it in her batter, and the batter was not bitter.
So 'twas better Betty Botta bought a bit of better butter.

Shorter Phrases:

Simply repeat the phrase a dozen or so times beginning slowly and getting faster as you go. Repeat. Repeat again. Rinse. Move on.

- Unique New York
- Upper roller, lower roller
- Two-toed tree toad
- Toy boat
- Three short sword sheaths
- Three free throws
- Susie sits shining ** (Potential profanity warning!)
- Swatch watch, wristwatch
- Stu chews shoes
- Six Sticky Skeletons
- The sixth sick sheik
- Scissors sizzle
- Shoulder surgery
- She sees cheese
- Seven sleazy shysters
- Sandwich, sane witch
- Rubber baby buggy bumpers
- Red leather, yellow leather
- Rear wheel, real wheel
- Really very weary
- Poodle parlor

- Pirate's privates
- Ocular broccoli
- Mud bug
- A minimum of cinnamon
- Irish wristwatch
- Imagining imaginary menageries
- Grip glue
- Good blood, bad blood
- Flies fly but a fly flies
- Flash message
- Exist amidst
- Double gum, bubble gum
- Crush grapes – Grapes crush
- Crash quiche course
- Chill, shake, serve
- Celibate celebrant
- Big black bugs bleed blue-black blood
- A big black bug bit a big blue bug
- Arnold Palmer
- Argyle gargoyle
- Aluminum linoleum

Variations: None, but there are hundreds more fun ones out there!

VIP:

Vocal	Interpersonal	Physical
Exclusively!	n/a	n/a

Skills:
- Diction
- Inflection
- Vocal Manipulation
- Volume

Bodega/Topeka

How to: My absolute favorite tongue twister game, so I had to make it a separate entry. This vocal warm up is a call and response game. Remember that with all tongue twisters, exaggeration with the lips, tongue, and mouth are key to development. The script goes:

Leader:	Group:
Bodega, Bodega, Bodega…	
	Bodega, Bodega, Bodega…
Topeka, Topeka, Topeka…	
	Topeka, Topeka, Topeka…
Bodega, Topeka, Bodega, Topeka, Bodega, Topeka, Bodega…	
	Bodega, Topeka, Bodega, Topeka, Bodega, Topeka, Bodega.

Repeat this in its entirety three or four times, first starting slow and then each time getting faster and faster. The final repeat should be at a breakneck pace!

Variations: None

VIP:

Vocal	Interpersonal	Physical
Exclusively!	A little bit.	n/a

Skills:

- Diction
- Inflection
- Team Building
- Timing/Pace
- Vocal Manipulation
- Volume

Section Three:
Mix 'em up Warm-ups

These three games are designed not only to engage performers and strengthen their focus, but also to mix up the order of the circle that the group is standing in. Maybe the performers end up in the same places every day and they need a shakeup, or maybe you want to do a Tune-up that requires people to change places. These are three of the ways to get there.

Dude!

How to: Every member of the group looks down at the floor. When the leader says, "Look up!" everyone must attempt to make direct eye contact with someone else in the circle. If the person happens by chance to also be looking back at them, both players shout, "Dude!" at the top of their lungs and trade places with other while doing some sort of amusing dance across the circle. Fast-paced fun!

Variations: Many! You could alter the word that is shouted to be something tied in with your group's work. Maybe require a different tone of voice or even dare to make it silent. Perhaps there is a particular physical move that players must use when trading places. This one has lots of room to play.

VIP:

Vocal	Interpersonal	Physical
A little, sure.	And fun, too!	Especially with elaborate dancing

Skills:
- Eye Contact
- Focus
- Inflection
- Stage Presence/Confidence
- Team Building
- Volume

Confuse-a-Cross!

How to: A wonderful game all about performer focus. The leader makes direct eye contact with another member of the circle, points at them, and walks to their position. The chosen player then has until the first person gets there to make eye contact with and point at someone else, to be able to vacate their spot. The process of pointing and exchanging can continue indefinitely.

Remember that this game is not about speed at first, but rather about communication and making choices. Keep the pace constant. The fact that it is silent can also add to the possible intensity of the exchanges. Once the group has it mastered, then you can start to speed it up. A really fast round of this one not only will get your performers focused, but might also give you a headache to watch.

Variations: Add sounds or specific gestures. Combine with "Zip, Zap Zop" or "Focus Circle." This one can be a lot of fun!

VIP:

Vocal	Interpersonal	Physical
Only if altered.	To the Nth degree.	Light, but effective.

Skills:
- Eye Contact
- Focus
- Listening
- Stage Presence/Confidence
- Team Building
- Timing/Pace
- Vocal Manipulation (variation)

Bippity, Bippity, Bop!

How to: One member of the group goes to the center of the circle. They then approach another member of the group and say one of three different phrases. The player standing in the circle must either

---

79

complete the phrase BEFORE the player in the center finishes OR remain silent, whichever is appropriate. The goal of the member in the center is to beat or trick the player in the outer circle and to switch places with them.

Center Player:	Outer Player:	Outcome:
Bippity, bippity bop!	Bop!	(must be said BEFORE center player finishes)
My hip when pop!	Pop!	(must be said BEFORE center player finishes)
Bop!	Silence	(if the player says anything, the center player wins)

This game takes a bit longer to mix people up than Dude! or Confuse-a-Cross, but it really emphasizes remaining in the moment and listening/responding to each other.

Variations: None.

VIP:

Vocal	Interpersonal	Physical
A smidge, perhaps.	Absolutely!	Depends on how the players trade places.

Skills:
- Eye Contact
- Focus
- Listening
- Team Building

Section Four:
Tune-up Warm-ups

Some of the best activities to use as Warm-ups are simplified versions of Tune-up activities. Why? These activities are guaranteed to overtly target basic principles specific to improv performance. Please note that since one of the important characteristics of a good Warm-Up routine is its speed (5 minutes or less) groups should already have spent some time with these as a Tune-Up BEFORE they are added into the Warm-Up rotation.

For a more detailed version of the complete Tune-Up version of the activity, please refer to Chapter Three.

What Are You Doing?

How to: One of the most famous acting exercises –for good reason. It hits space object work, listening, and focus with a vengeance.

For this game, players will pair up. The first player says to the second, "What are you doing?" The second player responds with some action (i.e."I'm brushing my teeth.") The first player then begins to mime the action that the second player described. The second player then asks, "What are you doing?" and the first player responds with a different action (i.e. "I'm feeding the chickens") which the second player must then mime. The action continually goes back and forth like this until the leader stops the game.

In this game a player is being asked to perform one action while not only holding a conversation, but actually describing a totally different action simultaneously. What a great exercise for working on the ability to split focus to two things at the same time.

Variations: Can be done in partners, in a line, or in a circle as a larger group.

VIP:

Vocal	Interpersonal	Physical
Some.	Yes.	Yes! – But MOSTLY this game is mental!

Skills:
- Focus
- Listening
- Mime
- Stage Presence/Confidence
- Team Building
- Volume

Magic Stick/Magic Ball

How to: It's all about space object work.

The leader mimes a "magic stick" (or magic ball, if you think that will get fewer snickers) and slowly, using only their miming skills, transforms the stick into a different object.

Once the object's identity has become evident to the rest of the group, the player then transforms it back into the original stick (or ball) and passes it to a different member of the group.

Variations: How I prefer to play. Instead of transforming the object back into a stick before it is passed, the object is passed as if it was that object (easy for a paper airplane, more difficult for a gorilla) and then the player that receives it will transform it back to a stick and then to the next object.

VIP:

Vocal	Interpersonal	Physical
Absolutely not!	A lot.	As physical as you can get

Skills:
- Flexibility
- Focus
- Mime
- Stage Presence/Confidence
- Team Building

Family Portraits

How to: In addition to being an excellent stand alone tune-up for younger performers, "Family Portraits" also can make a wonderful warm-up activity for improvisers at any level.

The group leader assumes the role of "photographer" and arranges the players into a family portrait pose, ala Sears (for a larger group, this could instead become a Class Portrait). The photographer then provides an attribute for the family/class that they must instantly display in a frozen pose (this is a photograph, not a movie). The attribute could be a profession, an emotional state, a physical quality – absolutely anything is fair game.

Examples could include:

- An angry family
- A teacher family
- A depressed family
- A superhero family
- A family without bones
- A doctor family
- A worm family

And so forth. There are virtually limitless possibilities.

A fun exercise that encourages instant characterization and teamwork.

Variations: You could make it a movie. You could combine it with the challenge Slide Show. You could add sound. There are several useful ways to mix this one up.

VIP:

Vocal	Interpersonal	Physical
No.	Yes, somewhat.	Very much so.

Skills:
- Flexibility
- Listening
- Mime
- Stage Presence/Confidence
- Stamina
- Team Building

Character of the Space

How to: A simple activity for ages 6 to 96 that can build some basic space work/mime skills

The players begin by wandering around the room. The group leader will then call out a particular environment (i.e. "Now you are walking on the moon!") and the players must all begin to move accordingly, as if they were on the moon. Although it is tempting to get vocal, try to keep this game entirely in the realm of the non-verbal. Once the environment has run its course, switch to a new one.

Examples of possible environments include:

- On the moon
- Under water
- In a bowl of popcorn
- On a frying pan
- On thin ice
- Through a muddy field
- On a treadmill

Etc., etc., etc. You get the idea.

Variations: When a player encounters another group member in the space, have them begin a quick improvised exchange (in character) appropriate to that particular environment.

VIP:

Vocal	Interpersonal	Physical
Only with the variation.	Some.	EXTREME!

Skills:
- Flexibility
- Mime
- Stage Presence/Confidence
- Stamina
- Team Building

3 Line Scenes

How to: The best tune-up to work the idea of "Yes, and…" (See **Rule #1 – Agree and Embellish**). Group members will create very short scenes containing only three lines of dialogue.

Players form two single file lines, stretching from the front to the back of the stage. The first two players step forward. The player from line one makes an offer – "You know, I sure do hate spiders." The player from line two then says something that advances that offer – "Well, don't freak out, but there's a spider on your chest."

The player from line one then says the final line that not only advances but also concludes the scene – "(Pounds their chest) There. Did I get it?" or "(Scream! Mimes picking it off and throwing it at the other player, who mimes it attacking their face.)" – As long as it advances the story, it counts as a line.

When the scene is over, players return to the rear of the opposite line. Let everybody go through the lines two or three times and move on.

Variations: Scenes could be done entirely non-verbally, if you would like to work on space object skills.

VIP:

Vocal	Interpersonal	Physical
Yes.	Yes.	Yes.

Skills:
- Diction
- Focus
- Inflection
- Listening
- Stage Presence/Confidence
- Team Building
- Vocal Manipulation
- Volume

Improv Fortune Cookie

The enlightened performer knows it is far
better to warm up than to burn out

CHAPTER THREE: IMPROV TUNE-UPS FOR TEAM AND SKILL BUILDING

This book began by covering various reasons why one should do improv. We then took a look at some of the greatest tools one can use to guarantee success and at some of the traps one can fall into that can guarantee failure. We walked through the various qualities of the ideal effective warm-up routine. So why then after all of that, didn't your group automatically hit the scene out of the park when they began to perform some specific short-form challenges? The answer is simple. Now that we've got the basics down, it's time to tune up.

So what exactly distinguishes a "Tune-up" from a Warm-up?

A Warm-up is a quick exercise that a group should do at the beginning of a practice or prior to a performance to help its members get in sync with each other – to get all of their brains working on the same plane, so to speak – so that as a team, they will be able to achieve greater success in performance.

A Tune-up, however, is an activity that a group consciously chooses to work on AS a practice, in a targeted effort to refine a specific improvisation skill (i.e. justification, endowments, space object work, etc.). Keep in mind, however, that just like a square can also be classified as a rectangle, a Warm-up or a Challenge can often be used as a Tune-up. It's all about the way the game is focused.

Perhaps your team has noticed that they are having difficulty actively listening to one another. You may decide to practice a few rounds of

Gibberish in an effort to force members to truly pay attention to one another's physicality and learn to listen with their eyes.

Maybe your group hits the occasional roadblock when faced with a challenge that requires players to make frequent offers from space. Perhaps a daily dose of Freeze Tag is the cure for what ails you.

The activities that are included in this section are intended to be used as an enjoyable way for your performers to work out their improv muscles. I have attempted to provide a checklist of many of the major skill areas that each activity targets prior to its entry. For an extended session, try combining a few Tune-ups that hit the same skill into a routine and see what piggybacks well on top of one another.

All of the games included in the next chapter, "Time to Get Up," can have a place in a solid team practice routine. Please note that in addition to the traditional skill builders in this chapter I have also included several of the Warm-ups and short-form challenges found elsewhere in this book that in my experience have proven to make excellent Tune-up exercises (especially in a workshop setting). So, get your performers up and moving!

And of course, remember that while the included activities are the ones that have proven to be the most successful for my improv students, they did not originate with me. The list belongs to the greater improv community at large and so by definition can never be fully complete.

So goof around with them!

Experiment! Use these activities as a jumping off point, but find what works for you. Pay attention to the notes I have provided about what skills specific exercises target and use those notes to help you to develop your own exercises.

In improv, as in all things, my advice is simple – don't be afraid to play.

3 Line Scenes (also a great Warm-up!)

Skills Targeted:
Concentration, Embodiment, Endowment, Justification, Listening/Being in the Moment, Mime, Physicality, Storytelling, Teamwork, Thinking Funny, Vocalization

Probably my favorite of all Tune-up exercises due to its incredible versatility, 3 Line Scenes are a fantastic tool to use in any workshop or practice setting.

The basic format of a 3 Line Scene is extremely simple. Participants begin by forming two single file rows. The player at the front of the first row will say the first line of a scene (a.k.a. make an offer), the player at the front of the second row will say the second line, and the original player from the first row will say the third, ending the scene. When finished, the players then go to the rear of the opposite row.

While 3 Line Scenes can be used to target many different skill areas, I particularly like to use them in workshop situations to help beginners become more aware of how to agree and embellish in order to advance the scene. In this situation, the format of a round would be as follows:

Line 1	Make an offer.
Line 2	*Agree* with the circumstances of the offer and *embellish* upon it.
Line 3	Maintain agreement and draw the scene to a close.

~ for example ~

Player 1:	Excuse me, sir, but how much are those rutabagas?
Player 2:	Well, they're typically $2 a pound… but if you give me your phone number, we'll call it square.
Player 1:	Humph. Not even if I was starving.

As you can see, this exercise follows a very simple format that allows for rapid fire reinforcement targeting a particular skill for groups of any size.

Hey, you said this exercise was versatile! How can I use it to strengthen other improv skills?

It's easy! I'll give you a few examples.

➤ Want to increase a team's ability to create understandable space objects?

Simply make the scene entirely non-verbal and have players agree and embellish using only mime.

➤ What about vocalization or endowment?

Try communicating everything through gibberish.

➤ Focusing on storytelling?

Remove all traces of humor.

➤ Working on groaners for a round of 185?

Require the third line of every scene to be a bad pun.

There's almost no limit to what a team can target with this activity with a little bit of creativity.

Character of the Space (also a great Warm-up!)

Skills Targeted:
Embodiment, Listening, Mime, Physicality, Spatial Awareness, Storytelling, Taking Direction

This is a ridiculously fun Warm-up activity that can also be used as a central component of everything from a beginning workshop with small children to an intense work session with experienced professionals. How cool is that?

Character of the Space begins by having every player in the group start walking around the room in no particular pattern, filling the entire area. The leader then provides an instruction that "changes" the environment that everyone is walking through.

Now you are walking on hot lava!

Now you are deep underwater!

Now you are swimming in a bowl of popcorn!

The players then continue to move throughout the space as if it was the new environment provided.

The basic version of this activity is entirely physical. Here, the game is all about how the players choose to adapt and use their bodies to communicate their new physical environments. This is a wonderful activity to use to help teach new improvisers – especially children – how to communicate story, character, and location using nothing but themselves. This is obviously an incredibly important skill in improv performance, yet for new performers it is frequently a huge stumbling block to overcome.

More experienced groups however, might really benefit from a session working with the advanced variation on the game. In this version, as two players meet they exchange a short bit of improvised dialogue based upon the current environment they find themselves in. Mixing this version with a round of 3 Line Scenes allows players to focus on the act of agreeing and embellishing while simultaneously being physical and is a wonderful choice that I highly recommend.

REALLY advanced groups (or any players that are trying to hone their skills until they become razor sharp, for that matter) can go a step even further. When the group leader notices a pair of players coming together, he/she can shout out "Freeze!" to stop everyone in the room apart from the two folks who are meeting. It then becomes their job to improvise a scene, developing characters and advancing a story based in some part upon their current environment. Once the leader thinks that the scene has progressed far enough, they can unfreeze the remainder of the group and the process can continue for as long as they see fit.

This is a fantastic activity to use in a workshop setting with groups that have a few miles on their tires as well as with the newest of the new.

Clap Circle Plus Focus

Skills Targeted:
Concentration, Listening, Teamwork

Good God and Hallelujah but if this isn't the best concentration exercise I've ever used!

At its most basic level, a game of Clap Circle is all about eye contact.

In it, participants must stand in a circle (obviously, based on the name) and then going around that circle, one player at a time must make direct eye contact with the person standing next to them. Then, communicating entirely through that eye contact, the two players must clap in perfect unison. The impulse then continues to be passed from player to player around the circle.

This by itself can be a great Warm-up for absolutely anyone or even a solid Tune-up focusing on eye contact and non-verbal communication for a novice group. It can even be a lot of fun! As players continue to become more and more advanced, the game can also be altered, giving players the power to reverse directions at will.

That's a BASIC Clap Circle.

NOW LET'S TAKE IT UP A NOTCH.

For a round of Clap Circle PLUS FOCUS, in addition to following the parameters of a regular Clap Circle listed above, players are also given a category (i.e. foods) that they must each provide one example of, with no repeats allowed within the group.

Now as the clap is sent around, players must also say the example provided by the person sending the impulse in pairs as they clap.

Players 1 & 2:	*(Making eye contact. Clap!) Bread!*
	(Player 2 turns to Player 3)
Players 2 & 3:	*(Making eye contact. Clap!)* Milk!
	(Player 3 turns to Player 4)
Players 3 & 4:	*(Making eye contact. Clap!)* Stew!
	(Player 4 turns to Player 5)

It helps the flow, by the way, if all of the examples that the players use are single syllable or at least short words – so don't let that one guy who always wants to pick something bizarre in an attempt to be funny have his way (Oh, and if you are that guy, stop it! – It's annoying.).

The addition of this single category already adds an element of focus and vocalization to an excellent exercise in communication, but we're not even close to finished.

LET THE FUN BEGIN!

After the group has mastered sending around their examples of foods, use one of the Mix-'em-up Warm-ups to change the player's positions around the circle. Descriptions of my three favorite Mix-'em-up Warm-ups (Bippity, Bippity, Bop, Confuse-a-Cross, and Dude!) are included in Chapter 2. Don't worry if only three-fourths of your players get moved – that's plenty.

Now send the chain of impulses around again, this time ping-ponging back and forth across the circle. Don't let players neglect making eye contact just because they've moved. If anything, it should now have become a more essential tool to the success of the game. It may take a few tries, but eventually, the group will get it.

ARE YOU READY TO MAKE YOUR BRAIN HURT?

Now that the group has mastered using the first category, it's time to add a second one to the mix (i.e. colors). Go around the Clap Circle again, this time each player giving their example of a color. Just as before, players should send an impulse around the circle using eye contact and say their example in unison as they clap. Send it around the circle a few times until they can do it fairly quickly.

Have they mastered this one? Good. Now is the perfect time to see if your participants still remember the first category. See if they can ping-pong it around the circle – just for fun.

Evil. Pure and simple.

Now mix them up once again.

TIME TO BRING ON THE PAIN!

Starting with either category, send the impulse around the circle a few times until the group can manage to do it with relative ease. Once you're confident that they've got the gist of it, switch to the other category. Once they've got that one down as well, it's time to finally get to the real work – sending both chains around...

at the *SAME TIME*!

Begin by sending one impulse around the group and letting it get established - I usually let it progress around the entire circle one full revolution. Now that the players have gotten into a rhythm, you can add the second category. You've now got two totally different patterns with two totally different categories going on simultaneously.

It will almost certainly immediately fail.

This is for good reason. You're asking your players to think about two different things at the same time while also listening for two different things at the same time. Talk about overload!

Inevitably, at least one member of the group will even be asked to respond to two different things at the same time when they receive both impulses simultaneously.

Once it drops – and it <u>will</u> drop – point out at least one strength about what the group did and get it going again. It usually takes me three to four tries before I can get both impulses to go a full rotation around a group. If your group has the stamina to keep on clapping (remember, they've been doing it for about half an hour by now, so the more frail among them might be complaining of having bleeding palms, or something), they can just keep going and going at this point.

This is easily the best focus exercise that I know of, plus it also forces players to truly listen to each other and communicate both verbally and non-verbally through their eye contact. Absolute perfection!

Chapter 6 includes a workshop format in which this activity is featured prominently.

Dr. Know-It-All (also a great Challenge!)

Skills Targeted:
Audience Interaction, Listening, Teamwork, Verbal Prowess

Sure, Dr. Know-It-All is a fun game to play during a performance, but with a younger group of performers, it can also be used as an excellent Tune-up!

The basic premise of the game is quite simple. Three players act as one character (Dr. Know-It-All) who will answer questions provided by the audience, with each performer contributing only one word of the response at a time – usually with very amusing results.

In a workshop setting however, rather than focusing on humor, this game can be a great introduction for newer performers (even small children) to fundamental improv concepts ideas like listening, teamwork, or giving and taking focus.

I have used this game successfully with groups of all ages, but honestly, I truly enjoy it the most with really young performers – first or second grade. Why? Mostly because of the genuine look of joy they get on their faces when it is their turn to be Dr. Know-It-All, but also because the exercise helps to lay the groundwork that improv is all about teamwork. And it can illustrate this in a way that any performer can understand, even at a very early age.

I also love to see the first time that the team's answer doesn't quite match up with what was going on in an individual player's head. The look on their face is priceless – and an amazing teachable moment.

I've actually had kids break character and turn to one of their teammates to tell them in no uncertain terms that what they just said was the wrong answer. There's no better time to instill the idea that each player can change the direction of the scene and it's everyone else's job to agree with that direction as well.

> *What a profoundly important lesson whether your*
> *players are six or twenty-six or sixty-six or*
> *two hundred and six.*

You can check out Chapter 4 for a more detailed description of how Dr. Know-It-All works when it is used as a challenge.

Energy Ball (also a great Warm-up!)

Skills Targeted:
Concentration, Mime, Physicality, Teamwork

The most basic of all of the physical Tune-up exercises, Energy Ball is a wonderful activity that can be used as an introduction to space object work for young performers, or as a nice refresher for your more seasoned players.

The game is almost absurdly simple. A typical round consists of nothing more than playing catch – it's just done <u>without</u> a ball. Just the act of miming the throwing and catching of the invisible ball in a believable manner is enough to teach the basic principles of mime (i.e. defining the shape & weight of an object, etc.) and to get your performers to start thinking about physicality.

But there's no reason that you have to keep the exercise that pared down.

With more advanced groups, there's nothing stopping you from changing the weight or size of the ball in mid-toss – or perhaps even changing the object entirely.

What if the players were now suddenly tossing a chicken or a dumbbell or a bear trap back and forth – how would that look different?

What would they need to do differently with their bodies?

How would they successfully communicate to an audience what the object is?

Typically, this is a game I use as a Warm-up activity, but in the right work session, it can be an excellent teaching tool to introduce players to getting physical.

Entrances and Exits (also a great Challenge!)

Skills Targeted:
Justification, Listening/Being in the Moment, Storytelling

A better game for teaching new performers the ancient art of justification, I know not of.

In a round of Entrances and Exits, a team is given either a set of variables or a platform upon which to base their scene and each player is <u>also</u> assigned an individual word. Anytime one of those words is used by any of the performers in the group, the player assigned to it must either enter or exit the scene, as appropriate, and *justify* the movement within the scene's context. In other words, as the game progresses players must constantly devise believable reasons to enter or leave – reasons that must simultaneously advance the story of the scene.

No small feat.

When used as a performance challenge (as outlined in Chapter 4), this justification is probably the biggest pitfall that performers face. Instead of thinking of their movement as an opportunity to provide an exciting offer to the other members of the scene, newer players tend to want to take the easy way out and give some random reason for their entrance or exit.

Now, don't get me wrong – used sparingly a little randomness can be a wonderful thing – but with a challenge like this that involves a lot of movement within the space of a three minute performance time, any more than two or three random exits will most likely annoy an audience (and these few are best when performed by the same player so that they can become a attribute of their character).

When used in a work setting, the game provides a wonderful opportunity for a group to slow down and focus on each other rather than the audience's reactions, and really think about <u>why</u> they are contributing what they are.

This is what makes Entrances and Exits such a strong choice as a Tune-up exercise. The three primary skills it targets – justification, listening, and storytelling – do not exist independently in a vacuum, but rather are all completely integrated together and must occur simultaneously for a player to be successful. In order to know when to enter/exit, one must be fully in the moment and listening intently to the other players. One must then be able to logically justify one's entrance/departure in a manner that concretely advances the story.

As a sidebar, when used as a Tune-up activity I would recommend providing the platform to newer performers so that their energies can be solely focused upon the three target areas, rather than on stringing three random variables together. As a team progresses, this aspect of a performance can then be added in.

It is also advisable to remind your improvisers to avoid the standard gimmick of forcing one player to enter and exit the scene constantly. Gimmicks can be great in a performance, but this is a time to work. Players should be completely focused on advancing the story while devising believable justifications.

If they can wrap their heads around that skill, they will have gained the ability to succeed in countless challenges.

Family Portraits (also a great Warm-up!)

Skills Targeted:
Embodiment, Mime, Physicality, Taking Direction, Teamwork, Vocalization

While a great stand alone activity for young performers, for most groups Family Portraits isn't so much a full-on Tune-up activity as it is a great intro to a full-on Tune-up activity.

In this exercise, the group leader becomes a "photographer" who will take a series of imaginary portraits of the remainder of the group. The photographer will assign a characteristic to the group.

You're an angry family.

Now you're a circus family.

Now everyone in the family has feet made of gunpowder!

The family members - or if you are working with a large group, the class for a class photo - must adopt a purely physical pose (non-verbal with no movement!) that communicates the attribute.

For a group of very young improvisers who are just learning the ropes, this activity could easily be enough of a workout by itself as it is a great introduction to essentials like embodiment and mime. However, don't neglect it just because you are working with a more advanced group.

Doing Family Portraits as a preamble to a round of the advanced variation of Character of the Space, for example, can be a wonderful match as it gets all of the players thinking correctly about how to accomplish the task of physicalizing that they are being asked to take on.

This is also an activity that can be spiced up a bit, if so desired. Try turning the photograph into a slow-motion film to add more of the element of teamwork. Or get rid of the physical component altogether and target vocal skills by becoming a recording engineer trying to create the perfect sound effect to communicate the assigned attribute.

Like many of the activities in this section, Family Portraits is a game that can be both incredibly fun and really beneficial for performers of any skill level.

First Line, Last Line (also a great Challenge!)

Skills Targeted:
Justification, Storytelling, Teamwork

In First Line, Last Line, improvisers are provided with two lines of dialogue. The scene must begin and end with these assigned lines.

Typically a challenge for well-practiced improv groups to use in performance, for the novice improviser First Line, Last Line works much better as a training activity. Why? Since the construct merely provides the starting and ending point of the scene, the game becomes all about the performers being able to successfully agree and embellish in order to advance the story. It doesn't get much more fundamental than that.

Players should work in pairs to create a 60 to 90 second scene. Each player is assigned one of the two lines and whether they will either start or end the scene with that line. The lines that are used for the team can be gathered in any manner that you like. They can be written in advance, provided by the rest of the group in the moment, or devised by some other means as you see fit. As the pair performs, they should try to ensure that every line of dialogue is an offer that makes the scene progress in some manner. In other words, their focus should always be on good storytelling

Any other endowments with which you choose to provide your players is entirely up to you (with really green improvisers it might be a good idea to also provide a character relationship or a conflict – or even a brief plot outline of a full scene, if they are total newbies), but remember that the ultimate goal of the activity is to force the performers to become self-reliant.

The more of this type of work that your improvisers do, the more confident they will become in their ability to advance a scene and live entirely in the moment.

Fortune Cookie (also a great Challenge!)

Skills Targeted:
Storytelling, Teamwork

Like First Line, Last Line, Fortune Cookie is a team challenge almost always intended to be used during a performance. However, in a work session it can also provide a wonderful opportunity for a team to practice their storytelling abilities. This activity can be done with a standard group of three to five performers or in pairs, if desired.

Instead of receiving a set of variables, a fortune cookie is opened and read aloud by the players. The team then must create a coherent scene that uses the fortune in some way (philosophical base, plot point, etc.). More often than not, the cookie will provide a fortune that contains a maxim (i.e. "Happy is the man who reaps a bountiful harvest") rather than a bit of action (i.e. "An exciting opportunity will come your way tomorrow"). Consequently, the value of this activity then revolves around the team's ability to create a great original story using the fortune as a theme.

When used as a skill-building activity with novice performers, a round of Fortune Cookie should probably not exceed 90 seconds. It's always a good idea to continue to remind performers to make sure that they consistently agree with each other and embellish upon every offer made. Everything that the players put out there must advance the scene towards a logical conclusion. To an improv performer, this type of challenge provides the best opportunity for both growth and creative expression.

You may choose to provide inexperienced performers with additional variables to aid their creation of a story, however, once they have some mileage on them it is important to force them to stand alone. That is the point, right? Frequent practice of this type of scene will really help your performers discover how to work together to develop a story.

Freeze Tag (also a great Challenge!)
(ALSO a great Warm-up! Stays crispy in milk!)

Skills Targeted:
Concentration, Individual Confidence Building, Justification, Listening, Physicality, Storytelling, Teamwork, Temporal Awareness, Thinking Funny

Freeze Tag was my personal introduction into the world of improv.

It was the favorite challenge of my seventh grade theatre class when we had "Improv Friday" and consequently we played it often. I wasn't very good (most of my scenes involved crawling on the floor searching for a contact lens, if I recall), but despite my shortcomings, I still had a blast. That's one of the biggest assets of Freeze Tag – it teaches great lessons about the fundamentals of improv while simultaneously being really fun – even if you aren't very good... yet.

A round of Freeze Tag begins with a short scene for two players. Once the premise has been established, another player calls out "Freeze!," replaces one of the players performing, and then begins a brand new, unrelated scene. The process continues indefinitely until the instructor decides that it's time to pause the merriment.

This process is all about offers – making them, accepting them, extending them to a logical conclusion, and developing a sense of story to prevent a player from an accidental denial.

In addition to dealing with offers, Freeze Tag also creates opportunities for players to work on justification, being funny quickly, and remaining physical. All in all, not too shabby for an exercise that even the most reluctant of performers will request frequently.

It is very important to help the inexperienced improviser develop a sense of the timing of beats of action in a round of Freeze Tag.

Each mini-scene within a round should last between five and ten seconds (two to five lines of dialogue), depending on the offer.

In my classes, one of two things consistently happens the first time we try to do the challenge.

Either the players are so enthusiastic that they jump all over each other – sometimes not even allowing fellow performers to make an offer at all before chiming in – or they are so timid that they allow the dialogue to go on and on, well beyond the moment's natural conclusion, until I finally freeze the scene for them.

In both of these situations, the student still needs to get a feel for the timing of the scene. Not coincidentally, once a performer has developed a sense of these beats, it can translate into a better understanding of their traditional acting as well.

Freeze Tag also provides a wonderful opportunity to work through the innate tendency that many beginning performers possess of remaining physically inactive. Since most offers will be based in some way upon a previous player's body position, it is incredibly important for performers to continually move. In Freeze Tag, this physicality provides the fuel for the other player's justifying fire, so to speak.

Speaking of other players making offers, it is important to make sure that you don't allow any single performer to hog the spotlight and keep freezing the scene over and over again and jumping in. We are attempting to foster teamwork, after all. But how does one manage to do this while not clamping down on the offending player's enthusiasm? It can be tricky, to say the least.

Personally, I discourage performing a round of Freeze Tag in a set order (i.e. around a circle) as a general rule because this completely goes against developing an intrinsic feel for that initial impulse – a feeling that you want to ingrain firmly into your beginners.

The other side of that argument is, of course, that making all of your students actually get up and go forces them to get used to the environment of constant offers that they must master to be successful at all of improv.

Honestly, however you choose to utilize Freeze Tag it is a pretty useful activity – so let your own judgment prevail.

More so than probably all of the other activities in this chapter, Freeze Tag doesn't really feel like work in a traditional sense. Not only is it a lot of fun to watch and do, but it also teaches a variety of important improvisation lessons.

Parting thought: *Do it often!*

Gibberish (also a great Challenge!)

Skills Targeted:
Justification, Listening, Mime, Physicality, Storytelling,
Vocalization

Originally one of the earliest of competition events, Gibberish has since evolved into a tool that players must be able to incorporate into many different improv activities. In fact, it is actually so useful that there has even become an entire subset of "Gibberish-Based Challenges" (i.e. Double Talk, Dubbing, etc.) that are wonderful, audience-pleasing choices to feature in any performance.

One should not ignore, however, the fact that Gibberish is also one of the best exercises to use to get players to focus on how to communicate and how to listen - without being able to fall back on the crutch of intelligible language.

In the setting of a work session, I recommend using Gibberish in its earliest incarnation. Players should create a standard scene based upon a provided platform, but communicate everything – every offer, every character attribute, every advancement – entirely through vocal nonsense rather than through words.

It is simply amazing what a performer is able communicate using only a gesture or a physical stance. It is even more amazing what can be communicated when that motion is combined with a strategically used non-verbal sound. Relying only upon one's verbal ability as the solitary means with which to advance a scene is not only lazy but, more importantly, it is profoundly boring to watch. With newer performers (and some seasoned ones too, for that matter) this is often a difficult hurdle to overcome – and not without good reason.

Have you ever had difficulty patting your head and rubbing your stomach at the same time? Metaphorically, this is exactly what improv is constantly asking its participants to do.

So many challenges require that a performer be able to focus on multiple things at once (i.e. Alphabet Game requires players to advance the story while also remembering and applying the alphabet). This division of mental resources can cause many teams of inexperienced players to become one of the most dreaded things in the world of improv...

a group of Talking Heads.

Forcing players to become comfortable with advancing a scene by using only grunts, ululation or some other degree of vocal nonsense combined with space object work can profoundly improve their ability to focus on story while simultaneously dealing with the parameters of a challenge during a performance.

Using Gibberish in a work session is not only about developing the ability to multi-task, of course. It is also a remarkably fun way to get your performers to start thinking about physicality and – perhaps more importantly – to loosen them the heck up. Even the funniest of beginners can quickly become intimidated when they are not allowed to rely on their strong suit – verbal language.

This is a great game to choose to help get players over some of their performance inhibitions.

Good Thing/Bad Thing (also a great Challenge!)

Skills Targeted:
Concentration, Justification, Listening, Storytelling, Teamwork, Thinking Funny, Verbal Prowess

I've used this activity frequently in both a workshop setting as well as in performance. It can be a great lesson about listening to other players and advancing a scene – plus it's always fun to see where the story eventually ends up.

Assemble players into a line of no more than eight across the performance area. Honestly, you could let the line go on as long as you wanted, but keeping it shorter requires players to provide more components to the story and therefore get in a little more practice.

The first player will begin to tell a story by starting with something good that happened. The second player advances the story by adding something bad. The third – something good, the fourth – something bad, and so forth. Personally, I like to use an odd number of players so that with each pass they are alternating between contributing good and bad events to the story.

Player 1	(Good):	I got $20 for my birthday to spend on comics.
Player 2	(Bad):	Outside the store I got stopped by a really scary guy who wanted my money.
Player 3	(Good):	He actually wanted to sell me an Action Comics #1, so I gave my money to him.
Player 4	(Bad):	But I was so sure it was a fake.
Player 5	(Good):	But it actually was real, so I sold it to the store for a million dollars.
Player 1	(Bad):	But the money made me feel empty inside.

Notice that this is purely a verbal game – nothing physical going on here at all. However, players <u>are</u> being asked to focus on two different areas at the same time – advancing the story, while contributing either a good or bad event to the plot. This makes for a great activity to use as a transition into others that focus on having players integrate physicality with their verbal contributions.

In a workshop, this can be a fun way to show new players how to construct a story, how to advance a scene, and especially how a player can create conflict while still agreeing with an offer that was made. In a performance, it can be really fun for the audience when players to try to outdo one another with the creative ways that they add bad things to the scene.

In either situation, it's an activity worth giving a try.

Hitchhiker (also a great Challenge!)

Endowment, Individual Confidence Building, Justification,
Listening/Being in the Moment, Mime, Physicality, Thinking
Funny, Vocalization

Yet another event that is typically used as a performance challenge, Hitchhiker can also have tremendous value in a workshop or practice setting as well. In this exercise, a "driver" picks up a "hitchhiker" (kids, don't try this at home) that has been endowed with some sort of a character stereotype. Through the course of a brief scene, the driver slowly transforms into the hitchhiker's character, pulls over, and then justifies their exit from the scene. The hitchhiker then slides over, becomes the new driver, and the game continues.

This is an activity that can be done with any size group – from the smallest to the largest. There are three primary areas that the challenge targets.

First: *The act of communicating a character QUICKLY!*

There are many different challenges that require a performer to take on an endowment and display it prominently. Some challenges, like Party Quirks for example, demand that one player communicate their character attributes to a different player without ever explicitly stating who or what they are. So how does one accomplish such a task? Simple! By developing one's ability to display and divulge character.

What better challenge could there be to practice this skill than one that not only allows, but requires the actor to play a stereotype?

In Hitchhiker, a performer must let both the audience and their fellow player know exactly who they are within the first few seconds that they are on stage.

Second: *The process of both vocal & physical TRANSFORMATION.*

It is the slow process of transformation from the character of the driver into the character of the hitchhiker that gives this challenge most of its entertainment value.

Watching as a conservative politician slowly introduces bits and pieces of the personality of a death metal band frontman into their character until finally the car has become a throbbing mass of poli-sci mosh pit glory can't help but grab one's attention.

But this is a difficult skill to master.

The driver has to REALLY be listening to the hitchhiker – both verbally and physically – and be able to pick up on, isolate, and then utilize the various character tics that they have on display. They then need to be able to use their bodies and their voices skillfully to communicate these attributes. They also have to have developed enough control to let the attributes creep in only one at a time, and let the audience revel in the slow burn of their process.

It takes a lot of poise and control (and practice) to be able to pull all of this off.

Third: *Devising original, entertaining, BELIEVABLE justifications.*

The final step in a round of Hitchhiker is for the driver of the vehicle to justify (in character, of course) a reason to pull the car over and exit the scene.

Since this is the final moment of stage time for the performer, and therefore it is important to leave the audience with a 'WOW!,' actors should want to invent something pretty funny here. But – and this is the kicker – it can't just come out of the clear blue sky. Like everything else in improv, it must be justified within the confines of the challenge and the context of the characters.

I can't tell you how often I've seen a team of inexperienced performers doing a round of this challenge fall into the trap of making an easy exit. The group has actually managed to accomplish the Herculean task of getting the audience to love their work, when suddenly a team member decides to pull over without warning and attempts to justify it with something lame that has no relation to the scene like "Man, I want some ice cream" or "I think I just saw Elvis!"

Unless the scene has been about how your character is lactose intolerant or you've been working the Blue Room in Vegas, these just won't work.

> *The audience will suddenly go silent, the performer's fragile spell of captivation suddenly broken.*

Because Hitchhiker requires such a blatant moment of justification, it is an excellent exercise to help a group Tune-up their skills. (For a real workout in justification, though, a round of Entrances and Exits simply can't be beat.)

Hitchhiker is a fun and effective workout for performers of all ability levels.

Use it with abundance!

Last Letter/First Letter (also a great Challenge!)

Skills Targeted:
Concentration, Justification, Listening/Being in the Moment, Storytelling, Verbal Prowess

At the risk of becoming repetitive, Last Letter/First Letter is a fantastic challenge to use in a competition, but can be an even <u>better</u> exercise to use in a workshop or practice setting (just as the previous five entries were, if anyone's keeping track).

In case you somehow haven't already picked up on it, LISTENING is one of the most important skills that an improviser must possess (and I've been mentioning it pretty frequently, so if you missed it, you might want to work on those listening skills yourself). Although there are many good exercises that can be used to improve a player's ability to listen, I can think of no other exercise that will do a better job than this one at forcing a player to truly pay attention to the specific act of doing it.

In a round of Last Letter/First Letter, a player will begin each line of dialogue with the last letter of the line that came before it. For example:

Player 1:	Have you seen the new line of coffee grinders?
Player 2:	Seen 'em? I helped to design 'em!
Player 1:	Man, what a sweet life you must have.
Player 2:	Ed, I'm not gonna lie to you – It is pretty great.

See why it's so effective? This game forces players to actively listen to everything that their partner is saying because they will have to use it themselves -- *immediately*. The stakes for maintaining concentration suddenly become very high!

As you can likely tell, especially when used as an exercise this challenge works best when it is done in pairs. When more than two players are used, performers (especially new ones) tend to get confused about whose turn it is and, on occasion, may even end up not contributing to a scene at all.

If a full-sized group was going to be performing this one in front of an audience for the first time, it might not be a bad idea for them to decide upon a running order for themselves (first, second, third, etc.) until they have mastered the art of giving and taking focus.

Although in principle I disagree with this amount of planning because it robs the scene of much of its spontaneity, first and foremost players have a responsibility to their audience to ensure that the story is consistently advancing.

Also, while you could have players construct an entire scene in this fashion just as they would during a competition or performance, in my opinion it's a little inefficient for a practice setting.

To really give your players the most opportunity for improvement, see what happens if you make this a TEN line scene, INCLUDING agreeing and embellishing, with a beginning, middle, and an end. The exercise now combines the elements of "Yes, And...," listening, and thinking in terms of a story – the three most important areas of all successful improv. Not too shabby, eh?

Machines (mostly a great Warm-up!)

Skills Targeted:
Concentration, Embodiment, Individual Confidence Building, Physicality, Spatial Awareness, Teamwork, Vocalization

Really, this one is primarily a Warm-up, but it's not one of the most famous acting exercises of all time for nothing. Even though it only takes a few minutes to do, Machines is a deceptively simple powerhouse that can deal rather effectively with several of the most important skills that an improviser needs to master.

It forces players to:
- work as a team
- relate to each other physically
- mime an activity
- vocalize
- maintain multiple simultaneous points of focus

…as well as get used to the idea that in improv, everyone's gonna look stupid sometimes. Plus it's really fun.

I don't want to bore you with a whole lot of extra, redundant, unnecessary, unneeded repetitiveness, so if you haven't done so already, go check out Chapter Two for a detailed description of the game.

Then use it.

Magic Stick/Magic Ball (also a great Warm-up!)

Skills Targeted:
Concentration, Listening, Mime, Physicality

The quintessential mime exercise!

In a round of Magic Stick or Magic Ball, one player begins by pretending to hold an imaginary (brace yourselves…) stick or ball. The player then transforms it into an object of their choice entirely through mime.

Traditionally, once the object's transformation is complete, the player will turn it back into a stick (to pass to the player next to them) or a ball (to pass to any player in the circle), who will then transform it into the object of their choosing. I, however, prefer to omit this reverse transformation step and simply pass the object to the next player in its current, more creative, form.

While the traditional method is perfectly fine to use, especially for younger players, by passing the mimed item instead of a stick or ball, we've gone beyond simple space-object work and have added an extra level of physicality to the exercise by throwing and catching the imaginary object. (Just picture how one would catch an elephant, for example!) Plus, players must now maintain a level of communication and listening with each other that just isn't present when every object transforms back into a safe and predictable standby.

Remember that like many of these Tune-up activities, Magic Stick/Ball is not necessarily meant to be a stand-alone activity. Rather it's a good part of a balanced improv breakfast. Try combining it with Character of the Space or Family Portraits to really build a lesson about physicality. Or try an abbreviated round of it during a quick Warm-up routine. It's a very versatile choice!

Anytime a group needs to practice their miming skills, this activity would be my go-to first choice for them to explore.

Mirrors

Skills Targeted:
Concentration, Listening, Physicality, Spatial Awareness, Teamwork

Despite the much deserved mockery that this particularly self-indulgent looking acting exercise receives in the movies (doesn't it seem like every time you see a scene that is supposed to be taking place in a really bad acting class they are doing a round of Mirrors?), it actually does have some merit – especially for improvisers.

In case you are unfamiliar with it, Mirrors is done by two players who are facing each other and are making direct, unflinching eye contact. The two players attempt to move in unison – one player becoming the leader and the other the follower. The trick, of course, is for the players to keep their movements completely synchronized with each other.

Although one manages to somehow feel simultaneously silly <u>and</u> pretentious while doing Mirrors (no small feat, I might add), to an improv performer, the value of the activity can be immense. To be successful, players must control their movements so that they are in complete agreement with each other and much of the information needed to maintain that agreement is being communicated via direct eye contact. I know I've written about this over and over again, but non-verbal communication between players is an incredibly important skill to foster.

Never stop working on it. Never. Ever.

Don't do this activity every day (unless you are really trying to thin out your improv herd – or get them to exclusively wear turtlenecks) but it certainly doesn't hurt anything to give it a whirl and see what sticks.

Questions Only

Skills Targeted:
Concentration, Storytelling, Verbal Prowess

While many groups typically choose this challenge to use during a performance, in my experience with students the results can be too unpredictable to risk it. When I emcee a performance or competition, I always try as best as I can to set up situations in which performers will be successful and build their skill base, not shut down from discouragement. Questions Only can, however, be used quite effectively to get players thinking of ways to advance a scene other than by using direct exposition.

The one rule of Questions Only is incredibly simple - everything must be stated in the form of a question (thank you Jeopardy!). Being able to effectively communicate meaning when confined to interrogatives sounds like enough of a challenge as it is, but to be able to advance a plot?

This is an excellent exercise to use to force players to hone in on how they tell a story.

Player 1:	Can you play a song for me on that piano over there?
Player 2:	What exactly did you want to hear?
Player 1:	Would you play me something to forget that I just got dumped?
Player 2:	Don't you think you're asking a lot of me?
Player 1:	What else can I do to forget how miserable I am?
Player 2:	Have you tried Hare Krishna?

It's incredibly hard for players to constantly advance the story of a scene when limited to only speaking in questions. New players will instinctively try to buck the format. Don't let them get away with anything!

Don't allow players to fall into the trap of making a statement followed by a question ("I don't know. Am I?").

Don't let them cheat by simply raising their pitch at the end of a sentence.

Certainly don't let them get by with just saying "Why do you think I…" for everything. That's just tacky.

The name of the game is Questions Only for a reason. Do what you can to help them keep moving the scene forward at all times.

Scene Beyond Words

Skills Targeted:
Concentration, Listening/Being in the Moment, Mime, Physicality, Storytelling

For advanced teams, Scene Beyond Words can be a wonderful challenge to use in performance. In my experience, however, the game is much more valuable to a team's progress as a Tune-up activity – so much so, that you'll notice I did NOT choose to include it in the list of challenges in Chapter 4.

The premise of the game is ridiculously simple – players just can't talk. That's it. This seemingly simple parameter, however, has a ridiculously big impact upon the scene.

As we all know, the performer's principle responsibility is always to tell a great story – but in this game the primary means of storytelling that players use has been stripped away from them.

How can I advance a story without speaking? You mean I can't even use gibberish?

There is a direct line between Scene Beyond Words and **Rule #4** – Be Physical. Everything in the challenge – and yes, I do mean everything – needs to be communicated using a player's body. The entire scene is storytelling through mime and space object work.

Telling a complete story through mime is tremendously difficult for new performers – and this is why Scene Beyond Words makes for such a great activity to use as a practice.

Most performers new to improv would be delighted if they just remembered to communicate the variables in a scene to the other players and the audience – and indeed they should be, as that is an incredibly important first step in their process. However, players need to be able to use those variables to tell a story – a story as fully developed as any other – and that is a skill that will take some time and effort to develop.

Scene Beyond Words is also a great activity to use if players are having difficulty following **Rule #2** – Stay in the Present. As soon as the luxury of using language has been taken away from them, most of the players that have been guilty of planning their scenes rather than performing them will fall right in place with the others in learning how to tell a story.

I can't claim that it's a guaranteed cure-all for a group that seems to fear action, but the simple act of having to communicate without sound seems to give players a heightened awareness of the need for solid, active storytelling.

Upon its initial appearance, this game will likely strike fear into the souls of new players, so I'd wait a little bit before I spring it on them. Once performers have gotten the improv bug in their system and are serious about really improving their skills, however, Scene Beyond Words would be right around the top of my to-do list.

Should Have Said (also a great Challenge!)

Skills Targeted:
Justification, Storytelling, Teamwork

Primarily used as a challenge in performance, Should Have Said also can be of great value in a workshop or practice setting.

In this game, players first and foremost must establish the context of their scene. Once they have a solid platform for the story to be built upon, the leader/emcee will periodically ring a bell as the scene progresses. Whenever the bell is rung, the last line of dialogue must be altered or replaced. The new line must then be immediately justified within the given circumstances of the scene.

Player 1:	But why were you looking through my window?
Player 2:	I was bird watching.
	(Ding!)
	I was fixing your siding.
	(Ding!)
	I... I've never stopped loving you.

What began as a moderately creepy exchange about a peeping Tom was, in the space of two dings, transformed into a potentially heart-wrenching tale of unrequited love. The more practice players have at justifying these changes (changes that essentially amount to an offer from space, by the way) to a scene, the stronger they will become at all aspects of storytelling in performance.

This is a really fun challenge to use in a practice session or workshop to try to drive that point home.

Story Ball

Skills Targeted:
Concentration, Listening, Mime, Storytelling, Teamwork

Story Ball is a very versatile game, used to force your performers to truly focus on storytelling. It can also be easily adapted to target different skill areas or to be effective for different age levels. I have used it successfully with not only my oldest of groups, but also with kids as young as kindergarten.

As the name implies, the game is all about effective storytelling.

One player, holding a ball, will begin telling a story but will cut off right in the middle of a key point. They will then toss the ball to another player who will immediately continue the story where it was left off.

The process continues until the story ends or the leader draws it to a close.

Player 1:	Once upon a time there was a man named Frank. Frank was always a pretty happy guy, but today was something special. Today he was...
Player 2:	Finally getting his teeth fixed. He had been ashamed of his teeth since he was a small child, and being such a

	happy guy, it was rough to be self-conscious when he smiled. Anyway, today he finally had his dentist appointment. But on the way to the dentist he...
Player 3:	Tripped on the sidewalk and fell down. It really hurt. Fortunately...
Player 4:	A beautiful woman stopped to help him up. "Are you ok?" she asked. "Nothing bruised but my ego," Frank replied, attempting to be witty. As she turned to leave, Frank stopped her, saying...

Notice that players can contribute bits of any length to the game. What's important is that all participants are fully focused on advancing the story and are intently listening to the other players.

With more seasoned performers, the game is the most effective when players are forbidden from being funny. As soon as the urge to impress each other with their razor sharp wit has been removed, it's amazing how well group members can focus on telling a good story.

With very young players, just keeping the story moving at all can be an accomplishment – small children don't always think in a perfectly linear narrative form. That's ok. Let them tell their story, however it turns out, and it can become a lesson on teamwork or giving focus.

That said, perhaps you have a particularly gifted group that is consistently quite good at advancing a story in their scene work.

GREAT!

The game can easily be adapted to require:

> ➤ *players to <u>always</u> be funny...*
> ➤ *or to follow an alphabetical pattern...*
> ➤ *or to include sub-vocal sound effects...*
> ➤ *or to be told entirely through gibberish – Ha! Try advancing a story clearly with that one!*

There is a lot of fun to be had with Story Ball.

Things I have learned from Story Ball:

- It's amazing how much second graders enjoy stories about pizza and poop.

- Performers of any age love to kill off characters -- only to then realize that leaves the story nowhere to go. Don't let them do it.

- No one – and I do mean <u>no one</u> – has very good aim while they are also thinking about telling a story. Make sure you are using a soft ball.

- Players always want Story Ball to become a round of Mad Libs. The point of filling in the last player's thought is to come up with something that makes sense, not something that is nonsense. Don't let it become random.

- I really like perogies.

This Is a Duck

Skills Targeted:

Concentration, Listening, Teamwork, Verbal Prowess

This Is a Duck is a really fun game that can help to improve listening and focus in groups of most skill levels.

Please note: despite its Brownie Camp Campfire sounding framework, it really is a bit too involved for truly young players. Unless you're trying to frustrate them, keep it away from the wee ones.

Grade Four to adult, however – Game On!

The players begin by sitting in a circle. One player is handed an object. As the object is passed around the circle, a bit of quick rhythmic dialogue is exchanged between players.

Player 1:	This is a duck.
Player 2:	A what?
Player 1:	A duck.
Player 2:	A what?
Player 1:	A duck.
Player 2:	Oh! A duck! *(Player 2 takes the duck.)*

As you can see the pattern takes exactly four measures of two beats each to complete. The second player then turns to the next person in the circle and repeats the pattern.

The pattern continues all the way around the group until everyone has passed the duck and all members have learned the rhythm. It may seem a little silly at first to your players, but remember – this is the tutorial level! They'll be thankful for being this explicit towards the end of the exercise.

Now start the pass again. This time when the duck gets halfway around the circle, introduce a second object. "This is a shoe." Now that two objects are being passed around the circle at the same time, players have to listen a little better.

Now it really starts to get interesting. Add two more objects at the halfway points between the two that are already being passed. "This is a ball." "This is a book." And so forth.

Eventually you should end up with as many objects as there are players in the game. Try to visualize how that works. Can you see why it's so awesome at increasing focus yet? Players have to be able to maintain two conversations and perform two actions at the <u>same time</u>. They are passing one object and receiving a different one simultaneously.

A moment of Player 2's dialogue, for example, would go something like...

Player 2:	*(to Player 3)* This is a duck.
	(to Player 1) A what?
	(to Player 3) A duck.
	(to Player 1) A what?
	(to Player 3) A duck.
	(to Player 1) Oh! A <u>shoe</u>!
	(to Player 3) This is a shoe.

Keep this up in the circle for long enough and somebody's brain is guaranteed to spontaneously combust.**

I should also add that usually when I choose to do this activity, I use objects that are actually the same as what we are saying they are as they get passed around (a small, stuffed duck for duck, for example.)

However, if you really want to get advanced on this one, try naming the objects as something <u>other</u> than what they are. Have players pass a ball and say it's a shoe. Or pass a pen and say it's a birdcage.

Anything that forces players to have to listen more carefully is only going to help them in the long run.

**Spontaneous combustion guarantee not valid in the U.S. or abroad.
Don't believe everything you read, ok?

What Are You Doing? (also a great Warm-up!)

Skills Targeted:
Concentration, Embodiment, Listening/Being in the Moment,
Mime, Physicality, Taking Direction

This incredibly well known theatre game is an improv "must-have." It manages to simultaneously workout a performer's physicality, listening skills and concentration all while being immensely fun. A trifecta of awesome!

TEACHING AND PERFORMING IMPROV

To participate, players pair up and take turns asking each other what they are doing. The player who asked the question then must mime the activity that the other player described.

As you can see...

Player 1:	What are you doing?
Player 2:	I'm brushing my teeth. *(Player 1 begins to mime brushing their teeth.)* What are you doing?
Player 1:	*(Without stopping brushing.)* I'm hopping on one foot. *(Player 2 begins to hop.)* What are you doing?
Player 2:	*(Still hopping.)* I'm painting a portrait. *(Player 1 begins to paint.)* What are you doing?
Player 1:	*(Still painting.)* I'm driving a Ferrari. *(Player 2 begins to drive.)* What are you doing?
Player 2:	*(Still driving.)* I'm reenacting every scene from *Gone with the Wind*. *(Player 1 begins to alternate between Rhett and Scarlett.)* What are you doing?
Player 1:	*(Still not birthing no babies.)* I'm constructing the universe at the subatomic level. *(Player 2 begins to play God.)*

And so on...

Notice that the game has a bit of an element of pimping to it as players try to devise new and unusual activities for their partner to be obliged to act out.

For my money, though, I think that the best element of the game is that players must fully commit to performing one action while being able to simultaneously think of and then verbalize that they are doing another. This is one of those games that can give you the best kind of concentration numbness. It's a thing of beauty.

In a workshop situation, I would begin with an example round and then have folks partner up so that everyone can be involved at the same time. If working with a team, then perhaps a What Are You

Doing? circle is a better match, in which players complete the activity as a group, performing the action given to them by the previous player in the circle. I've also used it as a group activity performed for others in which participants complete the exercise in a line formed across the performance space.

They're all good variations.

Yes, And ...

Not only is "Yes, and…" the most important concept in all of improv, having your performers (especially newer ones) explicitly present a literal rendition of the idea can also make for a great Tune-up activity.

The "Yes, and..." principle is the foundation upon which all of improv is built. It is the basic idea that in order to create story, players will always accept the offers presented by other performers and then add new information to build upon those offers. As I'm sure you've noticed, I personally like to call this idea "agree and embellish," but for the most part that's just because I prefer to be pretentiously wordy.

As an activity, a round of Yes, And... simply consists of two players creating a scene, however they are also required to incorporate the act of literally saying "Yes, and" to their fellow player as the plot develops.

Player 1:	So Mark, I haven't seen you around the bar lately.
Player 2:	<u>Yes</u>, you're right, I haven't been here. <u>And</u> that's because I've had to work so hard to pay off Johnny's medical bills.

Player 1:	<u>Yes</u>, they do charge an arm and a leg, don't they? <u>And</u> that comment would have been a whole lot funnier if Johnny hadn't lost that arm and leg in the accident.
Player 2:	<u>Yes</u>, it would have. <u>And</u> I just don't know how Betty and I will get by now.
Player 1:	<u>Yes</u>, it sure is hard. <u>And</u> how long has Betty been out of work, anyway?

You get the idea.

As you can see, because each player is required to actually use the words "Yes" and "And," they have no choice but to follow through on advancing the scene. Just look at how much information we learned about our two characters in the example in just five short lines of dialogue, even with the inclusion of a terrible joke.

Like Last Letter/First Letter, this game works very well when pairs are limited to an exchange of only ten lines. Try adding the extra challenge of seeing how much information a group can reveal to us about their characters in such a short space of time. Nine times out of ten your players won't disappoint.

This is an especially useful activity to use with new performers. It also pairs well with fish, red meat, and a round of 3 Line Scenes.

CHAPTER FOUR:
TIME TO GET UP! - THE CHALLENGES

I feel that I must preface this section of improv challenges (aka "handles") by stating that while I did specifically choose the games in this section to use when working with improvisers with limited or moderate experience (i.e. my target audience – secondary education students), this list should not by any means be considered to be all-inclusive.

With improv groups around the world constantly developing new work, the assortment of challenges that are out there has grown exponentially since I was first handed a meager list of ten when I was a high school student in Virginia (and that list was a bad photocopy of a 1981 list that originated at Vancouver TheatreSports).

The challenges that follow are the ones that I have found to be the *most* successful when I've worked with middle and high school performers over the years. I feel I should also again mention that the challenges contained in this section, unless otherwise noted, are not of my own creation, but rather are used extensively by the greater improv community at large.

This section is separated into two main categories of challenges.

I have called the first one "Team Challenges." These are games that are best suited toward a standard group of three to five improvisers.

The second category, "Large Group Challenges" contains those that work best with groupings of more than five – big surprise. Please note that when performed in front of an audience, the large group challenges should only be done with smaller groups (probably nothing larger than fifteen participants) or else either chaos or boredom will likely ensue. For those challenges that can work equally well in both standard and large group situations, I have tried to group them together with their most likely counterparts, or illustrated the differences in each section. I also tacked on a brief section of good tie-breaker challenges at the very end.

The term "variables" refers to any information provided by the audience.

A "standard set" of variables is made up of a location, occupation, and object.

Remember though, that variables can be (in most cases) anything at all that you like – brand of cereal, worst place for a date, nickname for a loved one, excuses for cannibalism – anything. They serve as the fodder for the scene, so the actors have some direction as to where they should take their story.

The questions used to get this information are referred to as "ask-fors," as in you are ASKing the audience FOR information (see Appendix D – Suggestions for Ask-Fors).

In the descriptions of each challenge, I have also attempted to note any differences between the class/workshop use of a challenge and that in a performance situation. Virtually every challenge included in this portion of the book is appropriate to use in either environment.

Also, unless otherwise stated in the description, all scenes should last between two and four minutes, based primarily on audience response.

Enjoy.

A COLLECTION OF IMPROV CHALLENGES FOR BOTH REHEARSAL/WORKSHOP AND PERFORMANCE/COMPETITION

Section One:
Team Challenges

Actor's Nightmare (aka "Playbook")

This game shares its name with the Christopher Durang play that dramatizes the recurring nightmare that afflicts virtually every actor - the "I'm in the middle of a performance of a familiar play, but I have absolutely no idea what I am doing" dream.

In this challenge, which is really only effective with a pair of performers, one player will read all of his/her lines from a script, while the other player must justify those lines within the context of the variables provided by the audience, forming a somewhat coherent scene.

Preparation:

You'll need to provide a script for one of the actors. In a class/workshop setting, just grabbing any play off of a shelf and flipping to a random page will do. For a performance, however, there are two bits of prep work that I highly recommend.

First, prepare the script for the actor on book by marking the starting and stopping point of the scene and highlighting the lines that they will read. If you don't know why, just ask anyone who has ever sat through a cold reading of a script with inexperienced actors. Whoa, Nelly! Since this will be in front of an audience, you don't want to leave anything to chance.

Second, to get the most bang for your buck, choose a selection that will be familiar to a large number of people in the audience – a famous scene from a famous play – or choose the climactic moment from a play that was recently performed in the area. By adding the extra element of familiarity to the spectators, you are doing everything that you can to help cement the success of the performers.

Performance:

In my experience, this one works best as a cross-team challenge. Get one player to represent each team (purely for non-competitive fun) and select who will be on the script and who must justify the lines. (Personally, I like to use a random method like flipping a coin or guessing a number to determine responsibilities.) Then get the variables from the audience.

While there are many possible types of variables that will work, just giving the players a list of nouns isn't really all that helpful. I find that to be the most effective in the shortest amount of time, players should be given a full platform, involving a relationship between the two characters and a conflict (i.e. best friends that like the same girl).

Providing the actors with a solid base upon which to build the scene will only strengthen their performance of a game based upon a gimmick.

Success:
A group is successful if they are able to justify the events of the scene in a manner that still makes some degree of sense – usually to the massive delight of an audience. I have yet to do this challenge publicly and have it not be a high point of the evening.

Use This Challenge For:
- Classroom/Workshop – Major Skills Practiced:
    o Justification
    o Listening/Being in the Moment
    o Teamwork (involves Chivalry, Finding The Game, etc)
    o Verbal Prowess
- Team Practice
- Single Group Performance
- Inter-Group Competition (Non-Competitive Round – cross-team challenge)

Alliteration

In this challenge, players are assigned a letter of the alphabet that they must incorporate into the scene by using as many words as possible that begin with that letter. A popular variation of the challenge is to assign each member of the team a different letter.

Preparation:
None

Performance:
This is a challenge for a single improv team. Get the letter (or letters) to assign the players from the audience. I find it works best when the letters are consonants – AND it seems almost obligatory that when each player is given a different letter, most of the performers should be assigned a common letter like r, s, or t, while one performer gets stuck with x or z. Then get a set of variables for them to build the scene around. The scene already has a built-in gimmick, so although audiences will remain lukewarm to an average performance, they will usually go wild for an all-out success.

This can also make for an interesting tie-breaker during a competition. Get one member from each team and assign both players a letter. Then split the audience in half and assign each performer to a portion of the audience. Give them the context for a sixty or ninety second scene and have the audience count the number of words used. The highest number wins.

Success:
The more words – the merrier! The single, daunting, measure of success for Alliteration is simply how many words that a player can use at a given time and still remain coherent. This is a very challenging game for most high school students, as their personal vocabularies are still very much works in progress. In fact, performers are often only able to provide a single word beginning with their assigned letter per sentence. Adults usually fare (slightly) better.

Despite its inherent obstacles, or perhaps because of them, a run-on sentence that ends up using a dozen words or more (i.e. "Sure Steve, suppose Sally steadfastly said sanctimoniously some sailors steadily sweat salty secretions. So?") will usually receive a thunderous reaction.

This is one that can almost make a young performer's brain explode from over-concentration, so don't let them forget to be physical. Even though the parameters of the challenge are verbal, the performers must still present an active and engaging scene for the audience.

Use This Challenge For:
- Classroom/Workshop – Major Skills Practiced:
    - Concentration
    - Listening/Being in the Moment
    - Physicality
    - Storytelling
    - Teamwork (involves Chivalry, Finding The Game, etc)
    - Verbal Prowess
- Team Practice
- Single Group Performance (only if mastered)
- Inter-Group Competition (Competitive Round – only with advanced groups)
- Inter-Group Competition (Tie-Breaker)

Alphabet Scene

In this challenge, each line spoken must begin with the next letter of the alphabet.

Preparation:
None

Performance:
After having tried this game with groups of many sizes, I can attest with absolute certainty that this is a challenge that works best when

performed by two players <u>only</u>. It is all but impossible for any but the most skilled professionals to produce anything more than a scene of talking heads once a third (or fourth, or fifth ...) player is added.

A typical Alphabet Scene could begin as such:

Player 1:	(A)	Al, I haven't seen you around here lately.
Player 2:	(B)	Been staying at home mostly.
Player 1:	(C)	Can't say I've seen your family, either.
Player 2:	(D)	Don't start with me, Martha.
Player 1:	(E)	Enough! I know you're two-timing me!
Player 2:	(F)	Fine! Do I have to say it?
Player 1:	(G)	Go on, get it out of your system.

And so on. The scene as performed above would conclude (naturally) when the players reach Z.

I personally enjoy getting a letter somewhere in the middle of the alphabet from the audience and using it as both the starting and ending point of the dialogue. In addition to the letter to be used, the audience should also provide a platform for the scene, preferably a relationship between the two performers and a conflict. The scene should take no longer than ninety seconds to present, and is often timed.

Although I prefer to use other challenges for this purpose, I've also witnessed Alphabet Scene effectively used as a tie-breaker. In this fashion, results are typically based on an audience vote for which team did the better job - so if you're not careful, things can easily get a bit muddy. Not a big deal for a single team performance or a mock-competition, but if groups are truly competing against one another, it's better to keep things as objective as possible.

Success:
This challenge is all about keeping the scene moving – advance, advance, advance! Audiences tend to be more impressed by a scene with a brisk pace, rather than one that is completely coherent and will

usually be very forgiving when a player says "exactly" as an X word or "Why" as a Y word. Consequently, it is imperative to avoid long pauses in the dialogue. If one player on a team is blanking on what to say ("I just can't think of a 't' word!), it then becomes the other's job to jump in and keep the action going.

This challenge is also a real "brain-buster," from a concentration standpoint. It always amazes me how quickly players forget the alphabet once they are asked to remember it in a high pressure situation, like at a competition or during a performance. Despite this wear and tear on one's mental faculties, players must somehow continue to be very physical and remain within the context of the scene. This, however, is much easier said than done, and for most players it takes a great deal of work to master. A team that can manage to perform at a quick pace while maintaining a solid amount of physical action is sure to be adored by one and all.

A Final Bit of Caution:
While certainly true for all of the challenges included in the book, it is extremely important that a team is well practiced at Alphabet Scene prior to attempting it in front of an audience. (I even knew an improv team that went so far as to have the alphabet printed upside down on their team shirts ... so they could read it while performing).

Use This Challenge For:
- Classroom/Workshop – Major Skills Practiced:
    o Concentration
    o Justification
    o Listening/Being in the Moment
    o Physicality
    o Storytelling
    o Teamwork (involves Chivalry, Finding The Game, etc)
    o Verbal Prowess
- Team Practice
- Single Group Performance
- Inter-Group Competition (Non-Competitive Round – cross-team challenge)
- Inter-Group Competition (Tie-Breaker)

Arms

While this challenge comes in many varieties, one thing remains the same in all versions – one player will need to provide the arms for another.

This can be performed as a monologue or any number of scenes.

Preparation:
- Variations One and Two require nothing.
- Variation Three requires many supplies to be ready – see performance description.
- Variation Four requires chairs.

Performance:
There are four basic variations to performing a round of Arms.

Variation One: *Arms Monologue*
In this challenge for two performers, one player will deliver a monologue of approximately ninety seconds based on variables provided by the audience, while firmly placing their arms behind their back. The second (non-speaking) player stands immediately behind the first and performs all the arm gestures for the monologue.

A great choice for classes/workshops, single team events, and inter-group non-competitive rounds.

Variation Two: *Arms Scene*
An Arms Scene is essentially just a standard improv scene based on variables from the audience.

With a group of four, the setup is easy – two players do all of the speaking in the scene and the two other players provide their arms. It becomes a tad more complicated with teams of three or five members, however, who have three options of how to proceed.

Option 1:	The group can get into pairs and leave the odd member out as a solo.
Option 2:	A pair of actors can work together, each providing one arm for the third.
Option 3:	One player can act as the arms for two actors who become a set of conjoined twins, often speaking only one word at a time as performers would in a round of Two Heads.

(The last option only works really well if the two performers are small-framed, or the arm provider has a freakishly long reach.)

Great for classes/workshops, single team events, and inter-group competitive rounds.

<u>Variation Three</u>: *Arms Assault*
This is the format of Arms that was popularized on the American version of *Whose Line is it Anyway?* and is done with three performers.

One player becomes a reporter/interviewer while the other two become the subject of the interview (one as the speaker, one as the arms). The interview takes place behind a table upon which an assortment of items have been placed – usually the messier and more edible the better (the necessary preparation I mentioned earlier). During the course of the interview, the person providing the arms essentially does all sorts of awkward or gross things to the person speaking (see *pimping* in the glossary).

This is a scene that can be hilarious, but should also be quick – keep it under two minutes. A rather unpleasant choice for classes/workshops, this version really only works well at single team events.

<u>Variation Four</u>: *Experts with Arms*
My personal favorite version of Arms, this one only works with a group of five improvisers.

Two players become experts on subjects provided by the audience, two players become their arms (this works best when seated, at least at the start of the scene), and the last player becomes the host of a talk show. The host interviews the two experts, opens the floor up for questions from the audience, or can even pause for a commercial break.

When done well, this is often one of the longer challenges in the course of a performance – often exceeding the five minute mark. This variation can work well in any of the different performance/workshop formats.

Other Variations:
It is easily conceivable that Arms could be combined with many other challenges to add an extra twist. Don't feel limited to simply what I've included here. Improv challenges are in a constant state of evolution – so play around with them, dang it!

Success:
Being successful with the gimmick of this challenge hinges upon a strong connection between what one person is saying and what the other person is doing. – the better the marriage, the stronger the audience response. It is important to note that either party can control the direction of the scene. The key is strong teamwork – the more convincing it is that the two people are actually one, the better. Oh, and let's not neglect the obvious (but always crowd- pleasing) tricks like scratching an itch, biting one's nails, or picking a player's nose.

It is very important to remain physical in this challenge – no small feat with the awkwardness of the positions the actors have to be in for this one. Dance-offs, modeling gigs, and the like are always fun.

A big word of warning needs to be interjected here, however. Inexperienced improvisers, when given an Arms scene, often immediately allow it to degenerate into a slap fight. While amusing for about two whole seconds, this quickly becomes off-putting for most audiences as they can't follow any story. Be sure to have a <u>no fighting</u> rule in place.

Use This Challenge For:
- Classroom/Workshop – Major Skills Practiced:
    - Audience Interaction
    - Endowments
    - Individual Confidence Building
    - Listening/Being in the Moment
    - Mime (Involves Space and Object Work, Naming, etc)
    - Physicality
    - Spatial Awareness
    - Teamwork (involves Chivalry, Finding The Game, etc)
- Team Practice
- Single Group Performance
- Inter-Group Competition (Competitive Round)
- Inter-Group Competition (Non-Competitive Round – cross-team challenge)

At The Movies

In this challenge, two players will become film critics who proceed to review either a single film or a series of multiple films. As they give their review, "clips" from the fictitious movie are enacted by the remaining group members. This challenge also can work well as a tribute to a fictitious actor or director.

Preparation:
Two chairs for the critics.

Performance:
The two critics should be seated center stage. In addition to a subject for the movie(s), get a relationship/conflict from the audience as an endowment for the critics (i.e. divorced couple arguing over who gets the dog). This conflict should come out only in passing and be related in some way to the movie(s) being reviewed. Once the scene and conflict have been established, the pair will begin describing setups

for specific scenes in the movie(s). The remaining players will act out those scenes.

As a general rule, the critics will give only a brief introduction to the clips, something like, "but then the mother-in-law arrived, and the movie just went downhill. Let's watch ..." and then let the players acting out the clip decide how the rest will go. A complete scene should usually have a total of three clips and then end with some sort of sign-off from the critics.

Success:
While it is very important to use the movie variables correctly, the central component to a successful round of At The Movies is the chemistry between the two critics. The dynamic that exists between the two of them provides a massive opportunity for laughs with this one. The challenge also provides a great chance to set up clips that border on the absurd, or are at least humorously embarrassing for the actors performing them. Letting the audience see you squirm just a bit can make them even more responsive when you eventually succeed.

Because of the more elaborate setup of this challenge, a typical scene runs around four minutes.

Use This Challenge For:
- Classroom/Workshop – Major Skills Practiced:
  o Endowments
  o Listening/Being in the Moment
  o Physicality
  o Spatial Awareness
  o Taking Direction
  o Teamwork (involves Chivalry, Finding The Game, etc)
- Team Practice
- Single Group Performance
- Inter-Group Competition (Competitive Round)
- Inter-Group Competition (Non-Competitive Round – cross-team challenge)

Body Leads

In addition to receiving a regular set of variables, in Body Leads each performer is also assigned a part of the body that all of the player's movement must originate from.

Preparation:
None.

Performance:
The presentation of this challenge is pretty straightforward. Players are on their own to develop a solid story using the variables provided while having the added burden of originating all movement from their assigned areas. There are two schools of thought, however, that players seem to use to attack the physical requirements of this particular challenge.

The first approach involves rampant justification – usually <u>over</u>-justification – of the body lead areas. The leaps of imagination involved in being able to successfully justify the absurdity of player's movements can lead to some absolutely hilarious moments. So what exactly is a believable reason for why you just pointed at my hairy mole with your butt?

The second approach is exactly the opposite of the first – intentional <u>under</u>-justification. The lack of explanation given for such bizarre movements can often be a source (albeit a frequently unreliable one) of great humor.

Success:
This is a challenge that is obviously all about physicality. Well to be more specific, it's about being able to maintain solid <u>storytelling</u> while also dealing with the enhanced level of physicality. It's no great bit of advice to say that each round should always have one team member originating movement from their ear or nose, a few members with spots on their arms and legs, and one from the butt – because

90% of the time, this is exactly what will happen anyway. (Or outside of a school environment, sometimes other obviously amusing locations on the body may be suggested.)

What might be useful, however, is how exactly to approach the justification issue. The greatest degree of success in this challenge seems to come when teams use a hybrid of the two methods described above – some moments of extreme justification within the body of a scene in which everyone is simply moving around in bizarre ways. This allows the most opportunity for zaniness to occur while still being easily grounded in a solid story.

When done well, this challenge can bring down the house.

Use This Challenge For:
- Classroom/Workshop – Major Skills Practiced:
    o Embodiment
    o Justification
    o Physicality
    o Storytelling (involves Making/Accepting Offers, Advancing, Extending, etc)
    o Taking Direction
    o Teamwork (involves Chivalry, Finding The Game, etc)
- Team Practice
- Single Group Performance
- Inter-Group Competition (Competitive Round)
- Inter-Group Competition (Non-Competitive Round – cross-team challenge)

Boris

In this fun and challenging scene, Boris is an invisible torturer performing some form of an interrogation. The other players are the victims of said torture.

Preparation:
None, but teams often want to begin tied to chairs.

Performance:
There are essentially two ways that a round Boris can be performed.

In the first version, all of the players on the team are being tortured and Boris is completely invisible – he doesn't physically exist, except to inflict some degree of unpleasantness upon a player. In the second, one of the players becomes Boris on an offstage microphone and actively interacts with the group.

There are also two ways that the torture itself can be played. It could be done as a rather dark scene, in which genuine pain is inflicted upon the characters, building tension and suspense, but the mood is lightened through the player's physicalization or by the information gleaned through the torture. That organization could also be turned on its head and the scene be constructed so that the information is serious, but the instruments of torture themselves are humorous (spatulas, turkey basters, the complete works of the latest generic boy band, etc.).

Success:
This is a rather difficult challenge for inexperienced players, simply because there is a lot going on in it. The framework is a bit more complicated than most, it calls for a lot (and I mean a LOT) of mimed action, and actors must be willing to have very intense reactions to the torture – many games end with players missing limbs, for example.

Consequently, while Boris is a fantastic game for advanced groups, *don't pull this one on a group of newbies.*

No matter what performance setup choices the team makes, the most important element of a good Boris scene is solid space and object work. This can be an exhaustingly physical scene for a group to do (when done correctly), but it can also have great rewards in terms of audience response. For a team to succeed in the manner for which the scene was designed, its members must be very adept mimes.

Use This Challenge For:
- Classroom/Workshop – Major Skills Practiced:
    o Embodiment
    o Justification
    o Mime (Involves Space and Object Work, Naming, etc)
    o Physicality
    o Spatial Awareness
    o Storytelling (involves Making/Accepting Offers, Advancing, Extending, etc)
    o Teamwork (involves Chivalry, Finding The Game, etc)
- Team Practice
- Single Group Performance (only with advanced groups)
- Inter-Group Competition (Competitive Round – only with advanced groups)

Categories

Either the entire team or each player on the team is assigned a category (i.e. cars, foods, etc) by the audience. They must incorporate as many examples of that category into the scene as possible.

Preparation:
None

Performance:
Overall a very straightforward scene based on variables from the audience. The single trick to a solid performance is to be able to continually advance the story while still using examples of the category.

This is a gimmick that, as far as entertainment value is concerned, will essentially take care of itself so long as the performers keep actively interjecting the category, so in order to keep the audience focused, the actor's attention should be placed firmly upon the story.

This is also a great tie-breaker. Get one member of each of the two tied teams to work together to create a two person scene based on audience supplied variables. Assign each of them a category. Also, divide the audience in half and assign each side the job of counting the number of examples mentioned by one of the players. The performer with the highest score after a ninety second scene is the winner.

Success:
Success in a round of categories is deceptively simple – just say a heck of a lot of examples of the category you are assigned, right? Of course, this is difficult, because as an improviser your primary responsibility is to always advance the scene. In other words, this is another challenge that asks the player to be able to think of two things at the same time (like Alphabet Game, for example).

The easiest way to succeed at any example of this type of challenge is simply to practice it a lot – primarily because you have to train your brain to be able to think in this "two-pronged" manner. Just like patting your head and rubbing your stomach is very difficult at first, with practice you can train your muscles to succeed at the task. Also, just like with the other "brain-buster" challenges, don't let your players forget to be <u>physical</u>.

Use This Challenge For:
- Classroom/Workshop – Major Skills Practiced:
  - Concentration
  - Justification
  - Physicality
  - Storytelling (involves Making/Accepting Offers, Advancing, Extending, etc)
  - Verbal Prowess
- Team Practice
- Single Group Performance
- Inter-Group Competition (Competitive Round)
- Inter-Group Competition (Tie-Breaker)

Chance of a Lifetime

In Chance of a Lifetime, an audience member is randomly selected and is questioned about something that they have always wanted to do, but haven't had the opportunity. The players then allow them to live out their fantasy through the magic of improv.

Preparation:
None, but chairs are often helpful.

Performance:
Always a ton of fun, this is a great addition to both single team shows and inter-group competitions (as a non-competitive round).

Simply choose an enthusiastic audience member and get them to come up on stage. Ask them a few questions to loosen them up – stuff about their lives, job, interests, etc. - then ask them the big one, "What is something that you have always wanted to do, but for some reason haven't?"

Once an answer is received, the group then works together to create a scene in which the audience member takes the central role and is allowed (read: forced!) to do the activity that they stated. This should be enacted as a full-fledged scene, with a solid story that contains a beginning, middle, and end, and climaxes at the performance of the activity. Because of the extended setup for this challenge, a typical performance runs five or six minutes.

Success:
Do everything possible to make the audience member look hysterical – the funniest person on Earth. The happier they are, the happier the rest of the audience will be. If the audience member is a great sport, then a little pimping is also a good idea. Have them perform some bit of awkward mime associated with the activity – the audience will eat up seeing one of their own succeed.

This challenge is always harder to do as an inter-group scene, simply because of the lack of familiarity with one's acting partners. The improv rules are always the same, though – give and take focus as needed. If a player has stellar ideas, they should voice them. If someone else does, the remainder of the performers should follow them full throttle. But whatever happens, the group must make sure to develop a strong story around the activity.

In other words, don't just jump out of the plane, but take the time to establish a scene around a character's fear of skydiving and subsequent triumph/celebration. If done well, this can actually get an audience cheering!

Use This Challenge For:
- Classroom/Workshop – Major Skills Practiced:
    - Audience Interaction
    - Embodiment
    - Endowments
    - Mime (Involves Space and Object Work, Naming, etc)
    - Physicality
    - Teamwork (involves Chivalry, Finding The Game, etc)
- Team Practice
- Single Group Performance
- Inter-Group Competition (Non-Competitive Round – cross-team challenge)

Counting Words

In a round of Counting Words, each of the players will be assigned a number between 1 and 10. Each sentence that the player speaks must contain that given number of words.

(Not to be confused with One Word Scene, in which the audience provides a word that becomes the only word that players can use in a scene.)

TEACHING AND PERFORMING IMPROV

Preparation:
None required, but taping signs with player's numbers on them can be a nice touch.

Performance:
This scene is really all about a pretty simple gimmick – the word limitation – so success in performance becomes all about telling a coherent story. Get a set of variables from the audience, then get the number of words that each player is allowed to say. Invariably, one team member will be assigned the number one and another will be assigned nine or ten. Occasionally, some wiseguy in the audience will yell out zero – use it! That player must then do everything as a very forceful mime.

Success:
This can be an incredibly fun challenge to perform and watch. Likely the hardest part for most new performers will be resisting the urge to allow one team member to drive the scene. Rather, players must learn how to allow the person saying only one word at a time to have as much control over the direction of the performance as the person saying ten. Each player must always focus on advancing, advancing, advancing.

Think about how cool it would be to be the person only saying one word. Literally every word you say is an offer!

Players really need to make sure that they stick to their number, though. Audiences will be keeping track, and if there is a player that consistently messes up, they can be very unforgiving. Also unless one can make it work as a joke, it is best if you don't have to count the number of words on your fingers – leave that to the audience who, once again, will always be checking the players work.

Use This Challenge For:
- Classroom/Workshop – Major Skills Practiced:
  - Concentration
  - Justification
  - Listening/Being in the Moment

- o Storytelling (involves Making/Accepting Offers, Advancing, Extending, etc)
- o Teamwork (involves Chivalry, Finding The Game, etc)
- o Verbal Prowess
- Team Practice
- Single Group Performance
- Inter-Group Competition (Competitive Round)

Dr. Know-It-All

Three players will become "Dr. Know-It-All," a character that literally does know it <u>all</u>, and will attempt to answer questions posed by the audience, each providing one word at a time.

Preparation:
Three chairs would be nice, but are not essential.

Performance:
Three players, either seated or standing, will form a line and become the character of Dr. Know-It-All. The remaining player(s) will take on the persona of a talk show moderator(s) who will explain who Dr. Know-It-All is and begin to solicit questions from members of the audience. If there are no other team members left to moderate, then the host will take on this role.

The performers playing the good Doctor will then attempt to address the questions posed by the audience, each speaking only one word at a time, trying to create complete thoughts by working together.

Player/Host:	Who has a question for Dr. Know-It-All?
Audience Member:	What can we do to stop global warming?
Player/Host:	Ahhh, an excellent question that concerns us all. Dr. Know-It-All, what <u>can</u> we do to stop the effects of global warming?

Player 1:	We...		
Player 2:		can...	
Player 3:			all...
Player 1:	wear...		
Player 2:		more...	
Player 3:			hats...
Player 1:	and...		
Player 2:		sometimes...	
Player 3:			eat...
Player 1:	lots...		
Player 2:		of...	
Player 3:			Candy!
Player/Host:	Eat lots of candy? Dr. Know-It-All, how will that help?		
Player 1:	It...		
Player 2:		couldn't...	
Player 3:			hurt!

After about five or six questions, the premise is a bit played out, and the challenge should be concluded.

This game is also a fantastic tune-up exercise for groups of any experience level. I've used it quite successfully with elementary-aged students who usually think it's a blast. Most of them get so excited when it's their turn to be the Doctor!

It is also a welcome game at any workshop where it can be a great way to illustrate to participants the importance of listening to each other and working together, in this case by creating coherent thoughts. The only difference between trying to make a complete sentence together one word at a time and making a complete story one offer at a time is the scope of the task. By demonstrating to players that they can easily be successful at agreeing and embellishing on this simpler level, you will help to build the confidence that they need in themselves to be able to succeed at their more advanced scene work.

Success:
It all depends upon listening.

Easily, the most important factor to being successful in a round of Dr. Know-It-All will be a team's listening skills. Players must be able to simultaneously listen to each other while maintaining a strong mental focus on the question that was asked. A player that cannot do this will be unable to answer a question to an audience's satisfaction.

However, just to make matters a bit more complicated, the best "answers" don't really answer the question honestly. Instead, while they are formulated as if they were a complete and coherent response, the content of that response should obviously be silly.

A good gimmick to try on the fourth or fifth question in a round is for the first player to quickly provide a single, definitive, one-word answer. It mixes up the rhythm and pumps a bit more life into the challenge. The team can then elaborate on the response after the fact.

Player/Host:	Dr. Know-It-All, how does one prevent a shark attack?
Player 1:	Spam!
Player/Host:	I'm sorry, did you say Spam? How would that prevent a shark attack?
Player 1:	Spam…
Player 2:	in…
Player 3:	your…
Player 1:	swimsuit.
Player 2:	They…
Player 3:	hate…
Player 1:	that…
Player 2:	stuff!

Dr. Know-It-All is a great exercise in teamwork and a great challenge to force some instant camaraderie among strangers.

Use This Challenge For:
- Classroom/Workshop – Major Skills Practiced:
    o Audience Interaction
    o Concentration
    o Individual Confidence Building
    o Listening/Being in the Moment
    o Storytelling (involves Making/Accepting Offers, Advancing, Extending, etc)
    o Teamwork (involves Chivalry, Finding The Game, etc)
    o Verbal Prowess
- Team Practice
- Single Group Performance
- Inter-Group Competition (Non-Competitive Round – cross-team challenge)

Dubbing/Double Talk

In a round of Dubbing, two players act out a scene onstage speaking only in gibberish. Two other players provide translations of their dialogue from offstage. This framework is the same for Double Talk, except in that version one player provides the voices for *all* of the other team members.

Preparation:
None

Performance:
Decide who will be translating and who will be speaking in gibberish. Then get a set of variables from the audience that must be used in the scene. One of the most fun aspects of this particular challenge is that both the gibberish-speakers and the translators have equal

opportunities for advancing the scene. In addition, there is a <u>lot</u> of justification work that goes on here.

Success:
The biggest key to success in Dubbing or Double Talk is for the gibberish-speakers to be sure to <u>wait for the translation</u> before continuing. For beginning performers, however, this is much easier said than done. Imagine having a conversation in a cavern and having to wait for the echo to completely finish reverberating before you can speak again. That's what performing this scene can feel like. There is a constant stop-start rhythm that players must get used to in order to be successful.

Another aspect to be aware of is that because the central players are always waiting for a translation, there is a tendency for them to freeze their actions frequently and to severely limit their movement to isolated areas of the stage. While it is advisable to remain on the same half of the performance space while being translated, that by no means gives a player permission to limit their physicality – if anything it needs to be increased to include heightened space object work, since they are only speaking in gibberish!

Also, as with all gibberish scenes, vocalization needs to be a big emphasis. Players cannot forget to use their tone of voice to let the audience know what it is that they are saying.

Lots of inflection combined with solid mime will significantly strengthen a Dubbing/Double Talk scene.

Lastly, performers can't neglect the give and take relationship between the gibberish-speaker and the translator. *Either* player has the exact same opportunity to advance the scene as the other AND the offers made should be <u>equally</u> divided between the two sides of this challenge.

And, of course, don't forget the familiar gimmicks of an extended bit of gibberish with a one word translation, or the opposite. Sparingly, these are always crowd pleasers.

Use This Challenge For:
- Classroom/Workshop – Major Skills Practiced:
  - Concentration
  - Justification
  - Listening/Being in the Moment
  - Mime (Involves Space and Object Work, Naming, etc)
  - Physicality
  - Storytelling (involves Making/Accepting Offers, Advancing, Extending, etc)
  - Teamwork (involves Chivalry, Finding The Game, etc)
  - Verbal Prowess
  - Vocalization
- Team Practice
- Single Group Performance
- Inter-Group Competition (Competitive Round)
- Inter-Group Competition (Non-Competitive Round – cross-team challenge)

Emotional Boundaries

In this particular challenge, the stage will be divided into either three or four zones (three would span across the width of the stage, while four would turn the stage into a grid). Each zone is then endowed with a particular emotion and as the players move about the stage they must adopt the emotion of the particular zone that they are in.

Preparation:
None, unless you would like to use tape to divide the stage into areas.

Performance:
Get a set of variables from the audience, and then get the emotional states. As a general rule, stick primarily to bold emotional choices, so that performers have some good meat to work with. Once that is completed, the scene is pretty straightforward, however, as with other "brain-buster" challenges that ask the player to think in a dual-

pronged method, it often becomes easy to abandon the story in favor of simply playing the emotion via huge reactions.

Success:
Emotional shifts should be very bold, BUT always in line with the story. Remember that the first question is always "Does this advance the scene?" not "Is this funny?" Simply playing on the emotional extremes will garner a player a few good reactions at first, then a whole lot of uncomfortable silence. Believe me – that's a very unpleasant feeling.

That said, it is also important not to let this scene simply become a lot of people yelling at each other, as can often happen with inexperienced improvisers. It gets really old, really fast. Variety is a major characteristic of what allows something to continue to be funny, so players need to be sure to utilize all of their vocal levels.

In addition to vocal variety, the players must work very hard to justify all of the action taking place during this challenge. Why did that actor suddenly get so angry, or nervous, or depressed? Every transition must make sense in something close to a logical fashion.

Use This Challenge For:
- Classroom/Workshop – Major Skills Practiced:
  - Concentration
  - Endowments
  - Justification
  - Spatial Awareness
  - Storytelling (involves Making/Accepting Offers, Advancing, Extending, etc)
  - Vocalization
- Team Practice
- Single Group Performance
- Inter-Group Competition (Competitive Round)
- Inter-Group Competition (Non-Competitive Round – cross-team challenge)

Entrances and Exits

... All the world's a stage,
and all the men and women merely players.
They have their exits and their entrances,
and one man in his time plays many parts.

- Jaques, *As You Like It*

In this game, each player is assigned a word by the audience that might come up in casual conversation. Whenever that word is spoken by another player they must enter or exit the scene as appropriate.

Both entrances and exits must be fully justified.

Preparation:
None

Performance:
First get a set of variables from the audience, and then get the assigned words. Each player should be given a different word that may or may not be related to the other variables. The group then begins a scene, making sure to use the assigned words frequently in the conversation.

The key point to remember when performing this challenge is to always justify every entrance and exit. Invariably, someone will be assigned a word that comes up a lot like "the" and someone else will get one that feels forced to use, like "antidisestablishmentarianism." Players should milk them both.

Success:
There are a few big areas that can trip up performers with this one.

Allow me to itemize...

Listening:

It is amazing to me how often a player's word is said and they simply don't do anything. Why? Most likely, because they are planning ahead for themselves instead of truly listening to the other performers. In the improv world, this amounts to (at least) a venial sin. All team members must be listening very actively for this challenge to succeed.

Justification:

Especially the first time a group attempts this challenge, justification tends to be an issue. Characters can never simply just enter or leave a scene; there must be some reasonable explanation provided that fits within its context. Of course, what's reasonable in the improv world may differ slightly from real life, so although believability is awesome, the audience will likely relish a few reaches into the implausible.

Pace:

As the scene goes on, it should also speed up. At the beginning, keep the entrances and exits coming at a relatively sane tempo. Justify everything completely. Now that a baseline has been established, it becomes OK to deviate from it somewhat. Speed up, reach a little further with the justifications, and generally have fun! By the end, it is almost required to use the gimmick of pimping another player into constant entrances and exits by saying their word several times in a row. If they can successfully justify all of their actions, the audience reaction will be borderline riotous! If a scene can end naturally after such a stream of activity, it should.

Always leave them wanting more.

Use This Challenge For:
- Classroom/Workshop – Major Skills Practiced:
  - Concentration
  - Justification
  - Listening/Being in the Moment

- o Storytelling (involves Making/Accepting Offers, Advancing, Extending, etc)
- o Teamwork (involves Chivalry, Finding The Game, etc)
- Team Practice
- Single Group Performance (only if mastered)
- Inter-Group Competition (Competitive Round)
- Inter-Group Competition (Non-Competitive Round – cross-team challenge)

Experts

In a round of Experts, players will become an expert on a topic selected by the audience. Another player then interviews them in a talk show-like format about the chosen subject.

Preparation:
Needs chairs.

Performance:
There are several different performance formats that can be used for Experts.

Variation One: *Expert Talk Show*
The most widely used format is that of a talk show – one with three guests on separate topics, all of which are received from the audience. The host, then, will typically find a way to tie the topics together in some fashion during the course of the scene. The discussion can be opened up to questions from the audience or not, depending on how the scene is progressing. If there are five team members, the fifth usually provides a walk-thru, becomes a relative of one of the guests, or serves as an audience plant (that may or may not storm the stage - Jerry! Jerry!).

This is also essentially the same format that is used for Experts with Arms (see Arms, Variation Four).

Variation Two: *Panel of Experts*

A Panel of Experts scene is similar to a Talk Show, except that all the experts are related in some way to a particular field and have been convened for a purpose assigned to them by the audience. The Experts sub-expertise can either also be assigned to them by the audience or (far more likely) endowed by the moderator. The group then proceeds to have a lively discussion about the topic and either solve the dilemma or reach a humorous impasse. It is up to the moderator to determine if this is a closed session (for just the players) or a town hall style meeting (which includes questions from the audience), but no matter which style is used, the scene must attempt to resolve the issue at hand.

Variation Three: *Group Interview*

This is essentially a Panel of Experts in reverse. Here a single individual (the expert, once again on a topic supplied by the audience) is fielding questions from a larger group of inquisitors. This could be a Senate hearing, a press conference, a job interview, or any other situation in which this could occur. Here the audience does not have the option to ask questions, but depending on the situation used, could embody another "character" that the interviewee is trying to impress.

Variation Four: *Experts with Arms*

See Arms, Variation Four – Experts with Arms.

No matter which format is used, it is important that a single team member becomes the "leader" of the scene, even if there is not a defined "host," simply for the purposes of pacing. This is typically a longer scene, clocking in around five to six minutes.

Success:
First and foremost, the players must always maintain their field of expertise with complete confidence. Even if their answer to a question asked is appropriately idiotic, their character must believe that it is quite profound. In other words, the player must always commit fully to their offers and consequently to the scene.

Especially their first time doing this challenge, many inexperienced performers may suffer from the "Jeopardy Syndrome" (you know the answer on your couch, but in the hot seat it's a different story) and blank completely when it's their turn to provide answers – which consequently can lead to their breaking character.

Also, many novice improvisers simply provide answers (usually humorous) to the questions asked and nothing else. However, since the audience craves storytelling, performers must create a <u>fully realized character</u> to give the answers, even if (or especially if) it is a familiar stereotype.

It is amazing how much more engaging a response is from Alfred, the doddering old professor, or Crystal, the former beauty queen now turned bag lady, than it is from Team Member X. Don't forget to also endow the host/moderator/inquisitors with characteristics, too. If these areas are emphasized, then a story, or at the very least a conflict, will have a much better opportunity to develop through the answers provided.

Use This Challenge For:
- Classroom/Workshop – Major Skills Practiced:
  - Audience Interaction
  - Endowments
  - Justification
  - Listening/Being in the Moment
  - Mime (Involves Space and Object Work, Naming, etc)
  - Physicality
  - Storytelling (involves Making/Accepting Offers, Advancing, Extending, etc)
  - Taking Direction
  - Teamwork (involves Chivalry, Finding The Game, etc)
- Team Practice
- Single Group Performance
- Inter-Group Competition (Competitive Round)
- Inter-Group Competition (Non-Competitive Round – cross-team challenge)

Fortune Cookie

A very simple premise for a challenge. A fortune cookie is handed to the players, opened and read aloud. The scene performed must then be based upon the fortune in some fashion (i.e. as the philosophical base, an event that takes place during the scene, etc.).

Preparation:
Needs a box of fortune cookies.

Performance:
Normally in this scene, no variables are assigned by the audience, however they could be added if so desired. The fortune cookie is opened, read to the team and the audience, and the scene begins. This is a very basic scene framework that simply takes the ask-for out of the equation and replaces it with a cookie. It should be noted, though, that audiences usually think this scene is pretty cool when it is successful.

Success:
The entire success of this scene depends upon the team devising a strong story with engaging characters. Fortune cookies usually provide a good maxim to use as a theme for a scene (i.e. "It is the wise bird that guards his own nest"), but rarely provide an action (i.e. "You will be visited by a mysterious stranger") so most of the scene's development depends upon solid teamwork. It may be advisable with inexperienced performers to also provide a variable or two from the audience so that they have a few idea starters.

In my experience, every single time a team has failed at this challenge it is been due to poor storytelling – not agreeing and embellishing. It is imperative that the group continually advances the scene. This is a fantastic opportunity to create something truly original, so don't let players waste it.

This challenge also makes for a great workshop activity. See the Tune-up section for more ideas.

Use This Challenge For:
- Classroom/Workshop – Major Skills Practiced:
    o Justification
    o Storytelling (involves Making/Accepting Offers, Advancing, Extending, etc)
    o Teamwork (involves Chivalry, Finding The Game, etc)
- Team Practice
- Single Group Performance
- Inter-Group Competition (Competitive Round)

Freeze Tag

Ah, Freeze Tag... the granddaddy of all improv challenges. Freeze Tag is probably the very first challenge that I ever attempted as a student and if you already use improv, it is likely one of the first that you use with your students. This is for good reason.

Not only is it a great single team or competitive challenge, it also is one of the best activities for teaching students all about offers.

In Freeze Tag, two team members begin the challenge by performing a brief scene. Once the scene has been established, another team member calls out "freeze!" and those that are performing freeze in their positions. The team member who yelled "freeze" then replaces one of the members performing and begins a brand new unrelated scene. This process repeats indefinitely.

Preparation:
None

Performance:
I find that it usually helps to provide the first pair a single variable as a (shaky) platform for their scene. Once that scene has been established, others team members can begin to yell freeze and start new scenes.

The average scene within a round of Freeze Tag should last between five and ten seconds. If there is a host or emcee, they should be the one to bring the round to a close once it has fully run its course. The time needed for a round of Freeze Tag can vary significantly depending on the number of players involved, but in front of an audience, I'd limit it to three minutes or so.

Freeze Tag also makes for a great non-competitive round in a multi-team evening. I usually use it as a "start of the evening's proceedings" activity, but it can work its way into a show in many different places quite successfully. It is also an extremely beneficial activity to use in a classroom situation (see Chapter Three: Tune-ups).

Success:
Freeze Tag is all about making and accepting offers. In a Freeze Tag mini-scene, one player makes an offer that establishes a situation or defines a goal. The other player agrees with the context and then the scene is usually over. Most mini-scenes should last from two to five lines of dialogue, depending on the circumstances.

An important skill to master to be successful in Freeze Tag is *timing*.

In my classes one of two things will almost always initially happen when we begin work on this challenge. Most of the time the players are so enthusiastic that they jump all over each other, sometimes not even allowing one another to make offers at all. Other times, though, they are so timid that they allow a scene to go on and on and on, until prodded by me to freeze the action and get in there.

Students need to develop a fully ingrained sense of the rhythm of a scene – a feel for the pacing of a beat of action – so that they can react appropriately. It should be no surprise that developing this sense of beats translates into a better understanding of their traditional acting as well.

The other common pitfall novice improvisers experience with Freeze Tag is forgetting to be *physical*.

Because the mini-scenes are so brief, there is a common tendency for players to remain a group of talking heads, rather than do a whole lot with their bodies. However, if performers limit their commitment to the scene's action, then the remaining players have no fodder with which to work to develop their own offers, which are usually sparked by some sort of interesting physical position.

All said, there are good reasons why this is such a common challenge to use. Not only is it a lot of fun to watch and to do, but it also teaches a variety of important improvisation lessons.

Use This Challenge For:
- Classroom/Workshop – Major Skills Practiced:
  - Concentration
  - Individual Confidence Building
  - Justification
  - Listening/Being in the Moment
  - Mime (Involves Space and Object Work, Naming, etc)
  - Physicality
  - Storytelling (involves Making/Accepting Offers, Advancing, Extending, etc)
  - Teamwork (involves Chivalry, Finding The Game, etc)
  - Temporal Awareness
  - Thinking Funny
- Team Practice
- Single Group Performance
- Inter-Group Competition (Non-Competitive Round – cross-team challenge)

Gibberish

In this scene, players may only speak in gibberish – an unintelligible language – to communicate everything.

Preparation:
None.

Performance:
Get a set of variables from the audience. The team must then devise a coherent scene using those variables in which only gibberish is spoken. That's it.

Gibberish is also used as a component of several other challenges, such as Dubbing/Double Talk.

Success:
The key to being successful with a round of Gibberish is to make sure that all communication is very clear. Since players cannot rely on the shared meaning of a common language, this is accomplished through solid mime (space-object work) and very deliberate inflection.

The typical problems that inexperienced players tend to run into all stem from a nervousness in really using gibberish. New performers often mimic the phonetic patterns of a foreign language or merely repeat the same set of nonsense sounds over and over and over again. To be truly successful in a round of Gibberish, a player must be utilizing a full range of sounds to their full comic and communicative potential – and in the process tell a compelling story.

Personally, I think that Gibberish as a stand-alone challenge works better as a training exercise than as an actual scene to perform for an audience. There are so many excellent lessons to be learned by using Gibberish in a class, workshop, or practice – how to tell a story, how to make offers without words, mime skills – the list goes on and on.

Most audiences, however, seem to have gotten a little more sophisticated as time has moved on (Gibberish was one of the earliest challenges, after all) and prefer an additional gimmick to be thrown in with the gibberish language. You can easily add the requirement of using gibberish to so many of the other challenges described in this book.

Use This Challenge For:
- Classroom/Workshop – Major Skills Practiced:
  - Justification
  - Listening/Being in the Moment
  - Mime (Involves Space and Object Work, Naming, etc)
  - Physicality
  - Storytelling (involves Making/Accepting Offers, Advancing, Extending, etc)
  - Teamwork (involves Chivalry, Finding The Game, etc)
  - Vocalization
- Team Practice
- Single Group Performance
- Inter-Group Competition (Competitive Round)

Good Thing/Bad Thing

Players will work together to tell a story, each providing one sentence at a time and alternating between adding a good thing or a bad thing that occurred in the action.

Preparation:
None.

Performance:
This is a challenge that works equally well in either a workshop setting or during a performance. When presenting it in front of an audience, I've typically used it as a cross-team, non-scoring, just-for-fun event.

Players will form a line across the performance space. The host will get a few variables from the audience to use as the platform for the scene and the group will begin to tell a story one sentence at a time. The first player will provide some context for the story in the form of a good event. The second player will continue the story by adding something bad that subsequently happened. The players continue to tell the story, going down the line and alternating between providing a good or a bad thing.

Player 1:	(Good):	This weekend, I went to go see my favorite movie.
Player 2:	(Bad):	But it was all sold out.
Player 3:	(Good):	But I was able to get tickets for the movie playing on the next screen.
Player 4:	(Bad): (Obviously)	It was *Twilight*.
Player 5:	(Good):	But in the darkness, I saw the girl of my dreams and she agreed to go out with me.
Player 6:	(Bad):	Turned out to be a guy.

And so forth. Typically, a round of this game will go through the line of players three times with the final performer bringing the story to a close.

The game can be played with as few as four participants, or as many as twelve. In my opinion, the ideal number to have is typically around eight, depending on the situation in which you are using it.

In a performance, I don't want to introduce anything that could cause performers to fail in front of an audience, so I will usually stick to an even numbered group – that way players are always providing the same type of information (either good or bad) throughout the entire story. In a workshop, however, I make sure that the group is an odd number to force players to <u>have</u> to alternate between providing good and bad information which, in turn, forces them to listen more intently to each other.

Success:
Like so many other challenges, success in a round of Good Thing/Bad Thing depends greatly upon a performer possessing good listening skills. Players must listen intently to everything that has preceded them in the story to be able to successfully provide their own section. A player that was planning their bit instead of listening and then produces a non-sequitur will not only annoy the audience, but will screw up everyone that comes after them.

Listen, listen, listen!

Also, it may come as a shock to those who have never played the game before, but it takes a surprising amount of focus to remember if one is supposed to provide a good or bad event for the story. This is the most frequent mistake made with this challenge, especially with newer performers. I can't even begin to count the number of times that players in workshops have stopped the momentum dead in its tracks to ask, "Wait. Am I a bad thing?"

The existential dilemma of that question aside, it is something that a player can never let happen during a performance. Group members need to stay focused and remain within the confines of the challenge consistently.

Use This Challenge For:
- Classroom/Workshop – Major Skills Practiced:
    - Concentration
    - Individual Confidence Building
    - Listening/Being in the Moment
    - Storytelling (involves Making/Accepting Offers, Advancing, Extending, etc)
    - Teamwork (involves Chivalry, Finding The Game, etc)
- Team Practice
- Single Group Performance
- Inter-Group Competition (Non-Competitive Round – cross-team challenge)

Half-Life

A one minute scene is played. The entire scene is then repeated in thirty-seconds. It is then repeated in fifteen seconds. It is then repeated in seven seconds. Finally, it is repeated in three seconds.

Preparation:
The facilitator needs a watch or timer.

Performance:
In a game of Half-Life, the host will get a set of variables from the audience. The team of improvisers will then create a story (hopefully one with a solid beginning, middle, and ending) using those variables that lasts exactly one minute. The host, who has been timing the aforementioned escapade, will then freeze the scene and the players will repeat the entire scene again in thirty seconds. Again, the host will freeze the scene and now the players must repeat it all again in fifteen seconds. The host will freeze the scene again and the players repeat the entire sucker in seven seconds. Finally, the host will stop it one last time and the players will do the whole shebang in a very frenzied three seconds.

Success:
This is a challenge that is all about two things – solid storytelling and being physical. If a team can do a solid job in those two areas, then the rest of the game will take care of itself.

When the team is performing the first minute-long scene, it is important that they do everything possible to ensure that they tell a great story – listening to each other, advancing each other's offers, etc. – being funny is completely secondary to storytelling to ensure the success of the challenge. Once the scenes start to speed up, the humor will come naturally.

Also, while telling the story players should make a point of using the entire stage and being as physical as possible. Why? This will then provide the team with benchmarks – those select moments that they can go <u>back</u> to in order to recreate the scene quickly for the audience. This becomes more and more important as the scene gets faster and faster – think about how quickly the three second version will go by.

This is absolutely one of my favorite challenges to use with my students because it not only hits on fundamentals, but it is also one for which success is within the reach of beginners, and excellence is possible for the advanced.

Plus, it's hysterical.

Use This Challenge For:
- Classroom/Workshop – Major Skills Practiced:
    o Individual Confidence Building
    o Listening/Being in the Moment
    o Physicality
    o Storytelling (involves Making/Accepting Offers, Advancing, Extending, etc)
    o Teamwork (involves Chivalry, Finding The Game, etc)
    o Temporal Awareness
- Team Practice
- Single Group Performance
- Inter-Group Competition (Competitive Round)
- Inter-Group Competition (Non-Competitive Round – cross-team challenge)

Hat Game

Each player wears a hat as they begin a scene in which no reference is made to the hats. The winner is the first person to get the other player's hat(s). A missed grab is a loss.

This makes for a very good elimination scene.

Preparation:
Hats, obviously. Preferably funny ones.

Performance:
The host will get a set of variables from the audience that the players will use as a platform for their scene, with the added requirement that they will also be attempting to grab the other players' hat(s) during the action. There really isn't much more to it than this.

In a multi-team competition, this challenge works best as a tie-breaker or as a special challenge for one member of several teams to take part in to try and win some sort of special prize. In a single team performance, there should always be something at stake for winning so that the audience will have a greater buy-in with the performance.

It should be noted that this challenge can be done very well with many other objects other than hats. I've also used it successfully with clown ties, wigs, red noses, and false mustaches – however, to avoid injury players with long fingernails should probably avoid the last two.

Success:
The biggest pitfall for many players is the fear of a missed grab. Often the concern is so great that it will cause them to freeze up entirely and not make a grab at all. In my experience, this is especially true when the challenge is being used as a tie-breaker, because of the high stakes of the situation.

To try and combat this (and after one particularly tedious scene went on for eight minutes before a player made an attempt at a grab), I instituted a ninety second time limit onto the scene (for two players – I'd double it to three minutes for four players). This kept the action going and the audience interested.

The key to winning the challenge is for one player to try to get the other players to move into some sort of subservient position to them. Just as height is one of the greatest tools a director can use to show dominance or control when blocking a traditional play, here being in a higher physical plane puts a player into place for making a successful grab.

Use This Challenge For:
- Classroom/Workshop – Major Skills Practiced:
    o Concentration
    o Listening/Being in the Moment
    o Physicality
    o Spatial Awareness
- Team Practice
- Single Group Performance (Be sure to add a prize!)
- Inter-Group Competition (Non-Competitive Round – cross-team challenge – A prize here, too!)
- Inter-Group Competition (Tie-Breaker)

Hitchhiker

A driver picks up a hitchhiker who is a larger than life stereotype of some character. Slowly, the driver will transform into the same character as the hitchhiker. Once the transformation is complete, the driver pulls over and exits. The hitchhiker then becomes the new driver, and picks up the next player.

Preparation:
Two chairs.

Performance:
The most unusual aspect of this challenge is that it traditionally uses no variables (although it conceivably could) as the actors decide on all of their own character attributes. Consequently, I find that it is more effective during a competition (as teams don't know what challenge they might get) rather than during a single team performance which a team could have prepared for.

In performance, the process of pulling over and picking up a new hitchhiker continues until every team member has had a turn as a hitchhiker (the first driver will become the final hitchhiker). When done well, this can be a really fun challenge for audiences and teams alike.

This is also a challenge that works beautifully as a workshop or team exercise – in which case it can be played with a specified number of players or be an open ended process that every participant will go through.

Success:
There are a few different areas that performers need to focus on to ensure success.

First, the main point of the challenge (at least as an exercise for teaching improv is concerned) is learning how to develop and display a character *quickly*. By limiting choices to stereotypical character archetypes with easy to identify attributes, the job of a novice performer is make bold choices in how they display those characteristics. If the character is obvious to the audience, then they will enjoy the scene all the more.

The second area that can be tricky is how the driver goes through the process of transforming from their initial character into the hitchhiker's character. In fact, I have witnessed some inexperienced teams that have completely forgotten this crucial step in performance. In a successful transformation, the actor will slowly pick up one attribute of the hitchhiker, then another, then another, until the transformation is finally complete, rather than making a drastic shift between characters.

Finally, this challenge provides a great opportunity to work on interesting justifications, as each driver has to include a good reason to pull over. These, of course, work best when incorporated well into the context of the scene, rather than coming out of the clear blue sky.

Use This Challenge For:
- Classroom/Workshop – Major Skills Practiced:
  - Endowments
  - Justification
  - Listening/Being in the Moment
  - Physicality
  - Storytelling (involves Making/Accepting Offers, Advancing, Extending, etc)
  - Taking Direction
  - Teamwork (involves Chivalry, Finding The Game, etc)
- Team Practice
- Inter-Group Competition (Competitive Round)
- Inter-Group Competition (Non-Competitive Round – cross-team challenge)

Human Prop

One improviser will become all of the props mentioned in the scene.

Preparation:
None.

Performance:
In this challenge, the team will perform a scene based on a set of variables provided by the audience. The gimmick here is that one member of the group will have the responsibility of embodying every single three-dimensional object that is mentioned throughout the course of the scene – in other words, they become all of the props.

It's a pretty simple gimmick, but it's physical, fun, and one that can involve a lot of pimping – and audiences tend to eat that up.

Success:
Obviously, the biggest key to success here is the willingness on the part of the player that is the human prop to be almost absurdly

physical when embodying the items that are mentioned. If they are able to successfully communicate those items to the audience, then a riotous response is all but guaranteed.

However, the prop player's elasticity is certainly not the only factor in determining if a team will do well.

Equally important is the *pace* of the scene and the manner in which the rest of the team names objects. I've actually had beginning groups that have performed a complete scene in which *not a single object* was mention by any of the players. That shouldn't even be physically possible. I mean...

just say a noun, for Pete's sake!

This left the remaining player standing around uncomfortably on the sidelines, probably thinking that they were the one doing something wrong. A perfect Human Prop scene will begin by mentioning a few items here and there as the players tell the story, but then gradually pick up speed – either forcing the actor playing the props to get more and more outlandish or alternate between objects at a faster and faster rate.

The obvious gimmicks that work well with any physically demanding scene still apply here, of course. Becoming a backpack, or a bib, or a pair of pants, or anything that forces the prop actor to get uncomfortably close to their fellow players will usually have an immediate payoff.

Likewise, embodying any object that puts the actor in a potentially embarrassing situation is almost always rewarded by the audience.

I remember one competition in particular in which a team performing Human Prop made the actor have to alternate from being a wheelbarrow, to a pogo stick, to a toaster (with finished toast popping out) and back again.

Guess which team won.

Use This Challenge For:
- Classroom/Workshop – Major Skills Practiced:
  - Embodiment
  - Individual Confidence Building
  - Listening/Being in the Moment
  - Mime (Involves Space and Object Work, Naming, etc)
  - Physicality
  - Storytelling (involves Making/Accepting Offers, Advancing, Extending, etc)
  - Teamwork (involves Chivalry, Finding The Game, etc)
- Team Practice
- Single Group Performance
- Inter-Group Competition (Competitive Round)
- Inter-Group Competition (Non-Competitive Round – cross-team challenge)

Infomercial

Two players are given a relationship by the audience (i.e. brothers, couple arguing, etc.) and act as the hosts of an infomercial for a product that the audience chooses. The remaining players are assigned attributes by the audience and must demonstrate those attributes as they give testimonials for the product.

Preparation:
Two chairs.

Performance:
The pair of players that are to be the hosts of the infomercial will sit in the two chairs center. The host will then get a relationship for the two to display during the scene from the audience. The audience will then assign endowments (i.e. slowly catching fire, in the middle of a snowstorm, a four year old child that lost their mommy, etc.) to the other players who are typically giving product testimonials one at a

time, on either side of the stage. Finally the host will ask the audience for a type of product for the infomercial to be about.

There are a LOT more variables that go into one of these scenes than most – which means lots of tummeling with the audience on the part of the host. It also means that there will be a lot of information for the team to remember. The host must therefore be very organized and specific in what it is that the audience is being asked to provide for the setup not to become tedious – and for the audience to be able to follow along during the performance.

Success:
Clarity, clarity, clarity. Right out of the gate, relationships need to be established, attributes need to be displayed, and so on. The scene should only last around two minutes, so the team can't waste any precious time with lengthy exposition.

Also, this is not a challenge that should be sprung on a team that has never practiced it. There are too many factors in the basic framework that the team must fully understand and know how to utilize before they try it in front of an audience. However, in the hands of a practiced team, this challenge can be a thing of beauty!

Also, while the structure might sound like it could be a good challenge for a group of individual members of various teams in a non-competitive round, I don't recommend it. Again, there are just too many factors that could go wrong.

Use This Challenge For:
- Classroom/Workshop – Major Skills Practiced:
  - Endowments
  - Justification
  - Listening/Being in the Moment
  - Mime (Involves Space and Object Work, Naming, etc)
- Team Practice
- Single Group Performance (only if mastered)
- Inter-Group Competition (Competitive Round – only with advanced groups)

Last Letter/First Letter

The last letter of Improviser 1's dialogue becomes first letter of Improviser 2's dialogue.

Preparation:
None.

Performance:
This challenge is based on a very simple but highly effective premise. The host will get a set of variables from the audience, as usual. During the course of a scene based on the supplied variables, performers will improvise lines of dialogue beginning with the last letter of the previous line. This is a challenge that for novice teams works best with a group of only two performers, but is easily usable for groups up to five members in size.

A scene might go something like this:

Player 1:	Oh my gosh, I love those pant<u>s</u>.
Player 2:	<u>S</u>top, you're just saying tha<u>t</u>.
Player 1:	<u>T</u>rust me, those pants are so YO<u>U</u>.
Player 2:	<u>U</u>nfortunately, they have a big hole in the kne<u>e</u>.
Player 1:	<u>E</u>veryone has those holes nowaday<u>s</u>.
Player 2:	<u>S</u>ometimes you know just how to cheer me up!

Success:
This is a scene that is all about – in a word – listening. Yes, players do still need to advance the story as that is always the number one priority in a performance, but to be successful with this one, players have to be completely in the moment, genuinely listening to everything that the other performers are saying.

Another key area to focus on when practicing is speed. Many beginning performers may have long (or what <u>feel</u> like long – dead air is a killer) pauses between lines of dialogue while they are processing what the previous player said and adapting the letter used to their own thoughts. The more a team has practiced this skill, and it <u>is</u> a <u>skill</u>, the faster they will become at the challenge. An ideal scene will be paced just a hair faster than the audience is thinking, so that they must catch up with the performers a bit. This will keep them on the edge of their seats and thoroughly impressed.

Also, just as with Alphabet Game, if a player is having a difficult time thinking of something, the other player(s) should never leave them and the scene hanging. Instead, players should always fill in any awkward silences that develop with their own contributions.

Use This Challenge For:
- Classroom/Workshop – Major Skills Practiced:
    - Concentration
    - Listening/Being in the Moment
    - Storytelling (involves Making/Accepting Offers, Advancing, Extending, etc)
    - Teamwork (involves Chivalry, Finding The Game, etc)
    - Verbal Prowess
- Team Practice
- Single Group Performance
- Inter-Group Competition (Competitive Round)
- Inter-Group Competition (Non-Competitive Round – cross-team challenge)

Media Challenges

The scene will be based on some kind of published material. This could be in the form of a newspaper headline (real or imagined), personal ad, letter to Dear Abby, TV Guide Synopsis, Movie or Video

Guide Synopsis, entry from Ripley's Believe it or Not, Guinness Book of World Records, etc.

Preparation:
The published material that the team will use.

Performance:
The scene will be based around an article/printed material that has been provided by the host, so for this challenge there will be no audience variables. The team will create a scene inspired in some way by the supplied media. Usually this takes the form of literally acting out the story of the material with embellishments inserted by the team throughout.

For example:

A Dear Abby Column...

in which a wife complains that her husband ignores her will typically inspire a scene in which a husband is guilty of an exaggerated version of the aforementioned ignoring, and will eventually conclude with the character of the wife following the advice given in the article – which may or may not have the desired result.

An Odd News Story...

about a man who was pulled over while operating a motorized bar stool while intoxicated will probably produce a scene in which we see the man getting drunk, choosing to drive his bar stool, getting pulled over and arrested by the police, and possibly an update on the story months later.

A TV or Movie Synopsis...

will likely create a scene that is a literal retelling of the events of the synopsis, but may bear little to no similarity to the actual film or TV show that was originally described.

An Encyclopedia Entry (Guinness Book, Ripley, etc)...

could go anywhere the team likes, provided that the information/event from the entry is used at some point during the scene.

Success:

As is true with all improv, the key to success in a Media Challenge scene lies primarily in the quality of the narrative. The team members must take great pains to ensure that a solid story is developed from the information provided. Also, it is equally important that key details from the source material are not omitted as an audience may be quick to voice their disapproval of a forgetful team.

Since the basic setup for this challenge provides almost everything that a team needs to craft a successful scene, this one <u>can</u> be used as sort of a "soft pitch" to a novice team. However, in the hands of experts, the fun liberties that the framework allows for can also make it one of the most enjoyable challenges to perform during the course of a show.

Use This Challenge For:
- Classroom/Workshop – Major Skills Practiced:
    o Endowments
    o Listening/Being in the Moment
    o Mime (Involves Space and Object Work, Naming, etc)
    o Storytelling (involves Making/Accepting Offers, Advancing, Extending, etc)
- Team Practice
- Single Group Performance
- Inter-Group Competition (Competitive Round)
- Inter-Group Competition (Non-Competitive Round – cross-team challenge)

Modern Fairy Tale

In this challenge, players will combine a well known fairy tale with either a film genre or even a specific movie. The scene will then use the characters and clichés from the film/type of film to tell the basic gist of the fairy tale.

Preparation:
None.

Performance:
The host will get two (and only two) variables from the audience – the fairy tale and the movie or film genre. After that, it is up to the team members to tell a good story. The host's job is to choose the suggestions that have the greatest and broadest audience appeal. A Fellini parody might amuse a few cinephiles in the audience, but re-imagining *It's a Wonderful Life* can make us all laugh.

In my experience, audiences generally tend to enjoy scenes that combine a specific movie with a fairy tale more than they do a genre, probably because performers can make more specific references during their scene. Why just mention a wizard or something when you can use countless Harry Potter references, right? Just as with all other variables, the more specific one can be in the setup, the better things will go during the performance.

Success:
This is probably a challenge best left to the most experienced teams. Simply the act of synthesizing the two bits of source material is enough to separate the wheat from the chaff.

The key to success, obviously, lies in integrating the correct amount of elements from both the fairy tale and the movie/genre. The fairy tale should always become the plot of the scene, and the film should be the twisted context. So the scene is still telling the basic story of the Three Little Pigs, but now the Big Bad Wolf is Don Corleone from *The Godfather*. (Actually, that could be a great scene! I'll have to remember that one.)

Personally, I have only used this challenge in competitions a few times, and only when I was sure that the team receiving the challenge was up to it. However, even with an experienced team there can be pitfalls. One competition in particular I can remember a team failing miserably at this challenge because one of the team members didn't speak up and say that they had never seen *Pulp Fiction* when the other team members all had. Consequently, it was pretty hard for them to do a Tarantino/Little Red Riding Hood mash-up. Always keep in mind that the players (especially those still in school) may have been exposed to a lot less pop culture than you might think.

Use This Challenge For:
- Classroom/Workshop – Major Skills Practiced:
  - Justification
  - Physicality
  - Storytelling (involves Making/Accepting Offers, Advancing, Extending, etc)
  - Teamwork (involves Chivalry, Finding The Game, etc)
  - Thinking Funny
- Team Practice
- Single Group Performance (only if mastered)
- Inter-Group Competition (Competitive Round – only with advanced groups)
- Inter-Group Competition (Non-Competitive Round – cross-team challenge – only with advanced groups)

One Word Scene

One word is obtained from the audience and will become the only word that players use in the scene.

Preparation:
None.

Performance:
The host will get a set of variables from the audience that the team must use in the course of their scene, but they will also get the additional variable of a single word that will be the only thing that the team is allowed to say. It then becomes the team's responsibility to tell a complete story and effectively communicate the use of all of the

variables to the audience, even though their vocabulary has suddenly become quite limited.

For a team of performers, this challenge is essentially the same as Gibberish, in that almost all communication will be done via inflection and space object work. It is important that teams take the time to effectively define the items that they are miming and likely use vocalization that exaggerates the emotional content being communicated.

Variation: *Personal Vocabulary*
In this version, a different word is assigned to each player. This opens up the rhythmic possibilities of the dialogue a bit more and makes it simpler for the audience to distinguish characters from one another. Performing the scene in this manner usually helps to encourage success with the challenge for a newer team.

Success:
Obviously, this is a challenge that will require a fairly sophisticated degree of physical and vocal control on the part of the performers. I would not suggest giving this one to a group of newbies performing in front of an audience for the first time.

However, it is also the responsibility of the host to make sure that the team is given a good word to use. Personally, to that end, I recommend that only longer, multi-syllabic words are chosen for performers at this level. A team of improvisers will have so many more options when using a word like "happiness" or "nightingale" rather than a word like "thud."

In addition, solid space object work is a must for this scene. As in all mime-heavy challenges, it is important that performers pace the scene a bit slower than reality and fully define the invisible objects that they are using.

Use This Challenge For:
- Classroom/Workshop – Major Skills Practiced:
  - Embodiment

- o Mime (Involves Space and Object Work, Naming, etc)
- o Physicality
- o Storytelling (involves Making/Accepting Offers, Advancing, Extending, etc)
- o Teamwork (involves Chivalry, Finding The Game, etc)
- o Vocalization
- Team Practice
- Single Group Performance (only if mastered)
- Inter-Group Competition (Competitive Round – only with advanced groups)

Options

At various points during this scene the actors will be told to freeze. The audience will then be asked to provide some vital piece of information for the story. The players must immediately incorporate the suggestion into the scene.

Preparation:
None.

Performance:
The facilitator will get a set of variables for the performers to base their scene upon. Once the context has been established (likely 20-30 seconds in) the host will begin to freeze the scene periodically. While the scene is frozen, the host will then ask the audience a question about what has just happened or what will likely happen next. For example:

> *Why did they decide to break-up?*
> *What are they having for dinner?*
> *Where should they go to find the missing tiara?*

The actors then must immediately incorporate the information provided into their scene.

This is a challenge that is a lot of fun for the audience because they get to see their suggestions quickly used by the actors – instant gratification – and is loved by performers because the constant pauses in the action give them a chance to play mental catch-up.

Success:
Options is actually a fantastic challenge for new performers because it takes much of the process of making offers out of their hands and places it firmly into the audience's – and does so as part of the basic structure of the challenge. Since new performers might remember to agree with each other, but often forget to embellish upon the offers other players make, this challenge helps to ensure that they will triumph.

However, much of the responsibility for the success of this challenge lies in the timing that the host uses when freezing and the suggestions chosen by the host to be incorporated. Sluggish freezing or using lame offers can make an Options scene painful, but keeping the action brisk and interesting creates a snowball of fun. In other words, you have the power to help the team succeed with this one!

Use This Challenge For:
- Classroom/Workshop – Major Skills Practiced:
  - Audience Interaction
  - Individual Confidence Building
  - Justification
  - Listening/Being in the Moment
  - Storytelling (involves Making/Accepting Offers, Advancing, Extending, etc)
  - Taking Direction
  - Teamwork (involves Chivalry, Finding The Game, etc)
- Team Practice
- Single Group Performance
- Inter-Group Competition (Competitive Round)
- Inter-Group Competition (Non-Competitive Round – cross-team challenge)

Party Quirks/Endowments

One player becomes the host of a party. The remaining players are each given an endowment and will act as the guests at that party. The first player then has to guess the other player's attributes within the context of a scene.

Preparation:
A means of letting the audience know what the endowments are. I use projections. Be sure to visit Appendix A for a list of 200 endowments that have been successful.

Performance:
The emcee can either get endowments from the audience or provide their own. The host of the party begins "setting up" refreshments and the like and will usually get one joke out in the first ten seconds or so. After that laugh (or groan), the emcee will buzz in guests one at a time. During the course of a scene, the "host" will attempt to guess the attribute assigned to the guest in normal conversation.

In performance, the hardest part of running this challenge is in letting the audience know what endowment is being used by the performer. You <u>could</u> put the performer playing the host into some sort of "cone of silence" and then get the endowments during the setup, assuming that the audience has a good memory.

Or...

What I have always done is to decide on a list of endowments far in advance and then made them into a PowerPoint slideshow (or overhead transparencies, if you go way back). The party guests are each given envelopes containing the endowments and enter in a pre-determined order as a tech operator advances the slides that the audience (but not the performers) can see. This could also be easily accomplished using a desktop projector or app instead, if you want to get the endowments from the audience either before the show or at intermission.

There are many other different Endowment-type scenes floating around out there, but this one is still my favorite.

Success:
Pace is the key to this challenge. Most of what makes it work is in the hands of the players, but some of it lies in the hands of the emcee and the rate at which they choose to ring to doorbell for the guests to arrive at the party. The entire scene should run about two minutes.

The player that is the host has the primary responsibility of ensuring that the scene develops appropriately. To that end, the host should NOT guess the player's endowments until the very end of the scene. If guests arrive, their attributes are instantly guessed and they leave, where is the fun for the audience? The best opportunities for humor occur not with the act of guessing (the easy road) but rather with the interaction between characters (the hard, bumpy, and winding road).

Ideally, once a character is rung into the scene, they should get a little interaction (maybe twenty seconds) with the host before the next guest arrives. The first guest should then go hang out on the sidelines and give focus over completely to the second guest and the host (**Rule #3** – Give or Take Focus as Needed). After they have had about twenty seconds of interaction, the first guest should interject something that ties everything introduced so far together, immediately after which the third guest should be rung in. After about twenty seconds of interaction with the third guest, it is once again appropriate for the first and second guests to take some of the focus again. Now that all the guests have arrived and after a bit more comic banter, it is finally an appropriate time for the host to begin guessing their endowments.

If a team has a fifth member, I have found that it is usually a good idea for the host to guess one of the players prior to the fourth guest's entrance. The audience can focus pretty well on a scene being pulled three ways, but the addition of a fourth creates confusion.

It is extremely important for a lot of unsaid communication to be going on between the guests and the host – a good deal of "Yes, I understand what you are now, thanks" or "I am totally lost." This is, of course, the sort of thing that a team develops with practice. Also, it is important that the host never outright guesses an endowment, but rather lets it become part of the conversation. In other words, the host never says "I think you're Elvis," but rather "There's an extra pair of blue suede shoes over there" or "If you're hungry, go help yourself to some fondue – you know, a hunk-a hunk-a burning cheese."

This is easily the most popular challenge that I use – so much so, that I always end every competition with the top three teams all doing it as the final "winner-determining" round.

Use This Challenge For:
- Classroom/Workshop – Major Skills Practiced:
    o Endowments
    o Justification
    o Physicality
    o Teamwork (involves Chivalry, Finding The Game, etc)
- Team Practice
- Single Group Performance
- Inter-Group Competition (Competitive Round)
- Inter-Group Competition (Non-Competitive Round – cross-team challenge)

Props

Two members from each team must come up with as many uses for a prop as possible.

Preparation:
Two sets of unusual props.

Performance:
I personally think that this works best as a non-competitive round with representatives from two teams just having a lot of fun, but it is

also a great choice for a single team performance or even could be used as a tie-breaker.

Get two members of each team to come up to the stage and present each pair with an unusual prop or set of unusual props. The players then quickly come up with as many uses as possible for the prop which they demonstrate through a few seconds of dialogue. The host alternates between teams for a few minutes and ends on an appropriate high note. Usually, this game is incredibly hilarious.

Success:
The biggest factor for success will lie in what the host has chosen for the prop to be used. While you are, of course, welcome to spend big bucks, I usually hit dollar and thrift stores to find my odd items, so you really can find them anywhere. The key is to search for pieces that, while they may have a very specifically designed purpose, are flexible or re-shapeable into new configurations.

I've had very good results with things like pool noodles, collapsible laundry baskets, unusual pieces of hardware, etc.

Basically, the more non-descript (or at least the less-obviously-descript) the objects are, the better. And don't TRY to find intentionally funny props. The humor should come from the performers. The best scenes will be inspired by items that might be odd, but not "joke store" funny.

The remainder of a team's success will depend upon the player's speed and willingness to jump all-in on an idea. The best thing to remember about a good round of Props is that the players don't have to build an entire scene around their ideas. It doesn't have to be an offer that is sustainable for three or five minutes. They are simply coming up with a quick premise that only needs to last them until the next team chimes in – about a whole five seconds.

It doesn't matter if the idea is trite, bizarre, or zany – it just matters that they keep coming, and coming, and coming.

Use This Challenge For:
- Classroom/Workshop – Major Skills Practiced:
  - Physicality
  - Thinking Funny
- Team Practice
- Single Group Performance
- Inter-Group Competition (Non-Competitive Round – cross-team challenge)
- Inter-Group Competition (Tie-Breaker)

The Purloined Letter

One letter of the alphabet, chosen by a member of the audience, no longer exists. It is replaced by a different letter chosen by a different audience member.

Preparation:
None.

Performance:
The host will get a set of three variables as a platform for the scene. In addition, the host will also ask the audience for a letter that they would like to see disappear and what letter they would like to see it replaced with. The team will perform a scene of about two to three minutes doing the best that they can to speak with this new linguistic configuration.

It is very important that the host make sure that the letter that is selected to disappear is a COMMON one. There is nothing interesting about a scene without a "Z" – unless the whole thing is about serving pizza to the zebras at the Zanzibar Zoo. Make sure that you choose a letter that shows up a lot. "T" or "S" or one of the other "always chosen on Wheel of Fortune" letters will do just fine. Heck, get rid of a vowel – that will throw 'em for a loop!

An obligatory word of caution, however, upon picking the replacement letter - if you are working in a school environment, be sure not to choose "F" or any letter that could obviously lead to a whole slew of profanity.

The last thing that you want is for your wholesome scene about Mother Duck and her Ducklings to turn into a Lenny Bruce rant.

If you're not in a school environment, however, the aforementioned is probably the <u>ideal</u> Purloined Letter scene.

Success:

While much of the success will simply lie in a team's storytelling ability, there are a couple little tricks or gimmicks that can be real audience pleasers. First, a few moments of difficulty on the part of a player in formulating their thoughts – if done well – can be quite funny. It gives the player the opportunity to "wink at the audience" a bit, without totally destroying the fourth wall like corpsing does – it just puts a tiny entertaining chink in it.

Conversely, a particularly rapid-fire stretch of substitutions can really get an audience revved up (and impressed). And let's not forget about pace. An ideal scene should likely start a bit slower than normal conversation and then gradually increase its speed until finally ending going a mile a minute.

Use This Challenge For:
- Classroom/Workshop – Major Skills Practiced:
  - Concentration
  - Listening/Being in the Moment
  - Storytelling (involves Making/Accepting Offers, Advancing, Extending, etc)
  - Verbal Prowess
- Team Practice
- Single Group Performance
- Inter-Group Competition (Competitive Round)
- Inter-Group Competition (Non-Competitive Round)

Remote Control

The host (or another player) owns the world's greatest universal remote control which they will use to manipulate the actors as they perform their scene.

Preparation:
None. Be sure to visit Appendix C for a list of some possible remote control settings.

Performance:
There are two basic ways to begin a round of Remote Control. The first is to base the scene on a set of variables that the audience provides. This will simply create a standard improv that the host happens to have control over. The second is to give the team a fake movie title (either already prepared or as suggested by the audience) that the team must then act out. Something that gives away half of the plot in a 1950's B-movie style (i.e. "It Came from Beyond the Living Room") probably works better than something simple (i.e. "The Letter").

Once the basic plot of the scene has been established (usually 20-30 seconds) the remote's owner may commence hitting buttons that impact the performers. Standard possibilities include the old tried-and-true classics "pause," "rewind," and "fast-forward," but let's face it, one can do pretty much anything they want with their remote nowadays, can't they? It can be loads of fun to change the channel, switch to a different language track, get the director's commentary, or skip ahead a few chapters in the DVD. Really advanced teams might be able to handle things like changing inputs to a video game unit, getting bored and checking out You Tube for a minute, or even the granddaddy of complexity, a picture-in-picture.

Usually the strongest way for a Remote Control scene to end is for the owner of the remote to announce that the next button push will be their last by saying something like "let's skip ahead and see how it all ends." That will then give the team a solid cue that they should wrap up all the action in the next ten or fifteen seconds, and the scene can conclude on a high note.

Success:
As with almost all of these improv challenges, two of the key words for success with Remote Control are *physicality* and *escalation*.

The performers must be as physical as possible at all times so that when the remote is utilized the humor will be automatic. Hitting "rewind" to watch a player walk backwards is one thing, but forcing them to do a reverse crabwalk over another player is a heck of a lot funnier. The owner of the remote should constantly be on the lookout for those awesome moments of physicality to exploit during the course of the scene.

As for escalation, just as increasing the pace from the beginning baseline of a challenge is very important in all short form improv, in Remote Control it is also important to increase the complexity of the buttons being pushed. If the first button changes the audio track from English to Swahili before the audience has even seen the actors on fast forward or rewind, there's nowhere for the scene to go. Consequently, much of the success of a round of Remote Control lies (literally) in the hand of the person operating the remote.

Use This Challenge For:
- Classroom/Workshop – Major Skills Practiced:
    - Embodiment
    - Justification
    - Listening/Being in the Moment
    - Physicality
    - Taking Direction
    - Teamwork (involves Chivalry, Finding The Game, etc)
- Team Practice
- Single Group Performance
- Inter-Group Competition (Competitive Round)
- Inter-Group Competition (Non-Competitive Round – cross-team challenge)

Scene Without "_____"

The possibilities here are literally limitless. The scene is played as if the world were without something (i.e. words, emotions, contractions, gravity, a word, love, parents, food, etc.).

Preparation:
None.

Performance:
The emcee will get a set of three variables for the team to use as the basis for their scene. In addition, the audience will also be asked to provide what the scene should be without. The team has to then accomplish what could be anything from a simple to a herculean task – to create a story using the environmental limitations provided.

Success:
There is no magic bullet to ensure success with this particular challenge, because the potential parameters vary so greatly that you never really know what you will end up with. Consequently, the advice here is the same as it is for most challenges – teams need to focus on story, story, story. As long as the audience has a clear story to follow and is engaged, then the simple act of telling that story in a world without "____" will be enough to keep them focused on the team.

Use This Challenge For:
- Classroom/Workshop – Major Skills Practiced:
    - Embodiment (Possibly...)
    - Mime (Involves Space and Object Work, Naming, etc)
    - Physicality (Probably...)
    - Storytelling (involves Making/Accepting Offers, Advancing, Extending, etc)
    - Teamwork (involves Chivalry, Finding The Game, etc)
    - Verbal Prowess (Possibly...)
- Team Practice

- Single Group Performance
- Inter-Group Competition (Competitive Round)
- Inter-Group Competition (Non-Competitive Round – cross-team challenge)

Sentence Scenes

These are scenes that are based in some way on a sentence provided by the audience. There are several varieties of Sentence Scenes.

Preparation:
Have audience members provide sentences on small sheets of paper either prior to the performance or during an intermission. Also, possibly a bell.

Performance:
There are many different forms of Sentence Scenes that can be performed. I have included in this section the three versions that I have used to the greatest degrees of success, but always feel free to use others or to create your own. Although all of these challenges work great as a part of a single team performance, the level of excitement that they generate can often pale in comparison to some of the other challenges used over the course of an evening, so I usually avoid them during inter-team competitions.

Prior to the performance (either as the crowd is entering or at a break), the emcee should approach several audience members and have them each write down a sentence on a scrap of paper. When it comes time to perform the scene, the host should go ahead and get variables from the audience as usual for the team to build their scene around. The host should also give the team members the sentences that they will be using, *without allowing them to be read*. Then as the team performs, in addition to telling a story, they must also incorporate the sentences provided in the manner appropriate to the variation selected.

Variation One: *First Line, Last Line*
One player is given a piece of paper containing the first line of the scene while another player is given a piece with the last line. The scene must contain all of the provided variables AND successfully justify these beginning and ending lines of dialogue.

Variation Two: *Sentence from a Hat*
Here, all of the sentences that were provided by the audience are tossed into a hat. A team member draws one of the sentences out of the hat and the chosen sentence becomes the basis for the scene. Usually, the scene will also end with a player saying this sentence.

Variation Three: *Sentence-Go-Round*
In this version, each team member is given a sentence by the host which they put in their pocket. Periodically during the course of scene, the host will ring a bell. Every time the bell is rung, one of the players must read their sentence as their next line of dialogue. The sentence must be fully justified by all players.

Regardless of which version is being used, there is a lot of potential for humor as the team tries to justify themselves out of the corner that the sentences just painted them into.

Success:
This is a challenge all about looking awkward and then suddenly being able to brilliantly validate everything that one has just said. Therefore it is a great challenge to use in a performance by a team that has mastered the art of justification.

As for specific tricks or gimmicks that one can use, the "looking awkward" part tends to be the most important aspect of the success of this challenge with an audience. They might find the sentence that a performer has just said to be ludicrous, so it is often a good idea for them to see that the actor also realizes that it's nuts for everyone to be in on the joke. This does not mean that the team should begin a session of unfettered mugging – this is really just a tiny wink at the audience to raise the stakes. Then, everyone in the room can enjoy the performer's ability to get out of the situation in a manner that makes some degree of logical sense.

Use This Challenge For:
- Classroom/Workshop – Major Skills Practiced:
    o Audience Interaction
    o Justification
    o Listening/Being in the Moment
    o Storytelling (involves Making/Accepting Offers, Advancing, Extending, etc)
    o Verbal Prowess
- Team Practice
- Single Group Performance

Should Have Said

At any point during this scene the players can be interrupted by a bell. When the bell rings, the last line of dialogue must be replaced with a brand new one.

Preparation:
A bell.

Performance:
The host will get a set of three variables from the audience for the team to use as a platform. Once the team has firmly established the story (around 20-30 seconds), the host can then begin to ring the bell as opportune moments present themselves in the action. Here is an example of how one exchange might look:

Player 1:	Have you ever seen a sunset as beautiful as that?
Player 2:	Never in my life. *(The host rings the bell.)* Of course I haven't. I'm blind, you idiot!

Of course, there's no reason why the host can't ring the bell more than once.

Player 1:	Why did you come all the way to Alaska to go fishing?
Player 2:	I don't know, it just looked so pretty in the brochure. *(Host rings the bell.)* I don't know, I just like the snow. *(Host rings the bell.)* I'm hiding from the mafia.

In fact, the host can ring the bell as often as they like.

Player 1:	What do you like to do on the weekend?
Player 2:	I paint, I sew – anything creative. *(Host rings the bell.)* Just sit around, mostly. *(Host rings the bell.)* Wait for you to call. *(Host rings the bell.)* They don't let me out of the cage much these days. *(Host rings the bell.)* I build things out of nail clippings. *(Host rings the bell.)* You go first. *(Host rings the bell.)* You'd know if you weren't so insensitive!

And so forth and so on.

This is also a great challenge to use in a Tune-up or workshop situation where the teaching focus is about making and acting upon offers. The facilitator can choose to ring the bell as they would during a regular performance, or they could choose to ring it whenever the team makes a bland or uninteresting choice. The bell can be an excellent tool to force the inexperienced player to up the ante a bit and make bolder choices in their improvisations.

Success:
This has been one of my favorite scenes to use ever since I began doing improv with students because it accomplishes several tasks at the same time. It…

- keeps players focused and in the moment
- forces them to listen
- requires them to make a continuous stream of offers

and is a heck of a lot of fun at the same time.

The challenge is essentially all about one player being able to continually make offers, then having the other players accept and immediately incorporate them into the scene. The primary indicator of success, therefore, will be the ability of the player to make as many offers as need be. The players have absolutely no idea when the host will choose to ring the bell during the scene, so to do well they must remain constantly on their toes and actively listening to both each other and for the bell.

This is a challenge that can be absolutely hysterical for an audience and is a continued favorite for students since the basic premise of the game is simple enough that a novice team can be just as successful as an experienced one at it.

Use This Challenge For:
- Classroom/Workshop – Major Skills Practiced:
  - Concentration
  - Individual Confidence Building
  - Listening/Being in the Moment
  - Storytelling (involves Making/Accepting Offers, Advancing, Extending, etc)
  - Thinking Funny
- Team Practice
- Single Group Performance
- Inter-Group Competition (Competitive Round)
- Inter-Group Competition (Non-Competitive Round – cross-team challenge)

Sit, Stand, Lean

A scene for three players. At all times, one team member must be sitting, one must be standing, and one must be leaning – and all three must be in constant motion.

Preparation:
Two chairs or stools.

Performance:
Note: For this challenge to work the team MUST have three players only.

The audience will provide either a standard set of three variables or a situation that the team will use as a platform. On stage are positioned two chairs or stools. Using those seats, the team must create a scene based upon the provided variables in which one member of the team is sitting, one is standing, and one is leaning at all times. In other words, whenever one performer moves, the other two players must compensate for that movement.

This challenge can be absolutely hilarious, provided the team isn't afraid to be physical. I have seen more than one performance that was destroyed by a team's physical reluctance. However, when the players fully commit to the premise and are in constant motion, this one is almost always a guaranteed crowd pleaser.

I have also used the four person version of this challenge (Sit, Stand, Lean, Lie Down) – but I have found that not only is it hard for student performers to concentrate on four places of the stage simultaneously, it is equally challenging for most audiences to do so as well. Consequently, I don't recommend using it.

Success:
As I already said, first and foremost a team has to be physical. A round of Sit, Stand, Lean in which no one is moving (or only moves a

little for that matter) will be ridiculously tedious to watch – movement is the whole point, after all.

After physicality, the second most important factor to success is pace.

Like most challenges with a single gimmick at the heart of its premise, much of a scene's success will depend on the team starting slow and then gradually increasing the rate of usage. For this challenge, begin by incorporating a smaller amount of movement early on in the scene, then slowly build in intensity, getting faster and faster until finally ending with a flurry of commotion.

As for gimmicks, the classic is for one team member to begin performing a fast-paced repetitive action that causes them to alternate between two of the positions. This, in turn, forces the other players to scramble all over the stage in their efforts to compensate.

Another good one is to let the audience see the team's confusion a bit, perhaps when a player forgets to move, thus giving the audience a little "we're in on the joke" wink.

Use This Challenge For:
- Classroom/Workshop – Major Skills Practiced:
    - Justification
    - Listening/Being in the Moment
    - Physicality
    - Storytelling (involves Making/Accepting Offers, Advancing, Extending, etc)
    - Teamwork (involves Chivalry, Finding The Game, etc)
- Team Practice
- Single Group Performance
- Inter-Group Competition (Competitive Round)
- Inter-Group Competition (Non-Competitive Round – cross-team challenge)

Slide Show

One player will present a "lecture" (academic, travelogue, etc.) during which all of the visual aids will be portrayed by the other players on the team.

Preparation:
None.

Performance:
This challenge has obviously been around for a while – it's still named Slide Show after all, despite the fact that very few of those performing it have ever even seen a slide carousel. However, it has stuck around for a very good reason. It is easily one of the most successful challenges that I have ever used, consistently delighting teams and audience alike.

The emcee will get a set of variables from the audience that will be used during the course of the scene as the team decides which player will be giving the lecture and who will become all of the slides. The audience will then provide a subject for the lecture and the scene begins.

The "lecturer" should begin with a quick set-up that introduces the topic for the scene and gets in at least one cheesy joke. They should then begin their "presentation" by "turning on" the first slide. he other players will then get into some sort of frozen position that the host will work to justify within the context of the lecture. The lecture usually consists of four or five "slides" and then concludes with a brief wrap-up by the lecturer.

Depending on the performance environment, the scene can be even more successful if the lights are blacked out between slides to add the element of surprise for the audience.

Success:
The biggest determiner of success for a team lies squarely in the hands of the performer chosen to be the lecturer. This player has the awesome responsibility of making all of the justifications needed during the scene and controlling the general feel and flow of the challenge. Also, with a few unusual exceptions, they will likely be the only team member able to speak during the scene, putting even more responsibility on the plate in front of them.

There are several good things that teams can do to help ensure success with this one. It's probably a bit obvious, but unexpected juxtapositions are a great tool to use here. Team members could get into a position that seems violent and then have the lecture be about the loving tenderness being displayed. Or the positions could be potentially offensive or suggestive, but the lecturer makes it all squeaky clean (or the reverse). Just like a Gibberish translation that is far different than what the player must obviously be saying, anything that defies our expectations tends to get a positive audience reaction.

A good gimmick to utilize is for the players to be frozen and for the lecturer to suddenly realize that the "slide" is either backwards or upside down. This is a bit of good natured pimping that audiences will eat up (so long as it's not overused).

Also remember, that now that we are living in the 21st century, we aren't limited to static images. Instead of a slideshow, the lecturer could easily be giving a PowerPoint or media presentation and can decide at will that a slide is actually an embedded video and turn things over to the other players for a while.

There are really so many different ways for teams to be successful with this scene. I have used it to unfaltering enthusiasm over the years and I highly recommend incorporating it into your own routines.

Use This Challenge For:
- Classroom/Workshop – Major Skills Practiced:
  - Justification
  - Listening/Being in the Moment

- o Physicality
- o Storytelling (involves Making/Accepting Offers, Advancing, Extending, etc)
- o Taking Direction
- o Teamwork (involves Chivalry, Finding The Game, etc)
- o Thinking Funny
- Team Practice
- Single Group Performance
- Inter-Group Competition (Competitive Round)
- Inter-Group Competition (Non-Competitive Round – cross-team challenge)

Sound Effects

As the scene is performed, a collection of sound effects that change from moment to moment will be heard. Players must adapt the scene to justify the sounds.

Preparation:
A collection of sound effects.

Performance:
The host will get a set of variables from the audience that the scene will be based on. After the context of the scene has been established, random sound effects will occasionally begin to play that the team must be able to justify.

This challenge is similar to Options in that the team must constantly work to justify the new information that they are being given. However, unlike Options, where the information is usually already related to the scene in some fashion, here almost every single sound will be an offer from space.

Personally, I have found that the best way to run this challenge is by preloading a set of sound effects onto a laptop that I, as host, have on stage with me. Then I can fire them off at opportune (or inopportune) moments as they present themselves. There are several good free programs out there that are great for running sound effects – including those that will assign effects to individual laptop keys. Pretty cool.

A technician could also be assigned to run the sounds off of a computer or CD, however that does require a bit more finesse on the part of the sound operator. While I have found that to be successful as well – and only when I have had that special technician that understood the rhythm and flow of improv – my personal recommendation is for the host to run them from the stage, if the resources are available to have them do so.

Success:
This scene is all about two of the most basic principles of improv – narrative and justification. As with all scenes, first and foremost the team must be focused on telling a solid story, and advancing it towards a logical (or illogical) conclusion. The challenge, however, presents the added requirement of being able to continue the story while justifying the unusual sound effects suddenly intruding upon the world of the scene.

Really, all that success at this challenge requires is an ability to accept a series of offers from space and then allowing them to continue to advance your scene.

> *"Well, of course there was a massive explosion in the closet – we've stored the larger ammunition in there for years!"*

> *"What do you know? Another rainstorm in the kitchen. We'll have to get the exorcist to fix that."*

The key is that the team never loses their momentum just because of a random sound effect.

This challenge is both a fun learning tool for new performers and is also ridiculously entertaining for an audience to watch with experienced ones.

Use This Challenge For:
- Classroom/Workshop – Major Skills Practiced:
    - Justification
    - Listening/Being in the Moment
    - Storytelling (involves Making/Accepting Offers, Advancing, Extending, etc)
- Team Practice
- Single Group Performance
- Inter-Group Competition (Competitive Round)
- Inter-Group Competition (Non-Competitive Round – cross-team challenge)

Space Jump

One player begins a monologue. A second player freezes it and then starts a new scene. A third player freezes that and starts a third scene and so on. Once all players have had a go and the final scene is established, the last player to enter finds a reason to leave. The players then revert back to the previous scene. One by one the players exit until we are finally back to the monologue, which the first player completes.

Preparation:
None.

Performance:
The setup makes it sound like this would be an incredibly confusing challenge, but in reality, once a team has practiced it once – it's a piece of cake.

The host should get a set of variables from the audience as usual for the performers to base their scenes upon, which they, in turn, should likely use only one at a time. However, even with this frugal variable usage, this will typically leave one or two of the mini-scenes variable-less. This isn't necessarily a bad thing, but it is something that should be taken into consideration by the performers.

The first player begins a monologue. This can be about one of the variables or anything else that their improvisational heart desires. After the scene has been established – usually about 20-30 seconds – the second player will yell out "Freeze!" and the first performer will freeze wherever they are in mid-position, just like in a game of Freeze Tag. The second player will then begin a brand new, unrelated scene for the two of them, while also being sure to justify the first player's frozen physical position. Once that scene has been established, the process continues again with the third player and so forth and so on until all of the players have entered the scene and the entire team is finally working together on the final scene.

Now the process reverses itself. The last player to enter will figure out a justifiable reason for their character to leave and once they have, the performers will immediately revert back to the previous scene. nce that scene has again re-established itself, the second to last player justifies an exit and the performers again revert back to the scene that preceded it. The process continues again and again until only the first performer is left onstage by themselves to finish their original monologue. The entire process should take just under three minutes.

Essentially, this challenge is simply a very structured modification of Freeze Tag.

Success:
The biggest mistake that a rookie team can (and usually will) make with their first attempt at Space Jump is to use up all of the provided variables in one of the short scenes, leaving the other players with no ammo to fire at their own scenes. This will likely, in turn, tend to slow down a novice player's impulses, as many really feel the need to rely on the audience suggestions for inspiration.

However, what would be a flaw for a new group also could be a great gimmick in the hands of an expert team. What if the first player used up all of the variables in an overly dramatic fashion during their original monologue scene, then broke the 4th wall a bit with a smirk or wink at their teammates, as if to say, "Have fun with this one, guys!" An audience would love it if that was done well, but flying solo without variables can be a risky gambit so it is best left to adept performers.

While audiences do tend to enjoy this challenge immensely when it's done well, it must be presented very clearly and performers must strictly follow the rules to keep their wandering attention.

Also, while any scene created by a novice team might tend to drag a bit – that is part of the nature of improv after all, hit or miss – in a round of Space Jump this will absolutely kill the rhythm of the challenge and will completely shatter the audience's laughter momentum. Teams have to make sure that they keep up the pace.

This is one of the first challenges that I ever did as an improv performer and there are some pretty good reasons why it's still alive and kicking.

An oldie, but a goodie!

Use This Challenge For:
- Classroom/Workshop – Major Skills Practiced:
  - Concentration
  - Justification
  - Listening/Being in the Moment
  - Mime (Involves Space and Object Work, Naming, etc)
  - Storytelling (involves Making/Accepting Offers, Advancing, Extending, etc)
  - Teamwork (involves Chivalry, Finding The Game, etc)
- Team Practice
- Single Group Performance
- Inter-Group Competition (Competitive Round)
- Inter-Group Competition (Non-Competitive Round – cross-team challenge)

Statues/Moving People

Two actors are molded by the audience. The scene will be based on their posed positions.

Preparation:
None.

Performance:
This can be an incredibly fun scene for an audience because it involves DIRECT interaction with the performers. The audience isn't just providing variables, but is actually physically moving performers around as they see fit.

Variation 1: *Statues*
In this original version of Statues, the performers are molded by members of the audience while the host gets a few variables. A scene begins in which all of the positions are justified – the original positions becoming the primary offer for the scene to be based around, and the provided variables adding a little more fuel to the fire. This version is very fun at first, but the audience interaction does wear off quickly, so teams must to be able to carry their own weight.

Variation 2: *Backwards Statues*
Essentially Variation 1 in reverse. In this version the host gets a set of variables from the audience while the players are molded by other audience members. The performers then break out of the positions and create a scene based upon the audience suggestions – which this time must <u>conclude</u> with the players freezing in the posed positions.

This version requires a good sense of non-verbal communication between team members so that they all end simultaneously. It is also a little more fun for the audience than Variation 1as it keeps them on the edge of their seats, waiting to see how the positions will eventually be justified.

Variation 3: *Bookend Statues*
Here, players are molded into positions by members of the audience. The performers justify their positions by basing a scene around them, however, the scene must <u>also</u> conclude with the players again frozen in the same positions as the start – or sometimes into each other's positions. In the hands of an experienced team, this one can be fantastic!

Variation 4: *Moving People*
Instead of being posed as a statue, in a round of Moving People the players essentially become robots – incapable of moving on their own impulse in any way.

In this challenge, audience members or other players manipulate performers like giant puppets as the scene progresses. This one is always an excellent opportunity to create awkward laughter as it puts performers and audience in constant physical contact. It allows for great gimmicks like players falling over, screaming about burning eyes because the audience member didn't make them do something trivial like blink, or even pimping the audience members a little (What if a character had to go to the bathroom or it suddenly became a love scene? Fantastic!). Tons of fun!

Success:
Almost every beginning team – no matter what positions they are placed in by the audience – decides that since they are now in an awkward physical stance, their scene must therefore be taking place in an exercise class. EVERY single time. Seriously – like clockwork.

While this flimsy context could easily sustain an awkward moment in a round of Freeze Tag – one that lasts about a whopping five or ten seconds – it is not a strong enough foundation for a fully developed two to three minute scene. As a facilitator, do what you can to ensure that your teams avoid this novice trap.

Other than the aforementioned pitfall, a team's success with this challenge will be based almost entirely upon their good justification work, storytelling, and teamwork – in other words, the same skills that help almost every other challenge – with the added component that one's physicality can never disappear from a performer's mind.

If they can tell a good story while being physical, a team will never lose an audience.

Use This Challenge For:
- Classroom/Workshop – Major Skills Practiced:
  - Audience Interaction
  - Justification
  - Physicality
  - Taking Direction
- Team Practice
- Single Group Performance
- Inter-Group Competition (Competitive Round)
- Inter-Group Competition (Non-Competitive Round – cross-team challenge)

Styles

Team members will perform a scene, adjusting the style/genre in which it is presented as the host calls them out.

Preparation:
None. See Appendix B for a list of 50 Styles that have been successful in performance.

Performance:
The host will get a set of variables from the audience as usual for the team to use as the foundation of their scene. Once the context of the scene has been established (usually 20-30 seconds) and a story has begun to develop, the host will then periodically freeze the scene and shout out a particular film, theatre, or television style (i.e. Opera, Ballet, Shakespeare, Western, Horror, etc.) or a combination of styles (i.e. Science Fiction-Newscast). The team must maintain the scene's

same basic plot but alter the style in which the story is being told. Once a group has gone through four or five different styles, they should then bring the scene to a close.

The host may get a list of styles from the audience, or they can choose the styles themselves. Appendix B is a great place to start!

Success:
The teams that perform the strongest rounds of Styles are the ones that manage to consistently advance the original story throughout all of the various genres they are given AND are able to pull off a satisfying ending. Both of these tasks are surprisingly hard for most beginning improvisers.

Even a really strong novice team will often abandon the premise that got them started as soon as the first style is thrown into the mix.

This isn't because this particular game is unusually challenging or anything. It is simply because it is yet another challenge that requires a performer to be able to think about multiple variables simultaneously – in this case the platform for the scene and the group endowment of the shifting genres.

There is also a tendency for teams – both beginning and expert for that matter – to want to make each style simply a one-off joke. While this can be a great gag to use once during the chain of different genres, the repetition is pretty tiresome for an audience and certainly doesn't improve your team's storytelling or justification skills. In other words, do everything you can to encourage new performers to try to "integrate the story with the style."

Use This Challenge For:
- Classroom/Workshop – Major Skills Practiced:
  - Concentration
  - Endowments
  - Justification
  - Listening/Being in the Moment

- o Mime (Involves Space and Object Work, Naming, etc)
- o Physicality
- o Storytelling (involves Making/Accepting Offers, Advancing, Extending, etc)
- o Teamwork (involves Chivalry, Finding The Game, etc)
- Team Practice
- Single Group Performance
- Inter-Group Competition (Competitive Round)
- Inter-Group Competition (Non-Competitive Round – cross-team challenge)

Superheroes

The audience will decide on a "world crisis" and the players, as a group of heroes with unusual superpowers, will work together to solve it.

Preparation:
None.

Performance:
The scene will begin with a single player onstage. This player will be assigned both an unusual super power (i.e. Chopstick Boy, Amazing Hair Woman, etc.) and an unusual world crisis (i.e. they've run out of Spam in Antarctica) to solve.

The single player will begin a short scene of usually no more than twenty seconds in which they both demonstrate their super power and "discover" the world crisis in some fashion – often through some sort of "crime-o-scope." The player then "realizes" that they can't go it alone – they will need the help of their fellow superheroes in order to remedy the situation.

One by one, the remaining players enter the scene. As they enter, the previous player will assign their superpower to them (i.e. the 1st player assigns it to the 2nd, the 2nd to the 3rd, and so on) and each will quickly do something to demonstrate it.

Once all of the players have entered the scene, they will work together using their various superpowers to somehow solve the crisis. Once the crisis is taken care of, the players will then exit the scene in reverse order, often with some sort of tag line, leaving the original player to provide a final wrap up for the audience.

The entire scene should last about two minutes, so all of this happens fairly quickly.

Success:
This is easily one of the most popular challenges that I use, likely due to the fact that it uses a very structured format which gives newer players something to brace themselves up with during a performance. It probably doesn't hurt that it's also ridiculously fun.

Almost every time I have seen a group fail at Superheroes, it was due to their team not following the basic structure of the challenge. o, the most important thing that players can do to guarantee success is to practice it enough so that the format is second nature.

It might seem obvious (but apparently isn't, since I mistakenly hear from someone at least once a week about how "you just can't practice improv") but this is the best advice for every single challenge in this book and beyond – practice!

> *Practice, practice, practice, practice, practice, practice,*
> *practice, practice, practice, practice, practice, practice,*
> *practice, practice, practice, practice, practice, practice!*

Practice until the team doesn't have to think about the structure of the challenge anymore. Remember that the more things that are floating around inside of a performer's head, the more directions that their focus is being pulled in. Taking one of those concerns out of the mix can do WONDERS for a team.

This should go without saying, but I suppose a little reminder can't hurt – it is imperative for a player to be as physical as possible when embodying the superpower that they are assigned. This is a great opportunity to get away with some gratuitous mugging and for once it actually be called for by the challenge – players should <u>revel</u> in it.

Being very physical with this game not only helps to communicate the assigned endowment, but frankly it just makes things fun for the audience – and if the audience ain't happy, ain't nobody happy.

Use This Challenge For:
- Classroom/Workshop – Major Skills Practiced:
    - Embodiment
    - Endowments
    - Justification
    - Listening/Being in the Moment
    - Mime (Involves Space and Object Work, Naming, etc)
    - Physicality
    - Storytelling (involves Making/Accepting Offers, Advancing, Extending, etc)
    - Taking Direction
    - Teamwork (involves Chivalry, Finding The Game, etc)
- Team Practice
- Single Group Performance
- Inter-Group Competition (Competitive Round)
- Inter-Group Competition (Non-Competitive Round)

Superhero Eulogy

A world-famous superhero has died. In this challenge several important people in their life will deliver eulogies at their funeral.

Preparation:
None necessary, but a podium and a row of chairs for players can be a nice touch.

Performance:
The only variable that the audience needs to provide will be the name of the superhero that has died. The host will then provide the basic setup for the scene, usually something along the lines of...

> *"Thank you all for coming today. Undoubtedly, we are all saddened by the loss of our beloved Captain Yo-Yo (or whatever is provided). Here are some of the important people in the Captain's life who would like to pay their final respects."*

At that point the host will back away and one by one each of the players will step up to deliver a eulogy for the deceased as a character that would have been close to them. Traditionally each speaker will take on one of the typical comic book archetypes.

These include:

- their arch villain
- someone that witnessed the development of their superpowers
- someone from their childhood before they knew that they had powers
- the person that was in love with them but only discovered their true identity after they died
- the person that accidentally killed them

... and so on.

Also, instead of the host giving the setup, a team member could easily function as a funeral director and provide segues between speakers in which they provide the endowments for the other players.

Success:
This is a very hard challenge for newer performers because it is essentially a collection of three to five short solo scenes. Young performers, especially high school students, are used to powering themselves by feeding off of the energy of the other players on their team. Consequently, once they are expected to perform all by themselves, many often become terrified. Even a relatively seasoned

group can freeze up when faced with as much alone time as this challenge provides.

This is a great scene to use in practice to help team members get used to performing by themselves because, despite the monologue format, it still has a solid structure of character types to fall back on. This "characterization shield" will help to prop up nervous performers who didn't realize that they were capable of tackling a solo scene. Consequently, this one can be fantastic preparation for an advanced group before they try to take on long-form improv challenges like The Harold. You heard me right – *it's a gateway scene.*

I would avoid giving this challenge to most groups of younger performers in performance unless you are certain that they are up to the challenge.

Use This Challenge For:
- Classroom/Workshop – Major Skills Practiced:
  - Endowments
  - Individual Confidence Building
  - Listening/Being in the Moment
  - Storytelling (involves Making/Accepting Offers, Advancing, Extending, etc)
  - Thinking Funny
- Team Practice
- Single Group Performance (only if mastered)
- Inter-Group Competition (Competitive Round – only with advanced groups)

Tag Team

Just like the name implies. Two players must remain onstage throughout the scene while the other players wait to be tagged on the sidelines to switch places. A fun, fast-paced challenge.

Preparation:
None.

Performance:
The host will begin by getting a set of variables from the audience for the performers to build the scene around. Two of the team members will remain onstage and begin a scene for two performers. Once the scene has been established (usually about 20-30 seconds or so) the tagging process can begin.

A player must typically justify a reason for their exit within the context of the scene and then tag one of the other players waiting just outside of the playing space. As the new player enters, they also must justify the reason for their entrance. The team has the option of having the tagged player entering the scene play either a brand new character (good for Beginners) or maintain the same character as the player that tagged them in (Experts only).

The process will continue with frequent tagging until the scene reaches its completion.

A good addition to make to the challenge (if the players will be maintaining the same characters) is to assign a specific hat for each character. This can help with audience clarity, plus it provides the bonus of added physicality as the hats are passed around during the scene.

Success:
Let's review the tagging process. There are two ways that a team can handle tagging each other in this scene. In the first, each player will maintain a consistent character throughout the challenge. This method essentially turns the game into a round of Entrances and Exits without the added variable of a trigger word – in other words, a pretty good way for newer performers to play.

In the second (and much more fun) method, the entire scene is built around the *original pair of characters*. As a player tags out, the new player must then continue the scene as the *same* character exactly where it left off – even if it's in the middle of a sentence. This method has the potential to be a lot funnier and also much faster paced, but it does take some skill to pull off well. Just think about the logistics of it. By the end of the scene, the audience will likely have seen every team member play <u>both</u> roles. This can be quite confusing for those watching unless the players give the audience something to latch on to for each character – an obvious vocal/physical characteristic.

A team that can master this will have the audience eating out of their hands. I also recommend the addition of the character specific hats.

A truly professional group could easily create a scene with four or more characters (distinguishable by their hats) that both players cycle through during the course of the scene. Wow! What a whirlwind of activity that scene would be.

In addition, it should be mentioned that just like most other improv challenges that have a physical gimmick similar to the tagging at their heart (i.e. Sit, Stand, Lean or Entrance and Exits), pace is extremely important for this one. The action should begin slowly and as the scene builds, the physicality – in this case the tagging in and out of players – should also increase in speed.

Use This Challenge For:
- Classroom/Workshop – Major Skills Practiced:
    - Justification
    - Listening/Being in the Moment
    - Physicality
    - Storytelling (involves Making/Accepting Offers, Advancing, Extending, etc)
    - Teamwork (involves Chivalry, Finding The Game, etc)
    - Vocalization
- Team Practice
- Single Group Performance
- Inter-Group Competition (Competitive Round)

Temperamental Director

One member of the team becomes a film "director." The rest of the players become the "actors" in a movie based off of audience suggestions. The director will periodically stop the scene and change the style/genre of the film. The actors then perform the scene over again in the new style.

Preparation:
None.

Performance:
For this challenge, the variables that the host will get from the audience will consist of a genre of movie and two bits of information to support it (i.e. if it's a heist movie, location and object to be stolen). The player that has become the director moves over to the side to observe as the other players begin to improvise a brief scene (lasting approx. thirty seconds) in which they use the audience's suggestions.

The director however, does not like their performance for some reason and will stop the scene abruptly, often harshly. The director improvises with the other players for a few seconds and then decides that the movie would be better if the performers instead did it with some modification (i.e. in a different style or genre, with different character attributes, etc.) The actors then re-do the exact same scene they did the first time, but with this new context. The process continues until they have gone through three style changes and finally the director likes the movie they have made.

Success:
This is a really fun challenge. Newer performers can be very successful with this one because it has a rigid structure that will support their choices, while experienced performers will relish the many opportunities that the challenge provides to shine. Plus, audiences tend to respond very well to it – a true improv trifecta.

It should be noted that the strongest performances of Temperamental Director will always abide by the following two guidelines. First, as the team performs the original version of the scene, their focus should be almost entirely on storytelling. They need to get all the details of plot and character out there as fodder to feed the rest of the challenge yet to come. Then, as the team repeats the original scene, the pace should begin to speed up and players can pick and choose what elements of the original will make it to the 2nd draft – almost the same as it works in Half-Life, another "re-do the same scene again" challenge.

Second, it is very important that the players establish some sort of a relationship between the director and at least one of the actors that can be revisited every time the scene pauses. Now instead of simply telling the performers "That was terrible, do it as a disco number!" the director can also allude to a back-story – maybe they used to date each other, maybe one of them married the other's ex, maybe they used to be college roommates – the possibilities are endless. Adding some tension to the relationship can only give the performers more material with which to work, and consequently succeed.

Use This Challenge For:
- Classroom/Workshop – Major Skills Practiced:
    - Endowments
    - Justification
    - Listening/Being in the Moment
    - Physicality
    - Storytelling (involves Making/Accepting Offers, Advancing, Extending, etc)
    - Taking Direction
    - Teamwork (involves Chivalry, Finding The Game, etc)
    - Temporal Awareness
- Team Practice
- Single Group Performance
- Inter-Group Competition (Competitive Round)
- Inter-Group Competition (Non-Competitive Round – cross-team challenge)

Town Meeting

One player will take on the role of mayor of a make-believe town and the rest of the team will become other important officials for the city. The audience decides on a reason requiring everyone to have gathered together and a "meeting" is held in which the performers take questions from the audience.

Preparation:
A podium and a set of chairs for the team.

Performance:
The only real variable that has to be decided upon by the audience is the crisis serving as the reason for why the "meeting" is taking place. If you like, the audience can also decide what the other officials are, but in my experience it's more fun if the game is played like a round of Superheroes and the other players decide what each other's official job is:

To answer that question, let's hear from our Chief of Police...

The Mayor will get the meeting started with a quick (twenty seconds or so) intro to the scene in which they will provide the needed exposition as to the nature of the crisis, and so forth. They will then ask the audience for a question about the topic which they will answer themselves. After they have answered the question, they will switch gears slightly and essentially become the moderator for the rest of the scene by directing the questions from the audience to their appropriate teammates.

Success:
This is not a challenge that I would ever give to a new team. Yes, it does have a solid structure to build upon and it has frequent audience interaction, but newer players have a tendency to either freeze up, or, bless their hearts, actually try to genuinely answer the questions the audience asks. While it is important that the players do reference the questions that are being posed, remember that, as with all improv, the

point is to entertain WHILE advancing the story. Completely genuine responses tend to neglect the "entertainment" requirement. Because this challenge consists primarily of longer solo responses, it's better left to performers with a few more miles on their tires.

That said, for an experienced group, this is a challenge that really gives them a chance to shine. Without tons of gimmicks to fall back on, Town Meeting is really all about the expertise of the individual performers. In a competition, this one can really do a great job of improvisationally separating the weak from the strong, so to speak.

Use This Challenge For:
- Classroom/Workshop – Major Skills Practiced:
  - Audience Interaction
  - Endowments
  - Justification
  - Listening/Being in the Moment
  - Storytelling (involves Making/Accepting Offers, Advancing, Extending, etc)
  - Taking Direction
  - Teamwork (involves Chivalry, Finding The Game, etc)
  - Thinking Funny
- Team Practice
- Single Group Performance (only if mastered)
- Inter-Group Competition (Competitive Round – only with advanced groups)

Two Heads

Two players will work together to become a single character, with each player speaking only one word at a time.

Preparation:
None.

Performance:
There're not really a whole lot of surprises with this one. The host will get a set of variables from the audience and the team will incorporate them into a coherent scene, with the added requirement that at least two of the players will be working together to portray a single character. Usually positioned with an arm around each other's shoulder, the players will each contribute one word at a time and the character must speak in complete sentences.

Other than that, this scene is pretty self-explanatory.

Success:
This is a game that for some reason is usually played with a team of four (with two sets of two players), but can easily be played with a group of three or five as well. In fact, I personally think that a group of three is the ideal number because having a single player as the other half of the conversation really speeds up the pacing of the scene – and pace is key to a scene like this.

The audience will have little tolerance for a scene that simply chugs along in a choppy rhythm unless there is a good laugh line at the end of every single line of dialogue. Having the single player in there as the scene's "straight man" reacting to the unusual situation both speeds the action and builds a bridge from the audience to the performers.

My recommendation would be to always include a single player no matter the number of players on the team. A team of four would simply have a three-headed character, and a team of five would have two two-headed people.

Use This Challenge For:
- Classroom/Workshop – Major Skills Practiced:
  - Concentration
  - Listening/Being in the Moment
  - Physicality
  - Storytelling (involves Making/Accepting Offers, Advancing, Extending, etc)

- o   Teamwork (involves Chivalry, Finding The Game, etc)
- o   Verbal Prowess
- Team Practice
- Single Group Performance
- Inter-Group Competition (Competitive Round)
- Inter-Group Competition (Non-Competitive Round – cross-team challenge)

Typewriter Scene (aka "Typist/Narrator")

One player will become an author writing a story. The other performers will then become all of the characters in that story and will act out what is being narrated.

Preparation:
A chair for the typist.

Performance:
The host will need to get a set of variables from the audience to use as the platform for the story. The player who is the narrator/author will usually sit off to one side of the performance space and will pretend to be typing the story that the other players are enacting.

Typically the author/typist/narrator will spend a brief period of time at the beginning (about 20-30 seconds) setting up the scene and providing exposition using the variables that the audience provided. During this opening set-up, the rest of the players will be acting out the location, etc. that the narrator is providing using mime and object work.

After this introduction to the scene, the players will begin to vocally interact with each other – and occasionally even with the narrator. Eventually a resolution will present itself and the narrator will conclude by doing something that brings the scene to a close.

Success:

I have seen so many novice teams fail at this challenge simply because they treated it as if it should have been a monologue for the "author" rather than a true collaboration between all of the performers.

The players acting out the story would all too often do a little bit, pause, wait for the narrator to say something else, re-enact what they just said, then pause <u>again</u> for the narrator to continue, and so on and so on throughout the entire scene.

Remember that the key to doing this game correctly lies in the give and take relationship between <u>all</u> of the players. The narrator can set up events that the players then have to justify and the players can go in unexpected directions that the narrator must then work to justify.

This challenge is not an opportunity for one player to be allowed to drive a scene. Every member of the team should be an equal participant in the story's development. While, yes, the narrator may be omniscient, *the scene should <u>not</u> play out like…*

Narrator:	And then the bear said, "Where's my honey?
Player as Bear:	Where's my honey?
Narrator:	To which the leopard replied, "Roar!"
Player as Leopard:	Roar!

It's repetitive, boring, and repetitive. (Get it?) A Typewriter Scene *should*, rather, go something like…

Narrator:	And then the bear said…
Player as Bear:	Excuse me, would you like to buy a subscription to Atlantic Monthly?
Narrator:	Which surprised the illiterate leopard greatly. He then replied…
Player as Leopard:	Do you see the fresh kill in front of me? I'm so sick of you people interrupting my dinner!

| Player as Bear: | What do you mean 'You people?! That's just ignorant, Mr. Leopard! |
| Narrator: | And as the bear ate the leopard he said... |

When every player has a voice, the scene has an almost limitless number of directions in which it can go.

Use This Challenge For:
- Classroom/Workshop – Major Skills Practiced:
    o Embodiment
    o Endowments
    o Justification
    o Listening/Being in the Moment
    o Mime (Involves Space and Object Work, Naming, etc)
    o Storytelling (involves Making/Accepting Offers, Advancing, Extending, etc)
    o Taking Direction
    o Teamwork (involves Chivalry, Finding The Game, etc)
- Team Practice
- Single Group Performance
- Inter-Group Competition (Competitive Round)
- Inter-Group Competition (Non-Competitive Round – cross-team challenge)

Section Two:
Large Group Challenges

185

185 is a game about telling really bad jokes – groaners, if you will. The performer's task is to make a "creatively bad" pun about an assigned word.

Preparation:
None

Performance:
Players should first be assembled into a line across the performance space. Simply get a noun from the audience, and then let the actors step forward to tell their joke. There is no set order for this challenge as players just act on impulse and whoever gets to the front first speaks. The framework for the joke is simple, and performers are allowed to modify it, if so desired.

---

185 _____ walk into a bar. The bartender says, "We don't serve _____ here." The _____ says, "(Insert Punchline)"

Noun: NUNS

---

185 NUNS walk into a bar. The bartender says, "Sorry, we don't serve NUNS here." The HEAD MOTHER replies, "You're forgiven, my son, alcohol can be HABIT forming."

Noun: SHEEP

---

185 SHEEP walk into a bar. The bartender says, "Get out! We don't serve SHEEP here!" So one of the SHEEP says, "Too BAAAAAAAD for you. Our tips are a SHEAR delight."

While in my experience, 185 tends to work best as a large group challenge, in the hands of an expert team doing a single group performance it can also be a great pace-changer during a show. It changes the dynamic of the performance slightly and allows for some great audience interaction – and variety is the key to keeping your audience's attention.

185 also makes for a great tie-breaker during a competition. Get one representative from each team (or the complete team is fine as well) and see who can make the most jokes in a set amount of time. You can even have the audience voice their approval or disapproval over the quality of the joke.

Success:
As you can tell from the examples, the greatest measure of success is a combination of how bad the pun was with how creative the usage is. Getting the audience to groan loudly and enthusiastically is wonderful, but occasionally one can actually earn cheers.

An audience is a MUST for this challenge. If you are using it in a class/workshop setting, then divide the group into two halves – performers and audience – that can flip-flop to become each others' audiences.

This is a challenge that will fall flat on its metaphorically personified face without the feedback of an immediate response.

Use This Challenge For:
- Classroom/Workshop – Major Skills Practiced:
  - Audience Interaction
  - Individual Confidence Building
  - Thinking Funny
- Team Practice
- Single Group Performance
- Inter-Group Competition (Non- Competitive Round)
- Inter-Group Competition (Tie-Breaker)

Conducted Scenes

Any scene that involves the players forming a line across the stage with the host pointing at who should be participating (ala a conductor) is considered a Conducted Scene. There are many different varieties of conducted scenes well-suited for either a performance or Tune-up session. These are the four that I have had the most success with.

Preparation:
None.

Performance:
Any version of a conducted scene will follow the same basic structural configuration.

The players will all form a line along the front of the playing space and the host will position themselves in front of the group. As the challenge plays out, the host will point at various team members when it is their turn to participate. These challenges typically work best with a smaller group of between five and ten players (eight seems to be perfect). It is also helpful for the audience's visibility if the host can get to a lower level than the players (what with sight lines and all).

Variation 1: *Conducted Story*
This is a great game all about players listening to each other and telling a story – consequently it also makes for a great Tune-up exercise! As usual, the host gets a few variables from the audience and the team will make up a story (with a beginning, middle and end) based on those variables. When the host points at a particular player, it is their turn to speak.

Players have no idea what the order of speakers will be, so they absolutely MUST be fully listening to the story that the other players are creating rather than pre-planning what they themselves will say.

In a performance, a player might only contribute a small section to the story or they might be chosen several times, depending on how the host decides to conduct.

No matter what kind of maestro the host turns out to be, he/she should always make a point of varying the timing of the moments that they choose to alternate between players. Some moments should transition at the ends of sentences, some in the middle, sometimes it's fun to go back and forth between two players saying one word at a time. As with so many things in life, mixing it up is key to success.

In a performance, the story should be wrapped up in under three minutes.

Variation 2: *Authors/Genres*

This game plays out exactly the same as Conducted Story with the addition that each player has also been assigned an endowment – in this case a particular author or a genre of writing. When working with younger players (or not very well-read adults) I'd personally recommend sticking to genres (rather than individual writers), or at least to a really well known book series. Anything from Harry Potter, to vampire fiction, to romance, to a how-to manual is fair game for this challenge.

The task is to maintain the same story throughout all of the different genres, much like a team would do in a round of Styles. This one is a bit harder than Conducted Story, but if the group is up to the task, it can be a ton of fun.

Variation 3: *Radio Stations*

Each of the players is assigned a different radio format (i.e. Heavy Metal, the Farm Report, Spanish Language Radio Disney, etc.) and they form a line across the stage. The host then becomes the radio tuner (for the few folks in the audience old enough to even remember what that is) and will alternate between the stations that for some reason are all broadcasting in their various formats about the same general subject, also provided by the audience.

Variation 4: *Orchestra Concerto*

In this fun challenge for advanced groups (or Tune-up for all levels) – and the host will actually get to become a real-life honest-to-golly orchestra conductor!

Each of the players will choose a gibberish sound with some sort of rhythmic pattern to it. The host will then "play" the group as they perform their sounds under his control. In a performance situation, both the host and the players need to be folks with a good musical background, otherwise the challenge will likely not result in anything worth watching. When done well, this game is ridiculously impressive; when done poorly, it is a failure of colossal proportions.

Success:

Just like for every other short form challenge in the book, it is obviously very important to incorporate a lot of humor during a performance that is using a Conducted Scene to keep an audience's attention. However, remember that what will make a team truly succeed at this challenge will not be a series of non-sequitur jokes, but rather the group's ability to listen to each other and maintain a solid storyline/consistent focus.

Conducted Scenes make for great Tune-up exercises because they all involve so much LISTENING to the other players on a team.

Listening is one of the most important skills that a good improviser will possess, yet it is also one of the most challenging abilities for newer performers to get a handle on. All of these different versions of Conducted Scenes (and remember, that there are many more out there – these are just the ones that I have had success with) rely very heavily on solid listening for a team to succeed.

A Conducted Story scene in which one player breaks off mid-sentence and the next player begins a new sentence instead of continuing where the previous player left off will garner the instant scorn of the audience. An Orchestra Concerto scene in which players aren't listening to each other will produce a big glob of mush instead of a song.

Even though it is an essential element of a successful performance, a helpful exercise to try in a Tune-up session is to forbid the use of humor in a Conducted Story. Once trying to show off for each other by being funny is taken out of the mix, players can really focus on the areas they should have been all along – on listening, on storytelling, and on teamwork.

Use This Challenge For:
- Classroom/Workshop – Major Skills Practiced:
  - Concentration
  - Endowments
  - Individual Confidence Building
  - Justification
  - Listening/Being in the Moment
  - Storytelling (involves Making/Accepting Offers, Advancing, Extending, etc)
  - Teamwork (involves Chivalry, Finding The Game, etc)
  - Vocalization
- Team Practice
- Single Group Performance (Orchestra Concerto only if mastered)
- Inter-Group Competition (Non-Competitive Round – cross-team challenge, not Orchestra Concerto)

The Die Game

An elimination round in which team members will attempt to perform a certain task determined by whatever version is selected. When a player fails at that task they must act out a scene dramatizing their own demise.

Preparation:
None. See Appendix E for a detailed list of 75 Die Game questions and 35 Zulu ideas that have been successful in performance.

TEACHING AND PERFORMING IMPROV

Performance:
Really any improv game that is used as an elimination challenge is already considered to be a Die Game by definition, even if the players don't perform a death scene – but honestly, where's the fun in that?

What follows in this section are the three most popular versions of The Die Game. In all three variations, the players will form a line along the front of performance area. Also for all three, when a player makes a mistake, the host will lead the audience in chanting three times, "Die! Die! Die!"

In my experience, the audience is usually very quick to point out a player's mistake and therefore is apparently filled with some sort of deep-seated subconscious blood lust. Freaky!

The player must then perform a short (5-30 second) scene in which they die in the manner of the audience's choosing. And please remember that the performance is supposed to be funny, so keep the methods of death light – death by vacuum cleaner, death by angry butterflies, or death by Perry Como are all good choices; death by horrific accident – not so much.

Also, this is a challenge that I use at almost every competition as an "end of the evening" sort of revelry. It gives the show some structure for the regular audience members and it gives your judges or crew time to tally things up to determine the winners. An ideal number of players is between eight and twelve. Any fewer and the game is too short, any more and it can become kinda boring.

Variation 1: *Story Die*
Although this is the best known version of The Die Game floating around the improv world (hence why I included it here), I have actually not used it in performance. Why? Well, mostly I was having too much fun using the other two versions, but also because it is exactly the same as Conducted Story with the addition of the elimination Die. There's nothing wrong with the challenge – it seems quite lovely. I just can't back up that feeling with an experience-based stamp of approval.

Here the host will get a title of a story and a genre from the audience and point at a player. After the foundation of the story has been established, the host will then point at a different player who must continue the telling of it flawlessly. A good host should develop a sense for the rhythm of the delivery and consequently will vary their pointing not randomly, but within the feel of the narrative – sometimes at the end of a sentence, sometimes in the middle, sometimes after only one word. If a player pauses, repeats a previous player, or makes no sense, the audience will begin their chant and the offending player must die. The story then continues without interruption until there is only one performer left standing.

Variation 2: *The Die Game*
While this version also goes by other names like "Question Die" that describe it more aptly, I simply refer to it as The Die Game because it is the primary version that I use.

The host will ask the players a question and they must answer it one word at a time going down the line as if the group were really one person. When the answer reaches the end of the line, it simply loops around and continues back at the beginning, becoming a record-breaking run-on sentence. Players have faulted if they pause, say more than one word, use a contraction, repeat what the previous player said, or make no sense. The audience will begin chanting "Die!" and the offending player will perform their death scene.

~~ For example ~~

Host:	Do you know the way to San Jose?
Player 1:	The…
Player 2:	way…
Player 3:	to…
Player 4:	San Jose…
Audience:	Die! Die! Die!
	(Player 4 steps forward.)
Host:	*(To Player 4.)* Sorry, that was two words. *(To audience.)* Method of death?

Audience:	Churro!
Host:	Alright, death by churro it is. Take it away.
	(Player 4 performs an elaborate scene in which she is comically attacked by an angry sentient churro, bent on revenge.)

I always use the sample question of "Why is the sky blue?" when giving the set-up to the audience and usually I will then use it as the first question of the game.

As the round progresses, the number of players slowly begins to dwindle and once it has been whittled down to the final two, they must face each other in a head to head competition. In addition to the other rules, if players break eye contact, it is now also considered a loss. This should be judged by the host who will stand behind the two players.

I always use the same final question for every game:

What is the meaning of life?

Eventually, one the players will make a mistake and we have a winner. However, since it is The <u>DIE</u> Game, when I use it *no one* is allowed to survive and the winner must also perform a death scene.

It seems appropriate to give the winning player some sort of prize – something silly is great, or I usually make a "Certificate of Life" suitable for framing and showing off.

Don't forget to check out Appendix E! Seriously Good Stuff!

Variation 3: *Zulu*
This is a really fun spin on The Die Game, suitable for groups who have had some well-punched dance cards in their past. I'd avoid giving it to newbies during a performance, as they often get a frightened deer-in-the-headlights sort of glazed expression when faced with it.

Here, players must come up with the name of something original that fits into a provided category. While one could probably use just about anything as that category, in my experience the two most successful are new products and film titles. When pointed at by the host, the player must quickly provide the name of something new that fits the assigned category.

A player has faulted if they pause, say the name of a product/film that already exists, repeats another player, or simply rearranges the words in the category's name. So for example:

Category: *Drain Un-clogger*

☺ Great Answers ☺	☹ Bad Answers ☹
Clear That Pipe!	Drain-O
The Flow-nator	Unclog My Drain

When a player faults, the audience will chant and the player will perform their death scene. The host should change the product type or film genre after every elimination. Like Die Game Variation 2, once there are only two players standing they must maintain eye contact, even the winner must die, and they should get a prize.

Remember that this is a lightning round and should go as fast as humanly possible. And, come on, go to Appendix E already! It also has a list of 25 Products and 10 Film Genres that have been successful in competition.

Any version of The Die Game also makes for a great tie-breaker in a competition. Simply get the two tied teams to form the line and whichever team the last player standing is a member of is the winner.

Success:
I wish there was some amazing secret tip that I could give players here, but really the two biggest keys to not being eliminated during a Story Die or regular Die Game are basic improv skills – actively listening to the other players and maintaining focus. Concentration is the word of the day, kids. For Zulu, though, I can't even provide that

degree of sketchy insight. It's a game that is all about "thinking funny" and frankly, having a quick wit is something that just takes lots of experience to hone to perfection.

However, the element of these challenges that keeps the audience happy isn't going to be the performance framework, but rather the quality of the death scenes. There is nothing worse (barring disease, famine, and reality television) than a player that just completely wimps out on their die scene. "Ahh, I'm dead. Flop." just isn't going to cut it.

Just as with any other improv scene, during a Die players should strive to establish and build a story – albeit a very abbreviated one – to frame in the main event of their demise with some context. The action should build in intensity, eventually leading to the climax of their death. Just because the Die is short doesn't mean that players are allowed to be lazy. They are being given the opportunity to perform a (5-30 second) solo scene, and they should treat it as such. If however, there have been several longer deaths in a row, a player should also have the insight to understand when to toss in a quickie to vary the pace for the audience.

Use This Challenge For:
- Classroom/Workshop – Major Skills Practiced:
    - Audience Interaction
    - Concentration
    - Individual Confidence Building
    - Listening/Being in the Moment
    - Physicality Storytelling (involves Making/Accepting Offers, Advancing, Extending, etc)
    - Thinking Funny
    - Verbal Prowess
- Team Practice
- Single Group Performance (except Zulu – only with advanced groups)
- Inter-Group Competition (Non-Competitive Round – cross-team challenge, Zulu – only with advanced groups)
- Inter-Group Competition (Tie-Breaker)

Freeze Tag (Large Group Version)

Although often used as a single team challenge, Freeze Tag also works extremely well as a large group activity – so much so that in performance it is the primary version that I use.

A pair of players will perform a brief scene. Once it has been established, one of the performers not in the scene will yell "Freeze!" and take the place of one of the pair. he player that entered the challenge will then start a brand new unrelated scene.

(For more details about Freeze Tag, look in the "Team Challenges" part of this chapter.)

Preparation:
None

Performance:
In general, a large group performance of Freeze Tag should play out exactly the same as it would for the single team version, except that there should be a long line of players across the entire stage area.

When I use this challenge in competitions, it is usually at the start of the evening as a "warm-up" for both the performers and the audience and involves one or more participants from every single team. I've also used it to great success in workshop settings with up to fifty players.

No matter what environment you are in, however, it's always a good idea to provide a few variables for the first pair of players to get the ball rolling.

Success:
There's no difference between what will make a performer successful in a large group setting versus the single team version. Players need to focus on making and accepting offers, getting a feel for the pace of

the overall scene, and being as physical as possible. It should be noted though that depending on how the challenge is being used, the host may need to do a bit of encouragement to get the audience to respond appropriately and enthusiastically to the performers.

After all, a good party is all about a good host – and it should always be a party.

Use This Challenge For:
- Classroom/Workshop – Major Skills Practiced:
  - Concentration
  - Individual Confidence Building
  - Justification
  - Listening/Being in the Moment
  - Mime (Involves Space and Object Work, Naming, etc)
  - Physicality
  - Storytelling (involves Making/Accepting Offers, Advancing, Extending, etc)
  - Teamwork (involves Chivalry, Finding The Game, etc)
  - Temporal Awareness
  - Thinking Funny
- Team Practice (Regular version)
- Single Group Performance (Regular version)
- Inter-Group Competition (Non-Competitive Round – cross-team challenge)

Good Thing/Bad Thing

See Team Challenges

Scenes from a Hat

Players will create a very brief scene (under five seconds) based around a premise that the host draws out of a hat.

Preparation:
Six to eight premises, pre-written on slips of paper and a hat. See Appendix F for a list of 75 awesome premises that have been successful.

Performance:
As with all of these large-group challenges, the scene begins with players forming a long line across the playing space. In my experience, for this game about a dozen performers is ideal.

The host will pull a premise out of an interesting looking hat. The premise will be something like "Unusual items found in your couch cushions" or "Rejected character ideas for Sesame Street" or "If teeth could talk." Players will then step forward on impulse and present their example of the premise as a very quick toss-out scene. Once the pace begins to slow down a bit, the host will select a different premise.

Also, Scenes from a Hat can make a great tie-breaker as well. Simply get one or more representatives from each team to come up and begin the challenge. The team that has produced the most examples of the premise in a 90 second period is the winner.

Success:
For performers, this challenge is all about quick wit without fear. Players need to come up with as many ideas as they can and present them as quickly as possible. In an ideally paced performance, one player should begin presenting their idea just as the laughter begins to subside from the previous player's contribution.

The host's primary responsibility during a performance lies in being able to sense when it is time to change the premise for the challenge. However, their most important job occurs long before the presentation when they select the actual premises that will be used. These premises must not only be good ones, but care must be taken to ensure that they are also suitable for your audience. This is a challenge that can turn R or X-rated without warning in an instant.

Obviously, for many groups the potential offensiveness of the challenge is not a problem. Heck, it is part of the reason why they would choose to be doing the game in the first place.

If one is working in an educational environment, however, the expectations are a bit different, so it is important to be purposeful when crafting the premises. In the school climate that I work in, there is an expectation that teams will likely approach the offensiveness level of "vague euphemism" but go no further as there are always lots of little brothers and sisters in the audience.

The entire challenge should last anywhere from three to five minutes, depending on audience response.

Use This Challenge For:
- Classroom/Workshop – Major Skills Practiced:
    - Concentration
    - Individual Confidence Building
    - Mime (Involves Space and Object Work, Naming, etc)
    - Thinking Funny
    - Verbal Prowess
- Team Practice
- Single Group Performance
- Inter-Group Competition (Non-Competitive Round – cross-team challenge)
- Inter-Group Competition (Tie-Breaker)

Bonus Section:
Tie Breaker Challenges

Occasionally during a competition there will be moments when the judging is just too close to call, a team deserves a second chance, or possibly there were several teams that deserve a shot at getting into a wild card bracket. This is where a tie-breaker type challenge will come into play. While there are certainly other challenges that one can choose to use as a tie-breaker, all of the ones listed below have been time-tested, audience-pleasing, field-narrowing successes.

185
Get one representative from each team and see who can make the most jokes in a set amount of time. Or you could do the same using the complete teams. You can even have the audience voice their approval or disapproval over the quality of the jokes.

Alliteration
Get one member from each of the tied teams and have the audience assign each of them a letter. Then split the audience in half and assign each player to a side of the audience. Give the players a few variables or a context to use to create a ninety second scene and have the audience in charge of counting the number of words used by each player that begin with the assigned letter. The highest number wins. Great audience participation!

Alphabet Scene
The most subjective of the tie-breakers, players from each team perform the challenge as usual and at its conclusion the audience votes for which player did the best job. This is fine to use during a mock-competition or single team performance, but I'd steer clear of it in an actual multi-team competition for which it is important to remain completely objective.

Categories

One member of each of the involved teams will come up to perform a scene together. Assign each of the players a category and provide them with either variables or a context to use as their platform. Split the audience into as many sections as there are players and assign a performer to each section. The audience will keep track of how many examples of the assigned category the player was able to use during the course of the scene. The player with the highest total after 90 seconds is the winner.

The Die Game (any variation)

Since by definition The Die Game is an elimination game, it's a perfect tie-breaker! Gather all of the members of both teams into a line and play as usual. The last player standing is the winner.

Hat Game

Get one player from every tied team and give each of them an unusual hat. The players are either given variables or a full platform and a scene begins in which they make no reference to the hats. The winner is the first person to get the other player's hat(s). A missed grab is a loss. The scene must be completed in less than ninety seconds.

Props

There are two good ways to use Props as a tie-breaker. In both methods at least two members from each team will come up and be handed an unusual object. In the first version, the winner will be the team that can come up with the most uses for that object in a thirty second time period, with a coin toss deciding which team goes first. The second method plays out just like the regular game and the audience decides which team's uses were the better ones. Like Alphabet Scene, I'd avoid the second version if it's for a true competition.

Scenes from a Hat

This can be done as a single player head-to-head challenge, or could be team vs. team. Get the players to come up and begin the challenge s usual. The team or player that can produce the most examples for the premise in a ninety second period is the winner.

CHAPTER FIVE:
HOW TO STRUCTURE AN IMPROV
PERFORMANCE

One of the best (or at least one of the most convenient) aspects of improv is its remarkable flexibility in performance. Whether you are planning a large scale inter-team competition or a more intimate show for a single group, every aspect of the performance can be adjusted to suit your individual needs. While this fact does extend to long-form improv performance as well, like the rest of the book, the focus of this chapter is strictly on short form challenges.

Let's begin by going over basic performance logistics that must be considered to guarantee a smooth performance. At the end of the chapter I have also included a section of sample forms, awards, and even a blank performance template.

We'll start by looking at a <u>single team</u> performance.

How is the room set up?
In its simplest of forms, all one really needs in order to do improv is a performance area on one side of the space and room for an audience on the other. Everything after that is pure gravy. I'll cover technical requirements in more detail later, but remember that you can get by with next to nothing if you need to. Improv has been around since tribes were re-enacting the hunt on the threshing floor – and they didn't exactly have a sound guy.

Who will lead the performance?
Typically, in a single team performance, one member of the company takes on the role of emcee while the other players sit in a designated

holding area. If your role within your group is solely that of a facilitator, as mine is with my students, then you have likely just nominated yourself to be the permanent performance emcee. Congratulations!

Who will perform?
There are two basic ways to determine which players will perform each challenge as they come up during the performance. In the first, the host can select the team members to go via a simple "This game is for Bob and Dave" tossed in as they describe the challenge to the audience in the setup. If this method is used, I would, of course, suggest that the selected players are adept at the particular challenge. In the Second, the players decide who will go, likewise based upon each player's strong suits.

Since you really don't want to slow down your performance with a discussion in front of your audience about which players will do what, many improv companies have this sort of thing already worked out amongst themselves. This group of players is the go-to for Half Life, this combination for Slide Show, this one for Experts, etc. It simply comes as a by-product of being well rehearsed.

What challenges will they do?
There are lots of possibilities here as well. Some emcees will choose a complete setlist in advance and it will be performed without deviation. Some will simply decide on games at will as the performance is in progress. Some will let the performers choose for them. Many emcees will use some sort of a randomizer to determine what games will be played – there's even an app for that! As with every aspect of your performance, my advice is that the more this process can be integrated into the actual presentation, the better.

SO... Why not liven it all up a bit and have the audience choose?

There are countless methods that could be used.

- They could choose from a posted list.
- You could create an improv challenge deck of cards and an audience member could simply "Pick a card. Any card."

- How about a series of numbered envelopes with challenges pre-written inside?
- A random member of the audience could get to choose the number and consequently what game will be played.
- Maybe there's a dart board with challenges posted on it on 3x5 cards.
- You could even create a carnival-style Wheel of Fortune game with a different challenge at every stopping point.

There are a million and one fun ways to determine what your show will be. Why not use them all?

What do I need to be careful of?
Technical concerns aside (we'll get to them later), there are very few logistical caveats that I can in good faith mention here. Every performance situation is different and consequently will have its individual problem areas that must be dealt with. Aren't you lucky! However, there is one mistake that universally has the potential to plague a performance, and in my experience is often neglected. But don't despair – with proper planning it is pretty easy to prevent.

> *It is very important that your team <u>does not fail in front of an audience</u>!*

I know – it seems obvious right? Trust me, it isn't.

First of all, your group MUST be fully prepared for the performance. I really don't mean to be insulting (honestly, I don't – I swear!) but it truly amazes me how often teams want to get up and perform improv without having done any real practice. The very fact that one doesn't have a script to use as a guide should demand it, right? Adequate preparation on the part of the performers is <u>essential</u> to a worry-free performance.

Please take note that I'm not advocating that players pre-plan for the show or anything like that. Pre-writing of any sort is diabolical and goes against everything that improv is about! What you should do, however, is ensure that only well-practiced games that the team has been successful with are options for the performance line-up.

This is also a good reason for having the company determine which members will perform what challenges. Every member will be very good at some games and weak at others, depending on what skills the challenge requires of them. Having a pool of a dozen performers in a group is wonderful, because as different challenges arise, different members with different strengths will get the opportunity to shine.

Newer improv performers tend not to understand the need for significant rehearsal time to produce successful improv and may try to fight you on it. Don't let them have their way. As the performance facilitator, the majority of your job responsibility is to make the group look as awesome as possible. A performance is <u>not</u> the time to be trying out a new challenge for the first time.

Let's move on to an <u>inter-team performance</u> or <u>competition</u>.

What's the same?
The basic set-up of the performance space can be absolutely identical for a multi-team performance as it is for a single team one. A holding area is needed for teams somewhere, with a performance space in front of the audience. The emcee should, of course, also have a designated area onstage. When I hold a multi-team performance, I reserve 1/3 of the theatre seating for the teams and the audience gets the rest.

So, what's different about an inter-team competition?
The biggest difference between the structure of a single group performance and that of an inter-team competition is the size of the team itself. In a single group performance, one can have a large pool of performers at their disposal and players can get up at will based on their strengths. In an inter-team competition format, the team must already be whittled down to a group of three to five players that will have to be able to do whatever challenge is asked of them.

How does one decide on which challenges to use in an inter-team performance?

Unlike a single team show in which an emcee has the ability to give only challenges that have been mastered by the group – nothing but soft pitches – there's no way to ensure that degree of familiarity for teams when they are coming in from all over a region. Consequently, my opinion is that it is in everyone's best interest to maintain a standard list of challenge possibilities that *could* be used in performance (guess what the inspiration for the chapter full of improv challenges was).

Whichever challenges you choose to include, there are <u>two parameters</u> that this list must adhere to.

First, it has to be short enough that teams can realistically be expected to have practiced all of them and to have been successful at the majority of them.

Second, it has to be long enough that the audience (who might be attending every competition that you hold) doesn't see the same challenges over and over and over again.

When I was a student and was doing competitive improv, the organizer's primary concern, I believe, was to be fair to all teams. Consequently, there was a challenge list of only ten games to practice. When a team arrived to compete, they would find out the one challenge from the list that would be used for <u>every</u> team in a particular round. Although, it is very fair to all of the teams competing to have them each attempting the same challenge, it is also profoundly boring for an audience to watch fourteen straight Space Jumps in a row. As you can surmise, the emphasis of these gatherings was much more on the *competitive* aspect, rather than on the *entertainment* value.

While I can certainly understand the desire to create an extremely formal and regimented competition, I knew that was not what I wanted to do when I decided to start one. (If that's something you are interested in, that's great! Do it! I don't think there's anything wrong with it at all – I just went in a different direction. And don't worry – everything in here still applies to you.) Yes, at the competitions I host, teams do win plaques and bragging rights, but I wanted the overall vibe to feel more like an improv party than an athletic association meet. Consequently, the organizational system I decided to use ensures that even teams that are eliminated from the competition proper still have opportunities to get up and perform. We also incorporate frequent audience interaction, occasionally feature guest performers, and while there are formal plaques for the top teams, there are also informal certificates and "prizes" from a dollar store.

Anyway, back to choosing challenges. The list that I use has about forty games on it and is made available to any team planning to attend. When preparing for a competition, I create a performance template from that list that includes more challenges for each round than I have teams coming. Then during the performance, I use the template like a menu and usually roll an oversized novelty die to determine which game a particular team will get. Yes, occasionally I still get a group that obviously has never practiced a particular challenge and might misstep a bit in performance, but total wipeouts are very few and far between.

How is the competition structured?
Obviously, one can structure a multi-group performance/competition in any number of ways, so get creative here! Do what you think sounds fun. Do what you think your audience will like. Do something that you've never seen before.

Here is the basic rundown of a typical competition that I host, as an example to get your own ideas flowing.

> ➤ The performance begins with a large group activity that every team can participate in. Most of the time, I call up two members of every team to participate in a round of Freeze Tag.

> ➤ After that, the competition consists of three formal scoring rounds.

➢ The first round includes every team and, depending on the number of groups competing, may also include a few non-scoring cross-team challenges that involve members of several groups working together. The round should last under an hour and then go to intermission, during which scores are tallied.

➢ The top five or six teams then advance to round two, which also includes a few non scoring challenges and lasts for around twenty-five minutes.

➢ While team's scores are tabulated, a non-scoring challenge like Scenes from a Hat or Chance of a Lifetime is used as cover.

➢ The top three teams then advance to round three which is always Party Quirks. (The one time I didn't end the performance with Party Quirks you'd have thought that I cancelled Christmas. Never again.)

➢ While the winner of round three is determined, I lead a quick Die Game with one member from every team playing, and then finish with awards.

The competitions I participated in when I was a student years ago were a much simpler two round structure. Every team did the same challenge in round one. The top teams then advanced to round two where they would also all present the same challenge (although a different one from round one). Formal scoring determined the winner. Once a team was eliminated they were pretty much done for the night, as evidenced by the highly whittled down audience left by the end of an evening.

How does one determine the winners?
Again, there are several ways that winners can be chosen. When I was a student, teams were scored on a 1-10 scale by three judges. When I began hosting competitions myself, I got judges from local improv troupes to come in and not only rate teams on a 1-10 point system, but

also provide detailed written feedback on performer's individual strengths and weaknesses.

I have since begun using an audience balloting system where every audience member is given a pencil and a ballot upon arrival and the votes are tallied at the appropriate times throughout the performance. Although teams do not receive the targeted feedback that professional judges provide, this method is in essence a direct democracy, and provides good incentive for every team to bring large cheering sections with them.

But there are lots of other possibilities, too!

- If the emcee is not affiliated with any of the teams, there's no reason why they couldn't be the one awarding points.
- Teams could face each other head to head with an audience applause-o-meter determining who advances to the next round.
- If you are not taking the scoring process too seriously, you could devise a completely random method that has more value as entertainment than it does as a true evaluation tool.

Like every single aspect of improv performance, the process of choosing the winners is fully customizable.

Are there other formats out there?
Of course! Many of the big improv groups (i.e. ComedySports or iO, formerly Improv Olympics) have their own performance structures (some long form, some short form) that work very well for them. As an example, the TheatreSports format pits two teams against each other (in essentially mock competition) with the emcee functioning as a referee.

It should be noted, however, that these specialized formats *belong to these individual groups*. In fact, in some cases (like TheatreSports) they are protected by law as intellectual property. Remember that part of the fun is figuring out what works for you. That's the best part about improv's malleability – after you have determined what you want the focus of your performance to be, you can truly create a fun and engaging structure to suit your specific needs, whatever they may be.

Moving on...

No matter what sort of performance you are planning, I'm sure that your list of logistical questions is topped with wondering what the technical requirements of the show might be. Here you go:

What equipment do I need?

As for truly <u>required</u> equipment – there isn't much. You can honestly get by with absolutely nothing if that's all you have, or you can make things as elaborate as you desire. To keep things running smoothly, however, it is important that you make sure to adequately consider the visual and aural needs of your performance space.

Visual:

If you are planning to do any challenges that require the audience to know information that your players don't (i.e. an endowment challenge like Party Quirks) you need some means of giving them that information. One of the large flip pads that are used in conference rooms can be great for this (it can also be a great place to record variables that a team needs to use as well), but only if your performance space is small enough for the folks in the back row to be able to read it – The last thing that you want is for blind Aunt Tilly and deaf Uncle Henry to start an invasive conversation about what the group will be performing.

As a teacher, almost all of my performances have taken place in larger spaces, like gyms and high school theatres. Consequently, the simple, low tech approach of a flip pad would not work for me.

Showing my age, when I began doing improv I used transparencies projected on a makeshift screen to communicate to the audience. It works very well (if you can still manage to find an overhead projector!) but does require a fair amount of pre-planning.

Once PowerPoint came along, I switched everything over to that. It still requires advanced planning for endowment challenges, but it looks a lot better and there's very little chance of operator error.

With all of the live projectors, document cameras, and even apps that are available quite inexpensively now, the possibilities of how one chooses to deal with this requirement have really opened up. As with all aspects of a performance, my advice is to try to make sure that getting variables or projecting endowments isn't simply a necessary evil that must be done in order to get to the actual entertainment, but rather is an engaging part of the performance itself.

Aural:
As for sound, again the possibilities are wide open. As you decide on what to include, you have three basic needs to consider:
- Music
- Sound Effects
- Performer Amplification

Let's start with **music**.

It's amazing what house music can do to set the mood of a room.

Many improv groups, especially those performing in a space with limited means, may choose not to use any because they simply don't have the capability of amplifying it adequately. Other groups that are trying to create the feel of a more formal competition environment may choose not to as well. Personally, since I have always wanted to create an "improv party" atmosphere, I have always relied heavily upon house music to get the audience into the right mindset upon arrival.

I always choose fun, upbeat music – mostly contemporary, occasionally funny, often covers – that we play slightly too loud to completely fade into the background. This immediately gets the audience to buy into the idea that the performance they are about to witness will be a lot of fun. It's always fun to watch as folks who are buying their tickets in the lobby try to sneak looks of anticipation inside the theatre as they hear the excitement of the music pumping inside.

What about **sound effects**?

There's never been a better time to use sound effects in a performance. You can get ridiculously elaborate at next to no expense if you desire. Gone are the days of painstakingly locating specific effects from an unwieldy LP or even CD library. You can produce buzzers, doorbells, explosions, and more with ease from a computer or smartphone. You can even have an entire library of files on these devices that you randomly pull out for a challenge like Sound Effects.

All of these audio clips are readily available and begging to be downloaded and used from free sound effects libraries online.

However, beyond getting the sounds themselves, there is a more important logistical challenge related to staffing that must be addressed.

Many professional improv groups can utilize as much sound as they like because they usually have a company member who is a dedicated technician. This individual is so ingrained in the improv world, that they have developed the same sense of timing and professional sensibilities as the performers. Consequently, they will be quite capable of not just merely providing technical elements, but doing so in such a way that they will create additional fits of laughter and heightened audience engagement.

If you are like me and are working in an educational environment, you will likely never have this uber-technician. The student operators that I get for improv change frequently, so they don't really get the opportunity to develop the timing needed to pull off that level of performance.

Even more to the point though is that for any multi-team improv competition (as I host) the technician will never have had time with every team, as most of them are strangers. This puts even more pressure on the technical elements, as their point is to enhance the performance for every participant, not just the home team.

Personally, I have kept things fairly low tech in performance, using a loud buzzer board as my primary sound effect producer. However, with an ample speaker system that I could control from the stage, as emcee I would be in an excellent position to provide very elaborate sound effects. If this is a goal for your group, I highly recommend that the facilitator be in a position to control all of the effects.

And don't forget that whatever you choose to do in the world of sound, you always need an adequate system of amplification appropriate to your performance space. While we're on the subject, this seems like an excellent segue to…

… transition to **performer amplification**.

This is easily the most important area of sound, and yet in improv it seems to be frequently neglected. Like I just said, it is imperative that your theatre/conference room/subway platform has <u>ample amplification.</u> If you are fortunate enough to be performing in a larger space, that means mics. Why? No matter how entertaining someone is, the audience cannot laugh at and respond to what they cannot hear.

As our competitions are in a large auditorium, we always provide a general, all-purpose sound plot. For us, that means the use of both shotgun mics above and floor mics below. Despite the fact that performers will be amplified, I still always spend a few moments discussing the importance of both volume and diction with them prior to the show. It doesn't matter if they are the funniest thing on two legs if no one in the audience can understand or hear what they are saying.

In smaller rooms this is far less of a problem area, however it still needs to be actively considered before one jumps into a performance. What will you do to ensure that the audience can hear players well enough to respond appropriately to the awesomeness of their performance?

What else do I need to consider when organizing a performance?

At the forefront of all your considerations (seriously – everything!), you've got to remember that the show you are putting on is a comedy and the most important aspect of comedy is **pace**.

Keep it moving *fast*.

I once allowed a guest emcee to run a competition since he was a professional that had flown in from a very well-respected improv company to run a workshop. Unfortunately, I assume because he was used to performing in a more serious long-form improv format, the concept of pace seemed to elude him and our typically just-under-two hour performance ran for over three and a half and had a dead audience begging to be set free. Not my proudest accomplishment.

Pace isn't the only tool at your disposal to ensure that your audience remains engaged. As you plan, you should also be thinking about variety. Just like a monotonous speaker will make an audience tune out, a show that only offers one type of performance can have a similar soporific effect.

One way I accomplish this variety is by intermingling cross-team challenges with the single team games every so often. It really mixes up the overall feel of a performance and can even provide some cover for logistical issues that you might need to accomplish (like tallying votes, for example). In addition, I think it's important to attempt to vary the challenges that are used from one performance to the next.

While consistency of structure is appreciated by an audience, seeing the same games show after show is no fun.

Well, that's about everything.

Whether you are planning to put on a single group or multi-team show, you have made a wonderful decision that you, your performers, and your audience will absolutely love. Now get started and go have some fun!

SAMPLES AND FORMS

Next, I have provided some examples of various files that I have found useful to help get you started. First is a sample competition line up. It includes a few notes to myself as the emcee as well as the overall structure and challenges. Additionally, I have provided forms, slides, and awards that have helped to keep me running smoothly.

Please feel free to use or adapt any of these materials to suit your needs. Enjoy!

Notes:

Performance Structure:
- Group challenges are used at my discretion based on time and pace to break up the flow.
- The list of challenges that are used in Round One and Round Two change from performance to performance.
- The Score column is used only if there are judges. If the audience is using ballots, this space is left blank.
- Some challenges on the list require a little preparation of materials (i.e. Horoscope, Odd News, Actor's Nightmare). Keep what's needed easily accessible during the show.
- Two challenges that are included require a large amount of prep.
  - Scenes from a Hat – I put them on small slips of paper and keep them in an envelope. Occasionally, I get additional audience suggestions at intermission.
  - Party Quirks – Most likely you will need to have decided upon the endowments prior to the competition. In addition, you need a means of communicating them to the audience and a list of the answers for the emcee.

Forms:
- Registration Form – We set up a table next to ticketing where teams register prior to going into a warm-up room. As emcee, I then use the sheet throughout the performance as a reference. After the show, the information collected goes into a database

that is used when the time comes to organize the next performance.

- Team Sign Up Form – I post this for local teams to sign up on, then as travelling teams let me know that they are coming, I add them to the list. Since I also allow at-the-door sign ups, the total number of teams that compete is usually three to five more than pre-sign up. Knowing that, I can plan more efficiently for a performance.

- Ballots – I have included the ballots that we use if we are basing winners on audience voting. Notice that the ballots get smaller as the competition goes on. We also ensure that eliminated teams still get the chance to perform in non-scoring rounds.

- Judge's Evaluation Form – For providing written feedback to teams if using formal judging.

- Awards – We award formal plaques to the top three teams, but no one should go home empty handed. Here are versions of certificates that I have used for both eliminated teams and the individual that won The Die Game. Additionally, other items like award ribbons, concession items, weird things from a dollar store can be passed out at will.

- Sample Slide Shows – There are four main slideshows, and three placeholders in a performance. Self-Advancing: Pre-performance, Intermission, and Final. Manual Advancing: Party Quirks. Still Image: All three placeholders (These are used during a round to keep the audience aware of the projection area, but have no movement so as to not distract from the performance). Note that Party Quirks includes an extra blank slide after each endowment.

TEACHING AND PERFORMING IMPROV

A Sample Improv Performance Structure

WELCOME and RULES of the competition.

Warm-up: 3 min or less Freeze Tag (2 members of each team)

60 min max - **Round 1 –**

Challenge	Team	Score
Town Meeting		
Hitchhiker		
Human Prop		
Options		
Should Have Said		
Remote Control		
Styles		
Emotional Boundaries		
Half-Life		
Modern Fairy Tale		
Experts w/ Arms		
Counting Words		
Media – Dear Abby		
Media – Odd News		
Sit Stand Lean (group of 3)		
---- if needed ---		
Temperamental Director		
Space Jump		
Purloined Letter		
Last Letter/First Letter		
Gibberish		
Boris		

INTERMISSION

INTER-GROUP CHALLENGE
185

20-25 min **Round 2**

Challenge	Team	Score	Total
Entrances and Exits			
Scene Without "____"			
Body Leads			
Typewriter Scene			
Double Talk			
Superheroes			
Alliteration			

Slide Show _____ _____ _____
Two Heads (group of 3) _____ _____ _____

GROUP CHALLENGE (to cover ballot tallying)
Scenes from a Hat – 2 players from each eliminated team

12 min **Round 3 – (3 teams – ALL GO ONCE)**

Challenge	Team	Score	Total
Party Quirks	_____	_____	_____
Party Quirks	_____	_____	_____
Party Quirks	_____	_____	_____

DIE GAME (to cover ballot tallying) – Regular Version, 1 player each team

END OF THE NIGHT AWARDS

Group Challenges List (use throughout)

** **Sound Effects – 2 people, 1 audience member**
Audience member makes sounds for players

** **Statues Variation 1 – 2 people, 1 audience member**
End in positions molded by audience

Alphabet Scene – 2 people

Chance of a Lifetime – 1 member of 5 teams, 1 audience member

The Good, The Bad and The Ugly Advice – 3 players

Radio Stations - 1 member from 6 teams

** **Horoscope – 3 people**
        Team member picks and audience member to determine sign

** **Actor's Nightmare**

                                        ** **first choices for tonight**

Tie Breakers (if needed):
Hat Game w/ ties
Categories

Team Registration Form

IMPROV TEAM REGISTRATION FORM

Team Name _____

Team School _____

Sponsor/Faculty Advisor _____

School Phone _____ **Advisor Email** _____

Team Member	**Email**
_____	_____
_____	_____
_____	_____
_____	_____
_____	_____

Ballots (Pass out only ONE ballot at a time)

Round One:

Team	Score	Team	Score	Team	Score
Team	Score	Team	Score	Team	Score
Team	Score	Team	Score	Team	Score
Team	Score	Team	Score	Team	Score
Team	Score	Team	Score	Team	Score

My vote for Round One Winning Team _____

Round Two:

Team	Score	Team	Score	Team	Score
Team	Score	Team	Score	Team	Score
Team	Score	Team	Score	Team	Score

My vote for Round Two Winning Team _____

Round Three:

Team	Score	Team	Score	Team	Score

My vote for Round Three Winning Team _____

TEACHING AND PERFORMING IMPROV

Judge's Evaluation Form

Improv Evaluation Form

Competition: An Evening of Improv Date _____

Team _____

(Score 1-10, highest)	Round One	Round Two	Round Three	Round Four
Met All Challenge Requirements				
All Team Members Worked Well Together				
All Team Members Agree and Embellish?				
Creativity Use of Humor				
Did the scene have a logical beginning/ middle/end?				
Average of all 5				

Additional Comments:

Eliminated Team Certificate

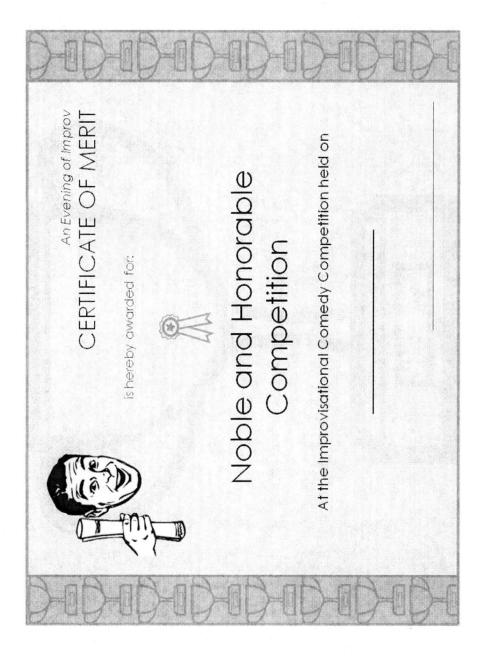

Die Game Certificate

Slide Samples from Various Years

<u>Pre-performance Slide Show</u> (self-advancing)

TEACHING AND PERFORMING IMPROV

Intermission Slide Show (self-advancing)

Final Slide Show (self-advancing)

<u>Party Quirks</u> (manual advance)

A superhero that is trying to figure out their superpower

Just got cut from the football team by the host

An overly attached boyfriend/ girlfriend

Ate something really spicy and can't find anything to drink

Place Holder (still image)

This chapter includes step by step walk-thrus of four of the different improv workshops that I have taught over the years. Each one that I have included is geared toward a group of performers at a different level of experience or with a different need.

While it's totally fine by me if someone (read: "you") would like to simply recreate any of them, I encourage you to tweak them, to edit them, to embellish them, to IMPROVE them – to modify them to suit you, your style, and your students.

We'll begin with the longest…

Workshop One:
Improv Camp

Middle School/High School/Beyond – 4 Hours + Performance

Please note: Although in the paragraphs that follow I will be describing an improv camp that I originally designed for use with a group middle school kids, this same format can work equally well for beginning performers of ANY age – be they high school, university, or even adult.

TEACHING AND PERFORMING IMPROV

For many years now I have been fortunate enough to be able to run an annual improv camp for sixth through eighth graders that takes place at the start of winter break in my school district. Not only has this camp been a huge boost for the level of interest in improv that my students possess upon entering high school, but frankly, it's also a heck of a lot of fun – I wholeheartedly recommend the experience of hosting one.

In a few short hours you obviously won't be able to cover everything of merit, but you can certainly hammer home some of the basic improv fundamentals that will help to guide your pupils as they progress (we spend quite a lot of our energy focusing on the **5 Rules of Improv**, for example). If you can give the participants a solid working knowledge of the basics while also providing for them a positive and fun day, hopefully you will be able to simultaneously ignite a spark of future interest.

Our basic day camp runs for four hours, beginning just after lunch (so we don't have to worry about feeding them) and is then followed up with an evening performance for their friends and family on our main stage. In my opinion, having the performance component of the camp is CRUCIAL to its success. Learning a bunch of improv theory is all well and good, but until it is put into practice, it cannot truly solidify for the kids. Plus, what good is training someone to be a better performer without giving them a chance to perform?

> *Although many try, you can't provide real actor training inside of a vacuum.*

Typically, our improv camp lasts from 11:30 AM until 3:30 PM, with the evening performance beginning at 7:00 PM and usually running for around one hour. We charge a fee to participate in the camp (combined with a drama camp for the elementary grades, it is our major fundraiser for the year) but not to those attending the evening performance – or as we sometimes call it – an <u>INFORM</u>-ance – to show off the newly acquired skills and the concepts we have covered to the students' family and friends.

Some of you reading this that are not used to working with middle school kids are probably thinking to yourselves, "Improv for four hours, straight? Are you kidding? With those squirrely guys?" Let me assure you that your fears are not unfounded.

Middle school students are a different animal from all others and I have the utmost respect for teachers that spend their careers working with this challenging age. Even in a fun setting like an improv camp they are, as I made you hypothetically say above, quite "squirrely" – initially. However, I am continually impressed each and every year by just how intensely focused and productive they can become by the final hour.

These are kids that are truly beginning to understand the concepts that we have been studying and are genuinely eager to work on putting them into practice.

For any other skeptics that might be lurking in our midst, let me also point out an additional bonus to working on improv with middle school students. Even though as a society we keep pushing kids to mature earlier and earlier, there is a marked difference in the level of inhibition that middle school kids have versus their high school counterparts. Being able to begin improv training before the horrific acne-ridden self-consciousness that often comes attached to a high school education can set in is an absolute godsend.

One more note: I usually vary up the running order of activities from year to year, but what follows below is a good indication of a solid Improv Camp agenda. As with everything else in this book, this should be a place for you to...

start from, not *end with.*

Please vary absolutely anything you like to suit your group's individual needs.

And remember – this workshop will work for *any age*!

0:00 - 0:30: *The Warm-up*

Once everybody has arrived, registered, and been given name tags, put everyone into a seated circle. I start by quickly introducing myself, since usually none of the students know me, however I don't have them introduce themselves. This would take up at least ten valuable minutes during which they could be learning something else, they have name tags, and frankly once they've been on their feet for an hour or so, we'll all know each other anyway.

Give a brief overview of what the entire day will consist of – five cent versions of some of the main concepts, the types of games you will do, and so on. If kids have a good idea where they are headed, they are probably going to be easier to convince to go along for the ride, right?

Immediately jump right into the action! For the warm-up, I always use four games – two of which are simply used to help students get to know each other and start feeling comfortable in the environment, and two of which are used to teach basic improv principles.

A good pairing of getting-comfortable activities is **"2 Truths/1 Lie,"** in which players must try to trick each other with a believable lie about themselves – a great icebreaker – and **"Human Knot,"** the old-school favorite of joining hands in a random pattern and then trying to untangle the chain. Incidentally, for camps with over twenty participants I recommend splitting the group into two smaller knots that are competing with each other to try and escape first. It just keeps things moving.

As for the two warm-up exercises used to teach principles, I'd start with the basics. **"Zip, Zap, Zop"** and **"Martha"** are great entry-level warm-up choices for this.

When teaching "Zip, Zap, Zop," be sure to emphasize the aspect of communication that is going on with the direct eye contact between players (I always describe it as boring a hole into the other player's skull with your eyes).

Improv performers have to be excellent communicators, not just through language, but also non-verbally – and this game is a fun way to introduce the idea to players. Be sure to switch the category a few times as you play. "Your name" or "their name" are both excellent choices to use at this early point of the day (another reason why I don't bother with introductions).

For Martha, highlight the listening skills that the participants are utilizing as well as how they are being physical and working together to achieve a common goal and create a scene.

Usually by the end of this first half-hour, they're hooked.

Summary:
- Put the group in a seated circle
- Provide an intro/overview of the day
- Play:
  o "2 Truths/1 Lie" – fun "getting-to-know-you" – at a distance
  o "Human Knot" – *really* fun "getting-to-know-you" – uncomfortably close
  o "Zip, Zap, Zop" – emphasizes communicative eye contact
  o "Martha" – working together to create a scene

0:30 - 0:45: *The Guidelines*

Now that you've gotten their attention, it's time to give their brains something to gnaw on for a bit. The next chunk of time should be spent covering the **Rules of Improv** (see Chapter One). Usually I have nifty handouts listing the rules that I pass out to the participants while I talk about them.

Although you should discuss all of the rules (maybe one minute each – don't belabor the point now, review it later!) I recommend putting the most emphasis on **Rule One: Agree and Embellish**.

Do this not only because it will be the focus for the remainder of this fifteen minute chunk, but also because it is the foundation around which all improv must be built. If your participants can't get a grip on this basic fundamental principle, then they will really struggle as they continue to learn.

> *It's just like learning math – when you miss a day because you got sick, you could be behind for the rest of the semester.*

To illustrate the point of **Rule One**, I suggest a strong round of the tune-up **"3 Line Scenes,"** in which players simply make an offer, embellish it, and conclude, creating what essentially amounts to a very short scene. As the participants work through the exercise, interject with your comments whenever a teachable moment occurs

How could he have embellished that offer even more?

What could she have said to agree more actively with the offer?

After students have each gone through the process a few times, this fifteen minute block is usually eaten up, but if you have the time, a round of **"Yes And…"** in pairs is also a great way to completely solidify the point. It can also be a good idea to hold on to "Yes And…" until later in the day so that you can review this fundamental concept prior to the participants practicing some of the various improv challenges in the final section.

Summary:
- Discuss the "Rules of Improv" (See Chapter One)
- Emphasize **Rule Number One: Agree and Embellish**
- Play "3 Line Scenes" – a couple times for each participant
- If time, play "Yes And…" - what the whole world of improv is built around

0:45 - 1:45: *The Big Idea*

This hour will be used to illustrate how important it is to make active choices as an improviser.

Novice performers will often fall into two categories – the first never want to make any offers at all, the second say so much that their fellow players can get overwhelmed. The need to make clear choices when given few or many impulses can be illustrated through several different exercises, but the two that follow are probably my favorite. Both of them are fun games, but the second one... ahhhh... if done right, can turn your brain to mush!

The first game to play is a rapid-fire round of **"Schwing!"** As you play, emphasize that even with a simple game like this there are still always five possible choices that each player can make for every single impulse that they receive – and each of those five choices will also have a different effect on the entire rest of the game.

> *When it comes to creating a scene, the number of possible choices that players can make as it develops becomes virtually limitless, and the impact of those choices immeasurable.*

Play a few rounds of this until the group is able to really go FAST and LOUD. I'd also recommend overtly mentioning the concepts of choices and impulses that you are attempting to illustrate a few times during these games, just to be sure that folks get the message.

Once "Schwing!" has been mastered, have the participants stand and do a round of a basic **"Clap Circle,"** reiterating the importance of making direct eye contact as a means of communication. Once a few passes of a clap circle have been completed and the participants are feeling more comfortable making direct eye contact, it's time to kick it into high gear by turning it into a **"Clap Circle Plus Focus"** (A thorough explanation can be found in Chapter Three – Tune-ups that provides much more detailed guidance on how to use it than here).

In a "Clap Circle Plus Focus" players are required to provide an example for a particular category (let's say "colors") as the clap is sent around the circle. Once the group has mastered the first category and can go around the circle at a breakneck pace, it's time to mix the players up. My two favorite Mix-'em-ups are **"Dude!"** and **"Bippity-Bippity-Bop!"**

After completing one (let's say "Dude!"), have the players again follow the same pattern from the first category – but now that they have been mixed up into a different order, the impulse is being sent back and forth all around the circle instead of just to the player on one's left.

Now add a second category (let's say "foods") and go around the circle, with players clapping and giving their example. Once they can also do this one well, do a second Mix-'em-up (let's say "Bippity, Bippity, Bop!"). Both categories have now been assigned and the group has been mixed up a second time.

Here comes the fun part!

Begin sending the first category around the circle. Once the pace has been firmly established, start sending the second one around as well. There will probably be a few dropped runs before the group succeeds at simultaneously sending both at the same time. Eventually, however, the group <u>will</u> be successful – they always are. I usually continue to try this until they can do at least three good runs back to back.

Remember that at some point, someone in the group will receive both categories at the same time, but – and this is the most important point to illustrate to your students this hour – the player cannot allow either of the categories to fall. This is the strongest concept that this activity can teach – the need to make and act upon choices, even when multiple offers come flying at you simultaneously.

Summary:
- Play Schwing! – FAST and LOUD!
- Play Clap Circle – Start with Basic, add Focus
  o Add color
- Play mix-em-up game "Dude!" – "Masters – spread yourselves!"
- Repeat Clap Circle with Color in new positions – Bouncing around the circle
  o Add Food
- Play mix-em-up game "Bippity Bippity Bop" – My hip went "Pop!"
  o Repeat food
  o Repeat color
- Do both Color and Food at the same time – their brains will have never hurt so good!
- Players WILL receive two impulses simultaneously – they must make a choice and act on one of them first.

1:45 - 2:00 – *The Bonus Round*

Sometimes there is a little extra time at this point, sometimes there isn't. However, when there is, don't ever let it go to waste. There are two other activities that I always have ready to go that can help to synthesize everything that your improv campers have worked on so far.

The first is the tune-up exercise **"Story Ball."**

Here participants will work together to tell a coherent story by contributing one or two sentences at a time before they pass the "talking ball" to a different player who then continues the story where they left off.

The players should be given <u>two caveats</u> before they begin, however.

TEACHING AND PERFORMING IMPROV

First, the story should NOT be allowed to be funny – at ALL. The focus here should be entirely on good, solid storytelling.

Second, players are forbidden from planning any of their plot twists in advance. When it is a player's turn, they must continue the sentence right where it left off and take it to its logical (or illogical) conclusion.

Limiting the players' ability to plan and to be funny prompts genuine listening to each other and provides an opportunity for participants to practice making choices and embellishing upon the offers of others.

The second is a tune-up/challenge called **"Good Thing/Bad Thing."**

In this game, players will form a line of eight people which will tell a complete story in one sentence increments. The first person will say something good, the second something bad, the third something good, and so forth.

For example:

Player 1:	(Good)	I decided to go to the amusement park!"
Player 2:	(Bad)	The lines were really long."
Player 3:	(Good)	But I got on my favorite roller coaster!"
Player 4:	(Bad)	It flew off the track."
Player 5:	(Good)	But it sprouted magical wings and flew!"

Again, players must be listening very carefully to the immediate offer being given to them in order to be successful.

Summary:
- A great time for reinforcement, if you have it!
- Play "Story Ball" – No planning! No funny!
- Play "Good Thing/Bad Thing" – responding to offers in the moment

2:00-2:15: *Bathroom Break*

It's time for a much needed rest. By now most of their heads probably hurt from the extended focus of the last portion of the camp (and your head almost assuredly hurts from their sheer enthusiasm.) I'd give them fifteen minutes and a snack/drink (which we provide for them at our camp), and then they'll be ready to get back in action.

2:15-2:30: *The Warm-up: Redux!*

Now that everyone has had a moment to blow off a little steam and decompress, they need to get focused again. Do a second quick warm-up routine, using either brand new activities or reviewing those from earlier.

This would also be a great time to incorporate **"Yes And..."** into the day if you were still holding on to it from earlier.

Summary:
- Play (choose a few): - Pick a card, any card – seriously, they're all good!
    - Zip, Zap, Zop
    - Martha
    - Shakedown
    - Bananas
    - Confuse-a-cross
    - Kwah!
    - Yes Let's
- Maybe "Yes And..." – the foundation on which it all is built

2:30-4:00: *The Work Session*

Now it's finally time for them to get to truly apply all that they have learned. First, review everything – FAST.

- ➤ Quiz them on the **Rules**.
- ➤ Remind them about eye contact.
- ➤ About "Yes, And…"
- ➤ About making choices.
- ➤ Make sure they understand that once an offer is out there, they have to run with it and make it as good as it can be!

Then start to play games. (Or, if you're writing a grant or something, "allow them to reinforce their newly acquired technical skills through practical application using short-form improvisational challenges" – feel free to use that.)

Don't throw anything incredibly advanced at them – keep it simple. Start with a round of **"Freeze Tag."** – it doesn't get more basic than that. Make sure that players are being as physical as possible, so that the others have something to build their scenes around. Also remind them that the scenes should ideally last between five and ten seconds – just long enough to establish a premise and embellish it a bit, but not long enough to get painful or awkward. Don't let them waffle on the sidelines and don't let them drive each other's scenes.

After a few minutes, start tackling some standard challenges. Below is a suggested list that I have found to be very successful when working with beginners. Obviously, you should feel free to incorporate your own selections into the list, but just make sure that any challenge that you decide to use provides the players with an adequate amount of structure. These are novice performers, many of whom have probably never even tried to do something like this before and without a solid set of rules to guide them, many can get lost or left behind.

As they are working, use those teachable moments to point out areas that they need to pay attention to such as avoiding a *split scene* – or any of the **7 Deadly Sins of Improv** (see Chapter One Part Two). This is where everything will start to come together and synthesize for them.

But remember - time is short.

Only allow one or two groups to do each challenge, or you'll never get through enough to prepare them for tonight's exciting performance.

- Space Jump
- Half Life
- Hitchhiker
- Options
- Should Have Said
- Remote Control
- Dr. Know It All
- Gibberish
- Human Prop
- Sit, Stand, Lean
- Superheroes
- Styles
- Experts w/ Arms

This work session will easily take the full 90 minutes with an enthusiastic group and could go on for hours upon hours if you allow it. That's probably why so many improv workshops that I see tend to be nothing more than someone leading kids through a series of games. It's fun, the kids love it, and it fills the time very well, but there just isn't that much <u>learning</u> going on. If you can do it, why not try to accomplish both goals at the same time?

With the final few moments that you have, take your charges through a round of **"The Die Game."** Not only is it a great activity to use at the end of performance, it's also a fantastic way to wrap up all of the enthusiasm that has been building throughout the day.

Before they leave, make sure that they understand the performance format for the evening and have them get organized into teams of three to five members (I like to let them choose, but you could put them into assigned teams if you prefer). Set a meeting time and place for all of you to gather about a half hour or so before the show and then turn them loose – former students hungry for knowledge, now fully nourished on an improv-rich diet.

Later – The Performance: *The Final Exam*

Once the participants have all assembled before the show, always – ALWAYS – review the main concepts that you focused on during the camp – the **Rules**, acting on offers, making choices, etc. Remind them quickly about the format for the evening, and then take them through a quick warm-up. Don't try to teach them anything new here, just do a quick review of a few of the warm-up games that they liked and maybe throw in one or two vocal warm-ups, since this will be in front of an audience, after all.

Next, find out what names the teams have chosen for themselves, and make a note of them on your template/running order for the night (as a place to start, on the page following this section is the template that I use for an Improv Camp Performance/Informance, for you to use or adapt). ay something inspirational to the players, enter the theatre and begin the show.

Start by greeting the friends and family that have come with a quick welcome and set up what exactly it is that they will be watching. (Just because they sent their kids/loved ones to your camp, don't assume that they know anything at all about improv themselves.) Give a quick explanation of the material that was covered during the camp so that they have some sort of an idea of what was going on all day. At least once or twice during this welcome, encourage some vocal audience participation to get them a little riled up – after all, this is improv, not a piano recital – it's supposed to get a <u>little</u> rowdy and you need to start the ball rolling. Plus, if you set the mood now, the audience will have stronger responses to the performers later, making them feel even better about their newly acquired improv skills.

After that, move into an activity that all of the performers can do together – **"Freeze Tag."** As the players walk to the stage, explain the principles of improv that Freeze Tag utilizes and, of course, toss in an amusing anecdote or two from the day. Like every game you use tonight, keep this introductory round to two or three minutes max.

Next start the challenges. I have a set of oversized novelty dice that I roll to determine what challenge a group gets. I roll a five, they get the fifth game on the list – and so forth. Doing something silly like this not only ups the fun factor for the evening, but it also brings it home to the audience that this really is completely improvised. If there were any challenges that were not successful for the participants as they tried them during the day, never let them be an option for the evening performance – as the facilitator, a huge part of your job is to help the performers look as good as possible.

Once a few groups have performed their challenges, I recommend adding at least one group challenge, the most likely candidate being **"Good Thing/Bad Thing."** Doing something this simple helps to break up the rhythm of the evening and also helps to actively demonstrate for the audience the principle of immediately responding to an offer.

Finish the standard challenges for the remainder of the groups, and then conclude the evening with an energetic round of **"The Die Game."** At first, a new audience may not know what to make of a theatre full of people chanting "Die! Die! Die!" at their children, but usually about a minute or so into it, everyone present is excited and laughing. Every student that participated in the camp should get a special certificate, as should the winner of The Die Game, and the kids leave the stage triumphant and victorious accompanied by the thunderous applause of their loved ones.

This is always one of my favorite nights of the year.

I bet it will be for you, too.

An Improv Camp Performance Template

Welcome/Intro/Overview of the camp's activities

Group Challenge: ALL Freeze Tag All Groups Go (circle one) once   twice   thrice

Used	Challenge	Group Name
__	Space Jump	_____
__	Half Life	_____
__	Hitchhiker	_____
__	Options	_____
__	Remote Control	_____
__	Human Prop	_____
__	Sit, Stand, Lean	_____
__	Should Have Said	_____
__	Remote Control	_____
__	Dr. Know it All	_____
__	Experts w/ Arms	_____
__	Gibberish	_____
__	Superheroes	_____
__	Styles	_____
__	_____	_____
__	_____	_____
__	_____	_____

Group Challenge – 2 players from each group

__ Good Thing/Bad Thing

Group Challenge – 2 players from each group

__ Die Game

Pass out Certificates

Group Names:

1. _____

2. _____

3. _____

4. _____

5. _____

6. _____

7. _____

Workshop Two:
Improv Fundamentals

Grades 3-5 (or adults that need to be reminded to be childish)
½ to 1 Hour

This is a really fun workshop that I have found to be very effective with the younger grades. It provides a combination of warm-up games, tune-up activities and challenges that emphasize the basic concepts of eye contact, teamwork, and telling a story.

Begin with a quick warm-up game. **Zip, Zap, Zop** is an excellent choice. Be sure to explain the importance of eye contact in improv, especially how it is a primary method that performers use to "talk" to one another. Make sure that your participants are deliberate and loud as they send the impulse around the circle, locking eyes with the person they are sending it to. They probably won't be the fastest bunch you've ever worked with right off the bat, but in my experience, they usually do a fantastic job with this game once they get in the rhythm.

Next, I like to get them moving around the room a bit. A game like **Character of the Space** is a great activity to try to get them used to tapping into their impressive imaginations in a constructive manner. The game begins by simply having the players start walking slowly around the room (after reminding them of basic safety rules like no running, no contact with other players, etc., of course). As they walk, it falls to you to change the environment that they are pretending to walk through (i.e. "Now you are walking on the sun!" or "Now you are underwater.") Don't let the game go on too long – about fifteen seconds in each environment should be perfect.

A good teamwork exercise that will also keep them physical is **Machines.** Begin by explaining the importance of teamwork in improv – in this case why it's important for each of the players to build off of each other and work together to create a unified machine.

Now get started by having one player begin to make a gesture accompanied by some sort of a nonsense sound. Allow the other kids to go up and join on to the machine one at a time as they feel the impulse – or if they are a timid group, you can always select the player who will join in next. Once all of the players have become part of the mechanics, it is your job to become the machine operator. You can make the machine speed up, slow down, or otherwise alter its pace or action as you like. Throughout it all, do what you can to ensure that the players are continually working together. Personally, I always enjoy ending a game of Machines by making the group's creation blow up.

Now that your participants have been both physical and focused, it's time to get to the real work. I like to begin with an area that children everywhere are familiar with – telling stories. Gather the group into a seated circle and take them through a round of **Story Ball**. Start with an explanation of the basic rules. A person will begin telling a story and then will pass the ball to someone else who must continue the story where it left off. Remind them that they are not trying to be funny, just tell a continuous story. You will likely also need to reinforce the fact that they are not allowed to plan their sections in advance – just continue the same story where the last person left off. And they are definitely not allowed to beam each other with the ball. Usually the kids I have taught excel at this game, although the topics of pizza and poop do seem to work their way into more stories than one might expect.

If they were successful with Story Ball, and my bet is that they will be, then the next logical step is **One Word Story**. Here we will simply go around the circle telling a story one word at a time. If the group needs a little help, it is fine to decide on a topic in advance for the story to be about. Again, usually the kids do a great job at this one, however, at least at first, some of them may have trouble not voicing their belief that the person after them said the wrong word (because it wasn't the one that they were already thinking of). Use this as a teachable moment. Explain that this is part of the magic of improv – there are always so many different directions in which a story can go, and just because you were thinking one way, that doesn't make it the only correct one. In fact, in improv usually the best moments occur when what we are expecting to happen... doesn't.

Everything that your participants have covered so far has been leading up to this next section –performing an actual improv challenge. I almost always use **Dr. Know-It-All** for this activity because it has a very simple format and is a solid way to incorporate all of the main concepts that we have illustrated so far. Here, three players will sit next to each other and become the character "Dr. Know-It-All" – a person who literally does know it all. Ask the group to provide a question and then pose it to the players, who must then work together to provide an answer that makes sense one word at a time. Have each grouping answer four or five questions and then change the players so that everyone gets a chance. This is a really fun game to use as the culmination of a good workshop.

Occasionally, you may get a group that is truly above and beyond in their ability, especially if the majority of its members are in fourth or fifth grade. When this happens, and **Dr. Know-It-All** comes a bit too easily for them, it may also be appropriate to try a round of **Freeze Tag**. The most basic of all improv challenges, it also provides a highly creative group of novices with a hearty taste of what doing "real" improv is like!

Summary:
- Circle and welcome
- "Zip, Zap Zop" – mention eye contact
- "Character of the Space" – don't forget safety
- "Machines" – relate to each other
- "Story Ball" – advance the story, don't be funny
- "One Word Story" – infinite choices at every turn
- "Dr. Know-It-All" – incorporates all the principles covered
- Perhaps "Freeze Tag" – a "true" improv challenge

Workshop Three:
Improv Basics

Grades K-2 – ½ Hour

Even the youngest of performers can enjoy improv training!

Although the games played with this group are decidedly simpler than the ones chosen for the older groups, the real difference from other workshops is actually philosophical. While it's perfectly fine (and actually a pretty good idea) to mention some of the improv principles that the different games cover, this workshop should primarily be an exercise in fun for the kids.

In other words, don't belabor the point. Simply mention the concept (i.e. "Performers have to be physical to show different characters or emotions with their bodies.") and then play the game. Give the kids as fun an experience as possible and as they grow up, they will keep coming back for more.

As with all other workshops, begin with a warm-up game. If you have the time, or will see the kids for multiple days, then doing something like "Zip, Zap, Zop" can be great. However, games like this can sometimes be a bit overwhelming for younger students, so if this is a one-off session, I'd keep it simple.

A great basic warm-up is **"Energy Ball."** Here players stand in a circle and simply mime an imaginary ball of energy that they pretend to toss to one another. There are no words to remember, but making eye contact with the person they are passing to is essential for success. This is a great game to use to hit beginning space object skills, teamwork, and interpersonal connections, while also establishing that the kids will be spending this time with you working with their imaginations.

After this, giving the children an opportunity to move around is usually a great idea. Most of the time, I do two games that piggy-back on each other a bit.

The first is **"Character of the Space"** in which the players walk through the room as if it was a series of different environments. Kids always have a lot of fun with this, but don't forget to remind them not to run or touch any other players.

After that I graduate to **"Yes, Let's"** with the minor modification that the workshop leader (YOU) will call out all of the actions that the players must do. Again, always a fun choice to use with the young-uns.

> *These games are great because they teach kids how to use their bodies as a communication tool without their even knowing it.*

Next we move back to the circle, this time seated, for a round of **"Duck, Duck, Animal."** This variation on Duck, Duck Goose is always a favorite for kids and while it certainly doesn't feel like anything even resembling work, it provides them with opportunities for both embodiment and object work – through imitation.

Here, instead of simply saying "Duck, duck, duck…" as the player goes around the circle, they must say a different animal each time. Then, instead of saying "Goose!" the player YELLS the name of another different animal and both the tap-er and tap-ee must run around the circle <u>as</u> that animal. You have to love any game that allows students to explore mime and impersonation while simply appearing to be fun.

Finally, we get to the culminating activity of the session, **"Family Portraits."** This is a simple and fun game that can work just as well as a warm-up or tune-up exercise for adult performers as it does for the kindergarten set. Group a few of the kids into a huddle as if they are getting a family photo taken ala Sears. Then, as the photographer, change the type of family that they are (i.e. a happy family, a sad family, a monkey family, a circus family, a rock star family, and so on.There really is no limit as to what types of families they can become.) The players must then strike a pose (remember that this is a photo, not a film) that instantly communicates the type of family that they are.

After this round is over, a simple wrap-up with a fond farewell and the wish to work with them again is all that is required.

Summary:
- Keep it FUN!
- "Energy Ball" – mime and imagination
- "Character of the Space" – don't forget safety
- "Yes, Let's" – modified
- "Duck, Duck, Animal" – fun impersonation
- "Family Portraits" – instant communication

Workshop Four:
Tips for Successful Improv

High School/Adult, assuming some experience – 1½ Hours

This is a fun workshop that hits on many of the basic principles of improv (just as all of the other workshops have done) while also giving participants the opportunity to put those ideas to the test. I have typically used this workshop with high school aged students at theatre conferences, but it can easily be utilized for any older group so long as they have at least a little improv background coming into it. While the workshop probably works best with between 20-30 participants, I once used it with a group of 110 and we had an absolutely fantastic time.

0:00-0:15: *Intro and Warm-up*

Begin with a quick welcome and introduction and provide an overview of what the workshop will cover:

> *Story good. Driving bad. Listen as you agree and embellish. Have fun.*

Thirty seconds later, dive right in to the first principle that you will be covering – that the point of all improv is *always to advance a story*.

In my experience, virtually everyone that has only done a little improv – just enough to know that they like it, but not enough to have really learned what it was that they were doing – has never even thought about telling a story. Most of them have gotten the improv bug by telling a few successful poop jokes, or just being a naturally funny individual, but have never actually learned anything about how to harness that incredibly enviable ability and use it consistently.

Remember that you will never, in the course of a mere ninety minutes, be able to fully teach your students how to advance a story to the point of mastery. Your goal with the workshop is to give the participants – who likely already have a vested interest in doing improv well – something to take home with them and use. If you can get them to actively think about what it is they are doing while they perform, many will attempt to hone their skill set on their own.

If you have been able to help facilitate this self-awareness, then you will have been successful.

After you have hammered home the point that improv is more than poop jokes and needs to have a story, begin with a warm-up game or three. While there are many activities that will work well here, my personal choices to use would be **"Schwing!," "Clap Circle,"** and **"Martha."**

As you play each game be sure to discuss the main point that each game illustrates:

Schwing!	the potential choices that are always available to performers
Clap Circle	the importance of eye contact and non-verbal communication between improvisers
Martha	working together to quickly create a scene and how every bit of input opens up new possibilities.

The most time that you should allow this eat up is ten or twelve minutes. In other words, keep it short and direct.

0:15-0:45: *Agree and Embellish*

Now that they've had the opportunity to be a little physical, it's time to go over the **Rules of Improv** (see Chapter One). I frequently find that students at this level tend, at first, to be a little standoffish when I present the Rules of Improv. After all, they've done just fine in the few attempts at performing that they did in drama class or at a party, so why should I be tying them down with rules? So typical of a teacher to take all of the fun out of something.

Consequently, I make a point of explaining how the few concise concepts contained in the improv rules actually FREE one as a performer. Almost anyone can be funny enough to succeed at improv once or twice, but using the rules as a constant guide will allow a performer to <u>consistently</u> succeed with only their wits.

As with improv camp, I spend the majority of this time dealing with **Rule #1 – Agree and Embellish.** It's the foundation of all improv, after all, and these guys not only have to understand it, but must also be able to actually do it to be able to succeed. Later in the session I will also spend a good chunk of time dealing with the importance of listening to your other players, but ideas like staying in the present and being physical I just mention during the teachable moments that invariably arise.

So what do I recommend for illustrating the idea of agreeing and embellishing to your students?

Why, **"Yes, And...,"** obviously.

Get a volunteer from the group to work with and go back and forth with them modeling the activity for everyone else. Have them make an offer and literally say "Yes" in response to it, then add a new twist to the action. Keep going back and forth "Yes, and-ing" each other for a minute or so. Try to take the scene to new and bizarre places, if you can. Throw in a few *offers from space* to keep them on their toes, but keep the scene moving. With you in there to control the direction that the action will go, you are virtually guaranteed a stronger result than if you simply chose two volunteers to demonstrate to the rest of the group.

Now that they have seen your example, get two volunteers that you didn't get the first time to do one of these scenes for everyone. This time, chime in with anything that will help the players in constructing their plotline – just illustrating the principle is good, but using it to create an engaging story is GREAT!

Now have the group members pair off and let each of the pairs try their hand at it. Float around the room and observe, breaking into the scenes where necessary to help folks out. If someone does something that is really awesome, make a mental note of it. After they have been doing this for a bit – try to keep it under two or three minutes – review with everyone what you witnessed. Discuss some of the great work that you saw them doing, and make a point of praising it. Mention some difficulty that you noticed and discuss ways to solve it. In other words, let them begin to help each other become aware of what they are doing as improv performers.

Now take this energy to the next level by going into a round of **"3 Line Scenes."** There are several different types of 3 Line Scenes available, but here you should do the same type that we used at

Improv Camp: Player One makes an *offer*, Player Two *agrees* with the context of the offer and *embellishes* it in some way, and then Player One *agrees* with the new offer and ends the scene. This is a strong, quick, and easy illustration of how important the concept of agreeing is. Inevitably someone will have difficulty advancing the scene forward. Don't just smile politely and let them get away with it.

Stop everything!

Help them (and everyone else for that matter) figure out a way to embellish upon the offer that was made. This can be one of the most valuable moments in the entire workshop.

0:45-1:00: *Learning to Listen*

Now comes the time to segue into the next content area – learning to listen. Being an excellent and active listener has a positive effect upon all aspects of improv performance. Everything from gaining the ability to embellish upon an offer, to learning how to give focus to another player, to staying in the present, to being able to tell what it is the audience wants to see all come back to a performer's ability to listen.

> *If "ACTING is REACTING" then*
> *"IMPROV is LISTENING."*

The best activity I know to illustrate this fundamental to performers is **"Story Ball."**

I know that this game may seem a bit too simple and childish for this more seasoned group of performers, but, especially once you have stripped them of the right to be funny, I can't think of any other activity that will get even a group of the boldest scene drivers to instantly begin to listen to everyone else. There are times when I have been using this exercise that you can actually see a moment of realization come over a performer's face – the incredibly rewarding "Oh! I get it now!" expression that means that you're doing your job.

Of course, they don't truly "get it," yet, not in the true sense anyway, but they may have just acquired the basic understanding of what they need to do in order to progress as a performer, and really that's what it's all about.

I have also incorporated a quick round of **"Good Thing/Bad Thing"** into this portion occasionally if time allows, however the basic skill set that this game teaches is exactly the same as "Story Ball" – the context has just been altered. If the group that you are working with could use some reinforcement or if you think that they might benefit from getting the idea presented to them in a different fashion, then by all means, include it.

1:00-1:15: *Game Application*

I like to spend the final half hour playing quick short form games with them. Short form improv is, after all, most likely responsible for getting them there in the first place and it is also likely to be their only previous improv experience. For the first fifteen minutes I like to play games from the suggested list below because they are easy to link back to the principles that have been covered. Be sure to explain the connections explicitly before and after (maybe even while) the players perform.

- **"Alphabet Game"** – This is a challenge that is all about listening to your fellow performer and being able to actively continue a story. It also is one that forces beginning performers to concentrate so much more than they are accustomed to that they often become *talking heads* and completely stop moving altogether. Thus, you can hit ALL of the rules of improv at the same time with this challenge.

- **"Options"** – Because this challenge involves immediately incorporating bits of information supplied by the audience as the scene progresses, for a performer it is all about *accepting*. This one is a great way to practice the principle in a non-threatening fashion.

- **"Typist/Narrator"** – A good choice to use because in a weak version of the challenge, the narrator *drives* the action, whereas in a strong one, there is a constant give and take between those acting out the story and the performer in the position of "creating" it. It may potentially be too challenging to use if the group has limited experience, but if they are up to it, it can be one humdinger of an exercise.

- **"One Word Scene"** – This particular challenge requires a different type of *listening/accepting* than most of the participants are likely used to. Here, they must use a single word to communicate a plethora of context to the audience <u>and</u> make all of their offers to each other <u>and</u> must be perfectly in tune with their teammates in order to effectively build a story. Perhaps a bit difficult, but a GREAT choice.

- **"Half Life"** – Most new performers mistakenly think that a good Half Life scene relies on frantic action. Not so. If a round of Half Life is successful, it is almost entirely due to the quality of the *story* that the performers came up with during the first minute of the scene. So long as that minute contains a solid story with a beginning, middle, and end AND the group is telling it in a physical manner, the remaining portions of the scene can't NOT be funny.

- **"Human Prop"** – While much of the fun of this challenge lies in pimping a fellow player into doing various potentially unpleasant or embarrassing things, it is also a great illustration of being *physical* WHILE *not abandoning story*. You can't really get a more obviously explicit example of the relationship between story and action than this one.

And OF COURSE, *use your own ideas*!

1:15-1:30: *It's a Free-for-all!*

Make sure to end the session on a less didactic high note. Let them revel in the fun and play whatever games they want – or if they're unsure of what to do, use the list contained in this book to help move them along. As they play, point out whenever someone does something really well that you have been working with that day. Give them some final moments to boost their confidence and leave with a "Wow!"

The real work is now up to them.

Summary:
- Intro – Improv is more than Poop!
- Warm-up
  - "Schwing "– Choices, choices
  - "Clap Circle" – Non-verbal communication
  - "Martha" – Make a quick scene
- Agree and Embellish – It's Rule #1 for a reason!
  - "Yes, And…" – With and without you
  - "3 Line Scenes" – Stop the scene to teach
- "IMPROV is LISTENING" (and occasionally making stuff up without a script)
  - "Story Ball" – Instant realization
  - "Good Thing, Bad Thing" – Same Skill, Different Drill
- Challenges, Your Choice - Apply the principles
- Challenges Their Choice – Leave with a "Wow!"

CHAPTER SEVEN:
A GLOSSARY OF IMPROV
TERMINOLOGY

The Funniest* Dictionary Ever Written
> * Moderately amusing at best. A thesaurus or even a rhyming
> dictionary when used correctly would likely have been a whole lot funnier.

Just like any other discipline, improv has terms specific to it that are used in its practice. What follows is a collection of some of the jargon used within the greater improv community. If we all speak the same language, we can communicate more easily, right? Here goes...

Accepting (aka Agreeing) – The simple act of agreeing with the offers made by the other players within a scene. When combined with advancing, accepting is the most important aspect of successful improv, as it is the only way for a group of performers to tell a story coherently. Accepting is the "<u>Yes</u>" in "<u>Yes</u>, and ..." **(See Rule #1 - Agree and Embellish)**

Advancing (aka Embellishing) – Progressing the scene forwards. Advancing is the constant "one-uping" of each other players must do to save a scene from stagnation. The two most basic fundamentals of improv are accepting and advancing **(See Rule #1 - Agree and Embellish)**. Advancing is the "<u>and</u>" in "Yes, <u>and</u>..."

Agreeing – (See Accepting)

Ask-for – A question asked by the host/emcee/facilitator of the audience in order to receive a variable, the information provided by the audience that will be incorporated into the scene. Scenes can require a wide variety of ask-fors or variables.

Beat – Just as in Stanislavsky-based acting, the term "beat" refers to a single unit of character action – in other words, the full use of a specific tactic in order to achieve a particular goal. As soon as a character's tactic or goal changes, we have moved on to another beat in the scene. No matter if a scene is improvised or scripted, it is always comprised of groups of beats.

Blocking (aka Denial) – One of the **Deadly Sins of Improv**, blocking refers to any time one improviser rejects a suggestion made by another team member - in other words, saying "No!" to an offer. This is something to avoid at all costs, as it goes against the most fundamental principle of improv **(See Rule #1 - Agree and Embellish)**. This term often confuses those that are new to improv, as it refers to the planned movement and composition of a production in traditional theatre.

Breaking the Routine – If a scene is stagnating, breaking the routine is a good way out of the rut. It simply refers to making an offer that takes the story in a new, possibly unexpected direction. Any new action, even the bizarre **(See "Offer from Space")** can be used to help make the scene advance.

Bulldozing – **(See Driving)**

Callback – **(See Reincorporation)**

Canadian Cross – In a Canadian Cross, a player enters a scene and performs some bit of action in a way that does not steal the scene's focus away from the other players, in effect becoming a piece of atmosphere or scenery. Similar to a walk-on/walk-thru in nature, however, those require an action that advances the scene in some way. A really fun gimmick, but don't go overboard with it, or it gets tedious.

Canceling – Anything that completely negates a previous action. As an audience needs a coherent story in order to follow the scene, canceling a previous action is a no-no. One of the **Deadly Sins.**

Challenge (aka Handle) – The framework around which the scene is built. Each challenge format has individual rules and requirements and may require different types of information to be gathered from the audience. It is the challenge that provides the scene's basic structure, therefore allowing an audience to be able to follow it.

Character Journal – **(aka Character Suitcase)** – Having a mental list/grab bag of fully developed characters that a performer can use at will during performance. The merits of this are highly debated, some arguing that having a few can't-miss characters to pull from at any time can only strengthen a performance, others believe that it can only hamper one's growth as an improviser. Personally, I believe that both statements are true and that the value in the use of this technique will vary greatly from individual situation to situation. Having a few characters that make frequent appearances at regular shows might be a good thing. Also, if improv is being used as a means of scripted sketch development, then dropping a familiar character into a new situation is highly appropriate. For a novice performer, having a familiar character to incorporate could only increase their level of confidence. However, a balance must be maintained between the new and the staid if one wishes to grow as an improvisational performer. If one simply repeats the same action over and over, they <u>will</u> likely become very good at it, but this will only come at the expense of the remainder of their developing skills.

Character Suitcase – **(See Character Journal)**

Chivalry – Being willing to defer to the ideas of a fellow player. A very important and challenging skill to master **(See Rule #3 – Give or Take Focus as Needed)**. An important aspect of chivalry is a willingness to allow your characters lose *status* if in the process it strengthens the scene as a whole.

Commenting (aka Stepping Out) – Very similar to "breaking the fourth wall" in traditional acting, commenting refers to any time a player breaks out of a scene to do something that references the fact that they are in a scene. As a general rule, this comes off as very amateurish, but in certain moments can be really funny. This is not to be confused with the asides sometimes called for by the occasional challenge format.

Complementary Offer – Any suggestion made during a scene that fits in well with the previous action. Making a complementary offer is a strong way to advance the scene, however it usually provides little, if any, conflict. This stands in stark contract with breaking the routine, although both are solid advancing techniques to use.

Conflict – Almost all theatre is about *conflict* – fighting against an obstacle to achieve a goal. Without conflict there is no action, and why would a play without action be worth paying money to go sit and watch? Improv is no different in this regard. Through incorporating conflict into their scenes, improvisers automatically have something solid to base a story around. It is also very important that the conflict, no matter how trivial it may seem to the average person, is a matter of life-or-death to the character. Virtually all forms of theatre are based on some sort of heightened action, so don't skimp on the conflict!

Corpse – Any time that a player breaks character and starts to laugh during a performance. As the name implies, it does tend to "kill" a scene. Just as an actor would never do this during a traditional theatre performance, as a general rule it should be avoided in improv as well, as it typically annoys the audience. Corpsing tends to crop up frequently on sketch-based shows going for a more spontaneous appearance like *Saturday Night Live* or *The Carol Burnett Show*. Other programs like *The Kids in the Hall* create a more polished feel by tending to avoid it altogether. Used very sparingly (read "genuinely") it can also be a very effective means to bridge the gap between actor and audience.

Denial - (See Blocking)

Driving (aka Bulldozing) – One of the **Deadly Sins of Improv**. When a player is driving, they have completely taken control over the direction of a scene. Since improv is all about teamwork, this is something a performer should never – and I mean NEVER, EVER -

do. It is also an *extremely* common problem among teams of inexperienced improvisers, who often may feel more comfortable deferring the control of a scene over to the "funny" team member. The more that a group practices, the more easily this can be avoided. **(See Rule #3 – Give or Take Focus as Needed)**

Edit – The act of stopping the action of a scene, either to add a new offer or to end the scene altogether. There are several different ways to edit a scene, some of which are a form of transition, some are a characteristic of a particular challenge, others are used as a means of providing structure to an otherwise chaotic scene. An edit can be done by either a performer or the emcee. An example of a game that utilizes frequent edits is Options, in which the host/facilitator frequently freezes the action to get information from the audience that must then be incorporated into the scene by the performers.

Embellishing – (See Advancing)

Embodying – The act of becoming anything non-human, usually either a piece of scenery or an object to be used in the scene. The challenge Human Prop for example, involves a player that must embody every physical object that is mentioned during the course of the scene.

Endowment – Any attribute that is assigned to a character, whether by the audience or another player. Some challenges like Party Quirks are all about deciphering what endowment a performer has received. Others, like Superheroes, involve characters that assign endowments to each other that will be maintained throughout the remainder of the scene.

Explore and Heighten – Essentially another way to say "agree and embellish" but sound a whole lot smarter. However, it should be noted that as the word "explore" implies, successful improv isn't usually about simply saying "yes" to an offer, but actually spending a little bit of time seeing how the action plays out.

Extending – The process of transforming an offer into the core of a scene. As a typical scene unfolds, an offer will be made at some point that gives a seasoned player an internal feeling of "Aha!" Extending is simply listening to that instinct, and then elaborating upon the idea, allowing it to develop.

Focus – Actually can have two different but interrelated meanings. First, focus refers to where the audience should be paying attention. An audience only has the ability to focus on one particular action at a time, so improvisers must avoid splitting the action into multiple places, as often happens with inexperienced groups of four players **(See Split Scene)**. Experienced performers understand how to both give and take focus **(See Rule #3 – Give or Take Focus as Needed)** – which is one of the most challenging aspects of improv. Second, focus can simply refer to the central premise of a scene – the offer that was extended. In other words, the audience's *attentive focus* should always be on a single central *dramatic focus.*

Gagging – One of the **Deadly Sins of Improv**. Any attempt to do something that doesn't come naturally from the scene's context, usually including the addition of stock jokes ("gags" - hence the name). I personally had a very bad improv experience resulting from my team gagging. In my first public improv performance (at age twelve, in a middle school tournament) my teammates and I, who had never taken the time to practice outside of a scene in drama class and frankly didn't know any better, decided to bring a few funny props with us to incorporate in our performance. The instant the first one appeared out of nowhere in the scene, we were viciously (at least in my twelve year old perception) booed by the audience and forced to make a hasty exit. I couldn't get off stage fast enough. (I know that I already told that story in Chapter One, but come on… it was seriously traumatic!)

The Game – A very challenging word to concretely define, because the very concept is about as abstract as they come. The "game" is essentially that vague instinctual notion of what makes a particular scene work – in other words, what's actually funny, or interesting, or engaging about it. Most improvised scenes are therefore essentially all about finding the game. An extremely important element of long-form improv, developing a sense of the game can also be very helpful for a short-form performer as well.

Gibberish (aka Jabbertalk) – Any language completely made up of nonsense sounds. There are several common challenges that require a performer to use gibberish (i.e. Dubbing or Double Talk). Inexperienced players often mimic the phonetic patterns of a foreign language or stay within a certain family of similar sounds. For gibberish to be really successful however, a performer must use a full range of vocalizations and, unless done for a particular effect, avoid the trap of dialect impersonation. It should also be noted that occasionally, even if unintentional, gibberish based on actual language patterns can appear to be culturally insensitive or even flat-out racist. So keep the nonsense random.

Goal – What a character in a scene is attempting to achieve. The struggle against an obstacle in the process of trying to achieve a goal is what provides a scene with conflict. Remember that no matter how trivial the goal may seem to us, to the character it must be the most important thing on earth. While the character may or may not succeed in reaching their goal during the course of the scene, they must always try to do so with every ounce of their being. Now we've got some action!

Gossip – Talking, talking, talking instead of doing, doing, doing. **(See Talking Heads)** Remember, **Rule #2** – Stay in the present? Scenes must always be active. Would you rather watch people having a conversation about an amazing expedition to see the Moon People of Cleveland Heights or a reenactment of it? Gossiping can also refer to a piece of offstage action or discussing events that have occurred in the past or will in the future – Most of these are also a violation of **Rule #2**.

Handle – (See Challenge)

Hedging – The improv equivalent of following up a home run with a bunt. Instead of choosing to undertake a specific action, performers simply engage in a conversation about what they could do. Hedging is gossip's long lost twin brother, out for vengeance.

Ignoring – Instead of accepting the offer of another player, it is treated as if it was never even made. This is one of the worst things a player can possibly do in an improv performance because unlike blocking, which at least acknowledges the offer's existence, ignoring the offer snubs and devalues the performer in the worst possible way.

Information Overload (aka Overloading) – Exactly as the name implies, information overload refers to times when too many offers have been introduced into a scene. This can be a significant problem, because it can lead to sidetracking, and makes finding a successful resolution to a scene very problematic, often impossible **(See Never-Ending Story)**.

Instant Trouble (aka Offer from Space) – Any offer made during a scene that seems to come out of nowhere. In most forms of improv, all offers should relate to the scene in some way, as that is a natural method of agreeing and embellishing. Although surprisingly indulgent of performer's whims at times, audiences crave a primarily linear storyline, so avoid this one, except in an improv emergency, when it's called for by the challenge, or when there is a definite need to break the routine.

Jabbertalk – (See Gibberish)

Justifying – Being able to explain, solve, or resolve every offer that is made. A primary job in both long and short form improv is to take seemingly incongruous variables and develop them into a coherent scene that an audience can follow. While actors will employ many different tools to make their scenes engaging, it is through how they justify the variables that gives a scene its coherence. In addition, some challenges like Actor's Nightmare revolve all around making justifications as the scene's primary gimmick.

Long Form – A type of improvisational theatre in which a longer play is performed. There are many different formats used in long form improv, some involving an extended stand-alone scene, some involving groupings of shorter scenes. Long form is significantly less gimmicky than short form and relies upon strong, honest characterization and narrative rather than humor for much of its success.

Masking – Essentially synonymous with the term "upstaging" in the traditional theatre, masking refers to any time a performer positions themselves in a manner that they either block an action that should be the focus of the scene or aren't completely visible themselves. This would, of course, be a bad thing. In traditional theatre, masking refers to the bits of scenery that hide what the audience shouldn't see (i.e. backstage, electrics, other actors, what the other actors may or may not be doing in the wings, etc.).

Mugging – Ever heard the old slang term "mug" meaning someone's face? In improv, mugging refers to when a performer simply makes funny faces and such, instead of genuinely accepting the offers made in a scene. While this may be fine in small doses in the hands of a very experienced player, it should be avoided at all costs by those still learning as it removes all traces of honesty from the scene.

Naming – Because improv performers communicate objects and locations through mime, it is very important to provide names for the places they "visit," things they "use," and sometimes even what types of characters they are playing. The audience will go along with just about anything that is put out there, but without naming the objects that are mimed, what to the performer is obviously a rake, to them could be a shovel, stick, dead body, fruitcake, or commemorative Statuette of Liberty.

Narrative – The story that is told during the course of a scene. Remember that all improv must be about a story, so when performers think structure, they must do so in terms of plot – exposition/setup, rising action, climax, etc. This is a do-or-die requirement of long form, but it is essential to quality short form improv as well.

Never-Ending Story – A scene that has so many elements introduced into it that it becomes impossible to bring to a close. The result of information overload, this is not a desirable occurrence.

Object Work – The act of miming the physical objects used in an improv scene. The things that are mimed are called space-objects.

Objective – (See Goal)

Obstacle – That which is preventing a character from achieving their goal. It is the struggle against the obstacle that provides a scene with conflict. Just about anything can be an obstacle - another character, a feeling, a social concern, even just the need to go to the bathroom can be effective (and funny) when used well.

Offer – Everything that a performer introduces into a scene, whether physical, verbal, or otherwise. Remember that all offers should advance the story in some way and that all performers should always agree with and embellish upon all offers **(see Rule #1)**.

Offer from Space – (See Instant Trouble)

Overloading – (See Information Overload)

Point of Concentration – (See Focus, second definition)

Post-Mortem (aka Post-Show) – A reflective discussion either by the players and crew or players and audience to discover successes, recognize problems, or explore a theme/idea contained in a production. Post-show discussions among improv team members are extremely important as they are the moments that will likely provide the greatest opportunity for growth. As many traditional theatres offer post-show conversations between actors and audience after selected performances of their "meatier" selections, why should improv be left out?

Plateau – If one were to construct a graph of a good scene, it would look like the face of a mountain because the scene is constantly advancing – going up and up and up. A graph of a bad scene, however, would look like a plateau, because it is stagnating – staying at one level – rather than advancing. A plateau made out of mashed potatoes would look Devil's Tower and would signal the arrival of alien life forms. Just saying.

Platform – The basic information upon which the entirety of the scene is built (i.e. location, characters, objective, etc). Without a solid platform, the players will most likely have a very difficult time advancing the scene. This is why it is important to always think in terms of narrative - build a story upon a solid foundation.

Playlist (aka Running Order) – The list of challenges that will be used during a particular performance. If specific variables or ask-fors are required by the game, they should also be included on a playlist. A playlist can be decided upon by the performers, chosen randomly, picked by the facilitator, or even selected by the audience in a variety of entertaining ways.

Pimping - One of my personal favorite improv terms, Pimping is forcing another player to do an action that they will likely find embarrassing or at the very least, generally unpleasant. Some challenges specifically call for pimping (i.e. Arms Assault). Other times, it is simply a fun thing to do to your teammates. Fun is the key word here; there should always be something of a sideways wink to the audience any time pimping is used. As with all gimmicks, do not do it too much, or it loses its effectiveness.

Postponing – Instead of accepting an offer and advancing the scene, a player chooses to stall (often by wimping or waffling). Postponing brings a scene to a plateau, a place of stagnation, rather than to a climax. Not very interesting to watch.

Raising the Stakes – Making an offer that makes a character's goal more significant in some fashion, either to them, to an opposing character, or to the scene in general. Raising the stakes is probably the easiest and consequently the most frequently used way to advance a scene.

Reincorporation (aka Callback) – The act of reusing an action or some bit of information from earlier in a scene, or even earlier in the show. This could be a moment that was particularly funny, something at the expense of the emcee, a topical reference ... anything. Essentially, Reincorporation is the long-lost cousin of "a running joke." However, just as with all running jokes, be careful with doing it too much. he third, fourth or even fifth time a player mentions his horrible diarrhea it may be funny, but by the twelfth, it's just plain annoying.

Running Order – (See Playlist)

Setup – The act of explaining a challenge to the audience and gathering any variables needed by using ask-fors. This can be done by a player during a single group performance, or by an individual designated as the host/emcee in any setting. A quick, clear setup is very important if you want the audience to have any idea what is going on. Without understanding the rules, how will they know what's funny?

Shelving – Saving an offer for later. Shelving is different from ignoring because when an offer is shelved by a player, initially it is actively acknowledged. It is only later that for whatever reason, it is set aside. However, just like when a film studio shelves a particular project, promising that the movie will be a surefire blockbuster the following fall, offers that are shelved rarely ever appear again during the course of a scene.

Short Form – A type of improvisational theatre in which short scenes are performed. Short form is the primary focus of this book as it is the format that is most commonly found in educational theatre. Although a much greater emphasis is placed on humor and gimmicks in short form improv, it still shares the same basic principles of strong narrative and characterization associated with long form. No matter which form is being used, the question is always, "Does this advance the story?" first and, "Is it funny?" second.

Sidetracking – Any time the central idea of a scene is arbitrarily altered. This occurs most often and easily through information overload, gagging, or mugging. Once a scene drifts off course, it can be very challenging to get it back on track.

Space-Object – The way improvisers refer to anything that is mimed instead of physically existing. Mime is extremely important in improv, since traditionally everything that is used (apart from a few chairs) is a space-object. It is through space-objects that most of the context of a scene is provided.

Space Work – Just as object work was defining the *props* through mime, space work is defining the scene's *environment* through mime. Again, context, context, context.

Split Scene – Any time that more than a single focus is allowed to develop during a scene. Something for all players to avoid, it is an especially tricky pitfall for inexperienced teams of four, who often will start two separate conversation pairs and end up creating a split scene **(See Focus)**. Knowing how to Give and Take Focus **(See Rule #3)** is a hard skill to master and takes time to develop, but actively avoiding Split Scenes is a great first step to take.

Status – The intrinsic value associated with a character, location, or object. Several of the earliest improv challenges involve a "status transfer," having one character lose value while another character's value increases (i.e. in a simple form, a beggar and king changing places). Many games still actively involve status in some way and, as it is one of the strongest ways to define a character for an audience, it should be emphasized by performers in virtually all scenes.

Stepping Out – (See Commenting)

Synthesis – Combining two or more things into a single idea. Synthesizing multiple variables is a very common way to make ordinary suggestions suddenly quite interesting. "A plumber" or "at a rock concert" are ok variables, but a plumber trying to unclog an angry rock star's toilet or a musical plumber that plays his own pipes are infinitely more interesting. This can be done by the emcee during the setup or even by the performers during the actual course of the scene.

Talking Heads – When a group of improvisers simply stand around talking instead of doing something active **(see Gossip)**. Remember that a scene should always be centered around physical activity, rather than a simple discussion. *DO*, don't tell.

Tilts – These are interesting ideas that aren't quite as bizarre as an offer from space, as they are still linked with the action, but they are dramatic enough to essentially *force* the scene to advance. "Tilt" can also be used as a verb, as in to "Tilt the scene" (to make it go in a new direction).

Tummeling – Playfully interacting with the audience, primarily during the setups. Tummeling is an important aspect of creating the fun, interactive atmosphere that is ideal for an improv show. A good host is an expert tummeler.

Uber-Mime – While it is extremely important to have strong details to all mimed actions, an uber-mime is one that is so detailed that the audience likely has no idea what in the world is happening. The key to successful mime is to latch on to the key characteristics of the object or action being mimed rather than to try to perfectly and accurately recreate an actual example of the item from nothing.

Variable – Any information gathered from the audience that will be incorporated into the scene. A variable is gotten from the audience through the use of an ask-for. Scenes can require a wide variety of variables or ask-fors.

Waffling – Another way that a scene can become nothing but a plateau of talking heads. A player that is waffling is simply not making concrete decisions, and consequently robbing the scene of action. The worst choice one can make about how to act on an offer is to fail to act on it at all. A **Deadly Sin**!

Walk-On (or Walk-Through) – <u>Exactly</u> what the name implies – the act of walking into a scene, making an offer that advances it, and exiting. Very, <u>very</u> gimmicky, but it can also be an extremely effective means of saving a scene that has plateaued, or adding a funny bit of business. Similar to a Canadian cross, however a walk-on is related to <u>and</u> advances the scene's focus and a Canadian cross is/does not.

Wanking – Doing something purely for an audience reaction rather than letting it grow naturally out of the scene. Not only is Wanking essentially a means of showboating, it goes against the fundamental principle of improv that all players must be actively advancing the story in a scene. I don't care how funny it is, wanking is not a good idea. Both gagging and mugging are examples of wanking. (I know that last sentence was a bit gratuitous, but where else but here could it have even been written?)

Wimping – The **Deadly Sin** of wussing out. A player acknowledges an offer, but then does not act upon it in the required fashion. Wimping is an extremely common problem with inexperienced improvisers, as they often have greater inhibitions and performance insecurities than their more seasoned counterparts. Waffling, gossiping, and so forth are all usually examples of wimping.

Improv Fortune Cookie

Fame and fortune await the reader who
masters the terms in this glossary

APPENDIX A:
LIST OF IMPROV ENDOWMENTS

The following is a list of endowments that I have used with successful results. Most of the following were written specifically for **Party Quirks,** but could easily be used for any other endowment challenge. Remember that there are absolutely no limitations on what could potentially be used as an endowment, however as you create your own, remember that attributes requiring a higher degree of physicality tend to be better at stretching a newer performer's abilities, as they often like to remain in the land of the verbal.

200 Endowments
That Have Been Successful

1. Trying to conceal their invisible friend
2. A salesman trying to sell everything at the party
3. Took a box of laxatives before the party
4. Convinced that they are invisible
5. An evil genius trying to take over the world
6. An astronaut who thinks the guests are a new life form he's discovered
7. A hungry dinosaur
8. The host on a five second delay
9. A group of circus performers
10. Can only communicate using charades
11. Thinks that everyone else is judging them
12. Can see people's death before it happens
13. A Russian spy who thinks that everything beginning with a "P" is funny (great when paired with ...)
14. Constantly using words that begin with the letter "P"

15. Darth Vader trying to ask the host on a date
16. Constantly going into monologues about what is going on at the party
17. Dora the Explorer on an adventure
18. Thinks that life is a musical
19. A detective investigating the host for a murder
20. A spy trying to record the party conversation with the tape recorder hidden in their teeth
21. A nun attempting to learn how to party
22. An astronaut preparing to launch tomorrow
23. Godzilla destroying a city
24. Slowly turning into a pirate
25. The world's dumbest thief
26. A grandma upset because the host never visits
27. Middle aged and still lives in their parent's basement
28. Slowly shrinking
29. A zombie attempting to eat the host's brain without being discovered
30. Mocks all of the host's actions
31. Stuck inside a pinball machine
32. Trying to hide their second head
33. Allergic to all physical contact
34. The seven deadly sins
35. A crazy chipmunk hyped up on coffee
36. A terminator trying to protect the host
37. Trying to conceal that they are pregnant
38. That guy who always tries to start a mosh pit
39. A cannibal that will only eat females
40. A caveman time-warped to the future
41. Only came to the party because their mom forced them
42. The king of the sewer people
43. Violet Beauregarde turning into a blueberry
44. An action figure coming to life and learning about how to act human
45. Poorly attempting to guess what character the host is
46. On a blind date with the host of the party
47. Can only speak in pick up lines
48. Thinks they are being pranked by the host

49. Trapped in a soundproof bubble
50. A bodybuilder showing off how strong they are
51. Made entirely of rubber
52. Thinks everyone at the party is really an evil robot in disguise
53. The lifespan from birth to death
54. Everyone represents a different country/state/city/etc.
55. A bird who thinks the host is their egg to protect from the other guests
56. Moves in slow motion, but talks in fast forward
57. The loser from next door coming over to find out what all the noise is about
58. Convinced that the host is a wise guru
59. Turns everything they touch into "art"
60. Slowly becoming dehydrated
61. Says the opposite of what they do
62. A parent trying to toilet train their kid
63. *The Wizard of Oz* in 60 seconds (or any movie, for that matter – BUT you must be certain that the actor is familiar with it)
64. In a high stakes poker game with the host
65. The world's worst lounge singer
66. Likes to speak in proverbs
67. Can make anything performance art
68. An extremely moody Ventriloquist
69. Models everything they touch – on the catwalk
70. An amateur fire eater
71. Thinks that everything around them is scripted
72. Only moves in slow motion
73. The reanimated corpse of Elvis looking for a fried peanut butter and banana sandwich
74. Thinks that they are in a dream
75. Afraid of using the restroom
76. Madly in love with whoever stands next to them
77. Romantically attracted to furniture
78. A malfunctioning robot
79. A cannibal trying to resist eating everyone
80. Can never sit still

81. Thinks the party is a renaissance festival
82. Can only speak in song titles
83. The type of lady that owns 200 cats
84. Trying to hide that they were just bitten by a zombie.
85. Switching back and forth between Hannah Montana and Miley Cyrus
86. Are living five seconds in the future
87. The most annoying person on Earth
88. A child that was just called to the principal's office
89. Terrified of the color blue
90. Attached to a massive amount of helium balloons
91. A crazy parent disguised as a student busting a high school party
92. Just inhaled a LOT of helium
93. Scared of everything soft
94. Everyone in a group is a different superhero
95. A bee that thinks the host is a flower
96. Narrating the party as a rap - with mad hip hop skilz
97. Voices all of their opinions as asides to the audience
98. In the middle of giving a performance of *Cats*
99. Afraid that they will spontaneously combust.
100. Thinks they are performing at a child's birthday party
101. Everything makes them crack up
102. A bird making a nest out of human hair
103. A caterpillar turning into a butterfly
104. Trying to hide that they are a dog disguised as a human
105. Speaks only in fortune cookies
106. The least funny person on Earth
107. Slowly turning into a computer
108. Acts out everything everyone else says
109. Protesting the party
110. A king in disguise testing the kindness of the host
111. Irresistibly compelled to hide behind the host
112. Can only speak in Shakespearian verse
113. A hunter resisting the urge to hunt the most dangerous game of all… people
114. A talent scout looking for the next big star
115. Ate something really spicy and can't find anything to drink

116. A witch secretly making a potion out of the other guests
117. A moustache salesman
118. A chicken with its head cut off
119. Has a crippling fear of feet
120. Just found some amazing treasures while dumpster diving
121. Thinks the guests are all residents of a nursing home
122. Afraid of hearing anyone else speak
123. A talk show host interviewing the "celebrity" guests
124. Screams every time someone says "the"
125. A rabid fan at a home sporting event
126. Thinks that the party is at a deserted camp site
127. Speaks entirely in Pig Latin
128. Always speaks with alliteration
129. A bride running away from her wedding
130. A preschool teacher explaining how parties work
131. Falls down after every four steps
132. Thinks that they are bilingual, but aren't
133. A Greek god
134. A soap opera actor reacting dramatically to everything
135. Can only speak like Dr. Seuss
136. Trying to fight their elbow fetish
137. The world's most optimistic person
138. Remarkably accident prone
139. Distracted by how attractive the host is
140. Won't admit that they have a mouthful of lemons
141. Can only speak in monosyllabic words
142. Just accidently drank a glass of glue they thought was milk
143. Trying to knock down a piñata that isn't there
144. Thinks that the host is their long lost brother/sister
145. Is inside a different natural disaster every 30 seconds
146. A world champion trick bartender
147. Thinks that they are the REAL host of the party
148. Seeking revenge on their ex, who happens to be the host
149. A carnival barker trying to get more guests to come to the party
150. Thinks that the host is a vampire and is trying to get him to bite them
151. Filming the "Making of" the party documentary

152. The Host's nanny
153. A real estate agent attempting to sell the house
154. The personification of a hurricane hitting the party
155. Getting revenge on the host for a terrible prank
156. Thinks the party is really summer camp
157. Thinks the party is a Spanish soap opera
158. Screams any time they are spoken to
159. Just got cut from the football team
160. Has a cheer for everything that happens
161. Barney the Dinosaur after he got out of jail
162. Easily distracted by shiny objects
163. Thinks the Fountain of Youth is in the host's basement
164. The host's grandmother
165. A caveman evolving into modern man
166. Has a mouthful of bees
167. A cowboy attempting to herd the guests
168. Pac-man running from the ghosts
169. A news reporter filming the guests using a hidden camera
170. Convinced that the everything is just a dream
171. A knight on a quest
172. Will die if they aren't touching another person
173. Knows everything
174. Slowly turning into a horrific science-fiction creature
175. Speaks entirely in clichéd romantic comedy quotes
176. The ghosts of the Beatles (yes, even the ones that are still alive)
177. Barbie looking for a new "Ken"
178. Dora the Explorer in her 50's
179. At their high school reunion (and so is their ex!)
180. Their spouse cheated on them with the host
181. Does an interpretive dance to go with everything that they say
182. Hitting on everyone they see
183. Can only speak in riddles
184. Secretly getting DNA samples of the guests
185. An annoying morning talk show host
186. A video game addict frantically searching for the remote
187. Wikipedia editor fixing the entry on the host

188. A psychic drawn to the party by unknown forces
189. Can only speak in grunts
190. Just got kicked out of a concert
191. Afraid that everyone is trying to bite them
192. A member of a boy band
193. Speaks only in texting abbreviations
194. Slowly being eaten by invisible insects
195. A greaser getting ready for a rumble
196. Fighting the irresistible urge to fall asleep
197. Really juiced up on steroids
198. Thinks they are at band camp
199. Slowly turning into a clown
200. The world's most awkward stand-up comic

APPENDIX B:
THEATRE, MOVIE & TV STYLES

The following is a list of TV, film, and theatre styles that I have used successfully with students. They are primarily used with the challenge **"Styles,"** but having performers become familiar with them will also come in handy for challenges that require players to provide their own scene endowments, such as **"Temperamental Director."**

As you are facilitating, always remember to stress that whenever a game calls for a change of style, performers can never abandon the storyline of the scene. Altering the style is simply a means to advance the action in an interesting fashion, and the player's job is merely to change the manner in which that story is being presented.

50 Theatre, Movie and Television Styles That Have Been Successful

1. Action Movie
2. Japanese Monster Movie
3. Science Fiction
4. Horror
5. Western
6. Ballet
7. Opera
8. Shakespeare
9. Cop Drama
10. Nature Documentary
11. Political Debate
12. Celebrity Roast

13. Sports Play by Play
14. Game Show
15. Newscast
16. Variety Show
17. Musical Theatre
18. Sesame Street
19. Spanish Soap Opera
20. Love Story
21. Documentary
22. Reality TV
23. Sitcom
24. Film Noir
25. Educational Documentary for Children
26. War Movie
27. Daytime Talk Show
28. Music Video
29. Spelling Bee
30. Experimental Film
31. Mime
32. Home Movies
33. YouTube Viral Video
34. British Comedy
35. Murder Mystery
36. Music Biography
37. Disaster Movie
38. Zombie Movie
39. Sports Bloopers
40. Absurdist Play
41. Cartoon
42. Hospital Drama
43. Summer Blockbuster
44. Political Talk Show
45. Circus/Side Show Acts
46. Paranormal/Haunted
47. Televangelist Show
48. Medical Show
49. Courtroom Drama
50. Commercial

APPENDIX C: LIST OF REMOTE CONTROL FUNCTIONS

The following is a list of various buttons that I have used with the challenge "**DVD/Remote Control**" with successful results. Just as when applying different "styles" to a challenge, remember that the <u>story</u> always must continue, no matter what button is "pushed." I also recommend that the emcee/facilitator always press "pause" between buttons to force the actors to stop long enough so that both they and the audience are able to adequately hear the context for the subsequent action.

And don't forget the great gimmick of having an actor repeat and rewind a very elaborate bit of physical business over and over (or even doing it in slow motion!)

The Basics
- Play
- Fast Forward
- Rewind
- Pause
- Slow Motion

Sound Related Buttons
- Mute
- Volume control
- Switching to any Foreign Language Track
- Turning on Subtitles

TEACHING AND PERFORMING IMPROV

Advanced Features
- The "Making Of" Featurette
- Director's Commentary
- Trailer for the Film
- Changing Channels (perhaps followed by...)
- Picture in Picture
- Jump to the Next Chapter
- A Deleted Scene
- Accidentally Changing the Video Input to a Gaming Console

To End the Scene
- Eject

APPENDIX D:
SUGGESTIONS FOR ASK-FORS

Variables are the pieces of information that the facilitator gets from the audience that will be incorporated into the scene by the performers. An ask-for is the question that the host uses to get the variable from the audience.

A "standard set" of variables is simply an occupation, location, and object - but why stop there? The very act of getting the suggestions is another opportunity to entertain, after all, so don't waste it.

Here is a list of possibilities that can be used as ask-fors to gather variables. As with everything else in the book, this list is not the final word on the matter, but rather a starting point for you to work from.

100 Ask-Fors
That Have Been Successful

1.	Give me a location.	** Standard Set **
2.	Give me an occupation.	** Standard Set **
3.	Give me any three-dimensional object.	** Standard Set **
4.	Where is the worst place to go on a date?	
5.	Where is the best place to go on a date?	
6.	Give me a make of car.	
7.	Give me a brand of cereal.	
8.	What is your favorite piece of furniture?	
9.	What is your favorite non-alcoholic beverage?	
10.	Give me a style of music.	

11. What is a common computer problem?
12. What is a common daily annoyance?
13. Give me a noun that starts with (any letter).
14. What is your greatest fear?
15. What is your greatest source of happiness?
16. Where is the best place to dispose of a body?
17. What do you want to be when you grow up?
18. What is the most useful invention of the past 100 years?
19. What is your favorite food?
20. Name something that would be interesting to put in a microwave.
21. What is the dumbest way you've ever gotten hurt?
22. What is your favorite rainy day activity?
23. What would you never do at a funeral?
24. Name a place you could travel to by foot (or by bike, or by plane, or by boat, etc).
25. What is the dumbest thing you've ever bought online?
26. What are hot dogs made out of?
27. What is your favorite color?
28. What is a relationship that can exist between two people?
29. What is a problem that could exist in that relationship?
30. Who is your favorite historical figure?
31. If you could go on a vacation to anywhere in the world, where would it be to?
32. Name a public building here in town.
33. What's a good pick up line?
34. What does green (or any color) taste like?
35. What is the most interesting thing you've ever found in your couch cushions?
36. Name something you can't eat.
37. If you could, who would you paint a portrait of right now?
38. What is the weirdest thing you've seen on YouTube?
39. What is hardest part about delivering pizzas?
40. What would be an interesting pizza topping?
41. What would a garden gnome do on vacation?
42. What is your favorite movie?
43. What is your favorite hobby?
44. Name any ingredient needed to make a cake.

45. What could be the subject of an interesting magazine article?
46. Name an item that would clog a vacuum cleaner.
47. We're going hunting later. What should we hunt?
48. Where is the worst place to go on your honeymoon?
49. Name an interesting article of clothing.
50. Name something that is not a fruit.
51. What does a Muppet do, once everyone has gone home for the night?
52. What's inside this box?
53. Name someone you wouldn't want to get a phone call from.
54. Name something that's a bad idea to do when dancing.
55. What is something you shouldn't send in the mail?
56. Name a product that would help to give a gerbil a bath.
57. If you had to spend the rest of your life in a Disney movie, which one would you choose?
58. If you were stranded on a desert island, what one thing would you bring with you?
59. What is a bad name for a children's band?
60. What did you have for lunch?
61. Name a reason that a man might send a woman flowers.
62. What country has the best pickles?
63. What animal would make a bad pet?
64. What is your favorite piece of outdated slang?
65. What is the weirdest thing you've ever found in your purse?
66. What frozen food would make the best weapon in a pinch?
67. What is the worst way to break up with someone?
68. In the movie version of your life, who would play you?
69. What does this button do?
70. What is the worst present to give your wife on your anniversary?
71. Name something that is (color).
72. What's a great game to play at a birthday party?
73. What animal would you never see on a farm?
74. What would the best book in the world be about? (Improv, obviously)
75. What is the opposite of a fish?
76. If you could buy any toy, what would it be?
77. Name any object that can fold.

78. Name an elective surgical procedure.
79. What is a word that sounds dirty, but isn't?
80. What occupation (i.e. Police) or object (i.e. Cars) would make a good band name?
81. If you could make anything out of papier-mâché, what would it be?
82. What would frighten the Jolly Green Giant (or other product mascot)?
83. What is something (other than a boot) that a cartoon character would catch while fishing?
84. What would be an unusual product to have its own superstore?
85. What fictional character would you like to have dinner with?
86. What instrument would you like to be able to play?
87. What animal are you the most afraid of?
88. What is/was your best (or worst) subject in school?
89. Name something (other than scissors) that you shouldn't hold while running.
90. What's your favorite flavor of ice cream?
91. What is your favorite present that you have ever received for your birthday?
92. Where would a cheapskate have a wedding reception?
93. If you could spend a day inside a video game, what game would it be?
94. What superpower do you wish you had?
95. Name a superpower that you would never want.
96. What's your favorite ride in an amusement park?
97. Name something you would find in a diaper bag.
98. What would be an interesting documentary subject?
99. I would now like to present the award for the Best _____.

100. What am I thinking of right now?

APPENDIX E: DIE GAME QUESTIONS & ZULU SUGGESTIONS

A **Die Game** is an elimination challenge in which players who fault for any reason must perform a quick scene in which they die in the manner of the audience's choosing (i.e. Death by Squeegee – nothing serious or actually fatal allowed here.)

In my favorite version of The Die Game, each player provides one word of the answer to a question asked by the emcee. If a player pauses, says two words, repeats what was already said, or otherwise makes no sense, they have faulted and are out.

75 Questions for The Die Game That Have Been Successful

1. Why is the Sky Blue?
2. So, how long has this been going on?
3. Do you come here often?
4. Do you want to know a secret?
5. What's another word for Thesaurus?
6. If you were a hot dog, would you eat yourself?
7. What is the perfect vacation?
8. Who stole the cookies from the cookie jar?
9. Does fuzzy logic tickle?
10. Hello, is there anybody out there?
11. What's the first thing that you do in the morning?
12. Do you feel lucky? Well, do you, punk?

13. Are you talking to me?
14. Can you handle the truth?
15. Houston, do we have a problem?
16. Buddy, can you spare a dime?
17. Does this outfit make me look fat?
18. Do you mind if I cut in?
19. If two's a couple and three's a crowd, what are four and five?
20. What is your biggest dream?
21. What's her problem?
22. Does a fish get cramps after eating?
23. What accessory would complete this outfit?
24. What do people like the most about you?
25. If sour cream isn't used by its 'best if used-by' date, does it turn sweet?
26. Is the grass really greener on the other side?
27. If a tree falls on a mime in the forest, does anybody care?
28. May I buy you a drink?
29. Why can't they make the whole plane out of the material used to make the indestructible black box?
30. How much wood would a woodchuck chuck if a woodchuck could chuck wood?
31. Are you going to eat that?
32. Do you know the way to San Jose?
33. Was it over when the Germans bombed Pearl Harbor?
34. Do you suffer from dry flaky skin?
35. Would you like to swing on a star?
36. Have I told you lately that I love you?
37. Do you believe in magic?
38. What's new, Pussycat?
39. Tell me, have you seen her?
40. Hey Joe, where you going with that gun in your hand?
41. Where have all the flowers gone?
42. Do the voices in my head bother you?
43. Are you ready to rock?
44. Will you still love me tomorrow?
45. Why do they call it a TV set when you only get one?
46. Would you care to answer a few quick questions to improve our service?

47. Do you have any gum?
48. Why can't we be friends?
49. Which came first – the chicken or the egg?
50. What color should I dye my hair?
51. If the members of the audience were laid end to end, how long would they be?
52. May I have this dance?
53. Do you want fries with that?
54. Is there any place like home?
55. Excuse me, does this come in blue?
56. Is she really going out with him?
57. What becomes of the broken hearted?
58. Baby, where did our love go?
59. Is anybody sitting here?
60. How many crows are in a murder?
61. What would you do with a million dollars?
62. What's up, Doc?
63. How much do you currently pay for long distance?
64. A train leaves Cleveland at 8pm going 55mph. How long before the passengers ask, "What am I doing taking a train?"
65. Who is your favorite superhero?
66. If olive oil comes from olives and corn oil comes from corn, where does baby oil come from?
67. Why do fools fall in love?
68. Who let the dogs out?
69. Who brought the hors d'oeuvres to the Donner Party?
70. Who wrote the book of love?
71. Who delivers the mailman's mail?
72. Shouldn't there be a shorter word for monosyllabic?
73. Should I stay or should I go?
74. What is your biggest fear?
75. Final Question: What is the meaning of life?

In a round of **Zulu**, each player provides the name of something new that fits into a particular category.

In my usage of Zulu with secondary students, the two categories that have been the most successful have been new products and film titles.

The name must be plausible and cannot simply repeat the category's name, nor can it already exist. For example, if the category was "Plant Food" then "Fert-o-grow Max" would fit, but "Miracle Gro" or "Food for Plants" would not.

This is a lightning round!

25 Suggestions for Products That Have Been Successful

1. Laundry Detergent
2. Furniture Polish
3. New Car Model
4. Weight Loss Pill
5. Toilet Bowl Cleaner
6. New Electronic Toy
7. Make Up
8. Shoe Manufacturer
9. Plant Food
10. Self Cleaning Litter Box
11. Get Rich Quick Scheme
12. Sunscreen
13. Muscle Building Supplement
14. All-You-Can-Eat Restaurant
15. Air Freshener
16. Hair Dye
17. Paper Shredder
18. Exercise Equipment
19. Construction Company
20. Drain Unclogger

21. Rat Poison
22. Laxative
23. Weed Killer
24. Energy Drink
25. Toothpaste

10 Suggestions for Film Genres That Have Been Successful

1. Paranormal (Can't Use the Word "Haunted")
2. Action/Adventure
3. Romance
4. Slapstick Comedy
5. Nature Documentary
6. Educational Children's Film
7. Western Musical
8. Alien Attack
9. Murder Mystery
10. Sports (i.e. Underdog Team Wins the League)

APPENDIX F: LIST OF PREMISES FOR SCENES FROM A HAT

The following is a list of suggestions that I have used for the game **Scenes from a Hat** with successful results. However, as with any other variable or endowment, they can certainly be adapted for use with other challenges or activities.

Have fun!

75 Suggestions for Scenes from a Hat That Have Been Successful

1. What a tree would say to a woodpecker
2. Games you can play with your toddler - but not your boss
3. If cats could talk
4. What your fruit is thinking
5. Things edited out of *Winnie the Pooh*
6. So, where exactly is Waldo?
7. What's buried in your grandmother's basement?
8. Unexpected bumper stickers
9. Things written on a public restroom wall
10. Unusual interpretive dances
11. What the host is thinking right now
12. What cows think right before they are slaughtered
13. What the person wearing the Chuck-e-Cheese costume is thinking
14. What actually lives on the other side of the rainbow

15. The worst ideas for a team cheer
16. The best excuses to use when you get caught sneaking in at 4 AM
17. Creative ways to get around a night club bouncer
18. Ideas for failed TV pilots
19. Things you shouldn't do on a construction site
20. The worst places for a ghost to be stuck haunting
21. Unused McDonald's menu items
22. The worst things to say at a wedding
23. What a bad private detective would say to stop a fleeing suspect
24. Unapproved uses for cottage cheese
25. Ill conceived ways to propose to your fiancée
26. Slogans for failed political candidates
27. Misguided new jellybean flavors
28. Creative ways to quit your job
29. New dance moves that haven't caught on
30. The worst products to sell door to door
31. Scenes deleted from Disney Movies
32. Things that you should never use duct tape for
33. Unusual things found in your couch
34. Bizarre late night infomercials
35. New electives being offered next year
36. Scenes edited out of *The Wizard of Oz*
37. Pick up lines used by leprechauns
38. Unusual subjects for a documentary
39. Ways you shouldn't break up with someone
40. What a mall Santa is secretly thinking
41. Things you shouldn't say at a funeral
42. The worst rapper on Earth
43. Things you shouldn't do with a rake
44. What the little voice in your head is saying right now
45. The worst excuses for speeding
46. What a bug is thinking right before it hits the windshield
47. Unusual country music lyrics
48. Scenes edited out of *The Lion King*
49. What a chair would say if it could talk
50. The worst excuses for not having your homework done

51. Bad presents to give to your grandma
52. Ways to not get that big promotion
53. Presents you should never give your teacher
54. How to approach _____ (Insert flavor of the month celebrity)
55. If Yoda told "Your Mama" jokes
56. Bad things to say while watching a romantic movie with your boyfriend/girlfriend
57. If dogs ran the world
58. Bad titles for a children's book
59. What clowns do on the weekends
60. Monkey pick-up lines
61. What a chicken thinks about you
62. What's on a fly's mind
63. What your TV would say if it were alive
64. What the mall Santa did to get fired
65. Things you shouldn't give as a wedding gift
66. What is hiding in the back of your freezer
67. Bad uses for Jell-O
68. What teachers do in their spare time
69. What a tootsie pop thinks
70. Offensive things to say to someone with a nut allergy
71. Unusual things to find in your shoe
72. What you shouldn't wear on the first day of school
73. Bad examples to use during a motivational speech
74. What your chewing gum is thinking
75. Unusual subjects for college courses

And 5 More Suggestions That Will Likely Produce Offensive (But Funny!) Results

1. Things to never say while waiting in the line for the bathroom
2. Worst places to find Monopoly pieces
3. Things you can say to your boyfriend, but not your friend's boyfriend
4. What's the secret in the "secret sauce"
5. Excuses the nurse just won't believe

INDEX OF:
ALL ACTIVITIES BY PAGE

Challenges

Warm Ups

Tune Ups

INDEX OF:
WARM-UPS BY SKILL (VIP)

Vocal Targeted Warm-ups

Diction

3 Line Scenes
Bodega/Topeka
Czechoslovakia (Sha-Boom!)
Gigolo
Pterodactyl
Schwing! (plus Bong, Bounce & Opa!)
Tongue Twisters
Wu, Wo, War, WOW

Inflection

3 Line Scenes
Big Booty
Bodega/Topeka
Czechoslovakia (Sha-Boom!)
Dude!
Gigolo
Ha, Ha!
Kwah!
Pterodactyl
Tongue Twisters
Wu, Wo, War, WOW
Zip, Zap, Zop

Vocal Manipulation

3 Line Scenes
Bananas!
Big Booty
Bodega/Topeka
Body Slap
Confuse-a-Cross!
Free Association
Ha, Ha!
Kwah!
Machines
Pterodactyl
Slap, Slap, Animal

Tongue Twisters
Wu, Wo, War, WOW
Yes, Lets!
Zip, Zap, Zop

Volume

3 Line Scenes
Bananas!
Big Booty
Bodega/Topeka
Body Slap
Czechoslovakia (Sha-Boom!)
Dude!
Duck, Duck, Animal
Focus Circle
Free Association
Gigolo
Jumping Jacks
Kwah!
Martha
Pterodactyl
Ride That Pony!
Schwing! (plus Bong, Bounce & Opa!)
Shakedown (from 8)
Tongue Twisters
What Are You doing?
Yes, Lets!
Zip, Zap, Zop

TEACHING AND PERFORMING IMPROV

Interpersonal Targeted Warm-ups

Eye Contact

Big Booty
Bippity, Bippity, Bop!
Clap Circle
Confuse-a-Cross!
Dude!
Energy Ball
Focus Circle
Free Association
Groupstop
Kwah!
Pterodactyl
Rainstorm
Ride That Pony!
Schwing! (plus Bong, Bounce & Opa!)
Shakes!
Slap, Slap, Animal
Zip, Zap, Zop

Focus

3 Line Scenes
Big Booty
Bippity, Bippity, Bop!
Clap Circle
Confuse-a-Cross!
Count-Up
Czechoslovakia (Sha-Boom!)
Dude!
Focus Circle
Free Association
Groupstop
Kwah!
Magic Stick/Magic Ball
Pterodactyl
Rainstorm
Schwing! (plus Bong, Bounce & Opa!)
Slap Circle (aka Slappy Hands)
Slap, Slap, Animal
What Are You doing?
Yes, Lets!
Zip, Zap, Zop

Listening

2 Truths/1 Lie
3 Line Scenes
Big Booty

Bippity, Bippity, Bop!
Clap Circle
Confuse-a-Cross!
Count-Up
Duck, Duck, Animal
Energy Ball
Family Portraits
Free Association
Groupstop
Schwing! (plus Bong, Bounce & Opa!)
Slap Circle (aka Slappy Hands)
Slap, Slap, Animal
What Are You doing?
Yes, Lets!
Zip, Zap, Zop

Team Building

2 Truths/1 Lie
3 Line Scenes
Bananas!
Big Booty
Bippity, Bippity, Bop!
Bodega/Topeka
Body Slap
Character of the Space
Clap Circle
Confuse-a-Cross!
Count-Up
Czechoslovakia (Sha-Boom!)
Duck, Duck, Animal
Dude!
Energy Ball
Family Portraits
Focus Circle
Free Association
Gigolo
Groupstop
Ha, Ha!
Half-Sheet
Human Knot
Jumping Jacks
Kwah!
Machines
Magic Stick/Magic Ball
Martha
Pterodactyl
Rainstorm

Physical Targeted Warm-ups

Stamina

Body Slap
Character of the Space
Clap Circle
Czechoslovakia (Sha-Boom!)
Duck, Duck, Animal
Family Portraits
Gigolo
Jumping Jacks
Machines
Rainstorm
Ride That Pony!
Shakedown (from 8)
Shakes!
Stretching
Yes, Lets!

INDEX OF: TUNE-UPS BY SKILL

Magic Stick/Magic Ball
Scene Beyond Words
Story Ball
What Are You Doing?

Physicality

3 Line Scenes
Character of the Space
Energy Ball
Family Portraits
Freeze Tag
Gibberish
Hitchhiker
Machines
Magic Stick/Magic Ball
Mirrors
Scene Beyond Words
What Are You Doing?

Spatial Awareness

Character of the Space
Machines
Mirrors

Storytelling

3 Line Scenes
Character of the Space
Entrances and Exits
First Line, Last Line
Fortune Cookie
Freeze Tag
Gibberish
Good Thing/Bad Thing
Last Letter/First Letter
Questions Only
Scene Beyond Words
Should Have Said
Story Ball
Yes, And...

Taking Direction

Character of the Space
Family Portraits
What Are You Doing?

Teamwork

3 Line Scenes
Clap Circle Plus Focus
Dr. Know-It-All
Energy Ball
Family Portraits
First Line, Last Line
Fortune Cookie
Freeze Tag
Good Thing/Bad Thing
Machines
Mirrors
Should Have Said
Story Ball
This Is a Duck
Yes, And...

Temporal Awareness

Freeze Tag

Thinking Funny

3 Line Scenes
Freeze Tag
Good Thing/Bad Thing
Hitchhiker

Verbal Prowess

Dr. Know-It-All
Good Thing/Bad Thing
Last Letter/First Letter
Questions Only
This Is a Duck

Vocalization

3 Line Scenes
Family Portraits
Gibberish
Hitchhiker
Machines

INDEX OF: CHALLENGES BY SKILL

TEACHING AND PERFORMING IMPROV

Scenes from a Hat
Should Have Said
Superhero Eulogy

Justification

Actor's Nightmare (aka Playbook)
Alphabet Scene
Body Leads
Boris
Categories
Conducted Scenes
Counting Words
Dubbing/Double Talk
Emotional Boundaries
Entrances and Exits
Experts
Fortune Cookie
Freeze Tag
Freeze Tag (Large Group Version)
Gibberish
Hitchhiker
Infomercial
Modern Fairy Tale
Options
Party Quirks/Endowments
Remote Control
Sentence Scenes
Sit, Stand, Lean
Slide Show
Sound Effects
Space Jump
Statues/Moving People
Styles
Superheroes
Tag Team
Temperamental Director
Town Meeting
Typewriter Scene (aka Typist/Narrator)

Listening/Being in the Moment

Actor's Nightmare (aka Playbook)
Alliteration
Alphabet Scene
Arms
At The Movies
Conducted Scenes
Counting Words
The Die Game
Dr. Know-It-All
Dubbing/Double Talk

Dubbing/Double Talk
Entrances and Exits
Experts
Freeze Tag
Freeze Tag (Large Group Version)
Gibberish
Good Thing/Bad Thing
Half-Life
Hat Game
Hitchhiker
Human Prop
Infomercial
Last Letter/First Letter
Media Challenges
Options
The Purloined Letter
Remote Control
Sentence Scenes
Should Have Said
Sit, Stand, Lean
Slide Show
Sound Effects
Space Jump
Styles
Superheroes
Superhero Eulogy
Tag Team
Temperamental Director
Town Meeting
Two Heads
Typewriter Scene (aka Typist/Narrator)

Mime

Arms
Boris
Chance of a Lifetime
The Die Game
Experts
Freeze Tag
Freeze Tag (Large Group Version)
Gibberish
Human Prop
Infomercial
Media Challenges
One Word Scene
Scene Without "_____"
Scenes from a Hat
Space Jump
Styles
Superheroes
Typewriter Scene (aka Typist/Narrator)

TEACHING AND PERFORMING IMPROV

Teamwork

Actor's Nightmare (aka Playbook)
Alliteration
Alphabet Scene
Arms
At The Movies
Body Leads
Boris
Chance of a Lifetime
Conducted Scenes
Counting Words
Dr. Know-It-All
Dubbing/Double Talk
Entrances and Exits
Experts
Fortune Cookie
Freeze Tag
Freeze Tag (Large Group Version)
Gibberish
Good Thing/Bad Thing
Half-Life
Hitchhiker
Human Prop
Last Letter/First Letter
Modern Fairy Tale
One Word Scene
Options
Party Quirks/Endowments
Remote Control
Scene Without "_____"
Sit, Stand, Lean
Slide Show
Space Jump
Styles
Superheroes
Tag Team
Temperamental Director
Town Meeting
Two Heads
Typewriter Scene (aka Typist/Narrator)

Temporal Awareness

Freeze Tag
Freeze Tag (Large Group Version)
Half-Life
Temperamental Director

Thinking Funny

185
The Die Game
Freeze Tag
Freeze Tag (Large Group Version)
Modern Fairy Tale
Props
Scenes from a Hat
Should Have Said
Slide Show
Superhero Eulogy
Town Meeting

Verbal Prowess

Actor's Nightmare (aka Playbook)
Alliteration
Alphabet Scene
Categories
Counting Words
The Die Game
Dr. Know-It-All
Dubbing/Double Talk
Last Letter/First Letter
The Purloined Letter
Scene Without "_____"
Sentence Scenes
Two Heads

Vocalization

Conducted Scenes
Dubbing/Double Talk
Emotional Boundaries
Gibberish
One Word Scene

INDEX OF: CHALLENGES BY USAGE

Class or Workshop Setting

185
Actor's Nightmare (aka Playbook)
Alliteration
Alphabet Scene
Arms
At The Movies
Body Leads
Boris
Categories
Chance of a Lifetime
Conducted Scenes
Counting Words
The Die Game
Dr. Know-It-All
Dubbing/Double Talk
Emotional Boundaries
Entrances and Exits
Experts
Fortune Cookie
Freeze Tag
Freeze Tag (Large Group Version)
Gibberish
Good Thing/Bad Thing
Half-Life
Hat Game
Hitchhiker
Human Prop

Infomercial
Last Letter/First Letter
Media Challenges
Modern Fairy Tale
One Word Scene
Options
Party Quirks/Endowments
Props
The Purloined Letter
Remote Control
Scene Without "_____"
Scenes from a Hat
Sentence Scenes
Should Have Said
Sit, Stand, Lean
Slide Show
Sound Effects
Space Jump
Statues/Moving People
Styles
Superheroes
Superhero Eulogy
Tag Team
Temperamental Director
Town Meeting
Two Heads
Typewriter Scene (aka Typist/Narrator)

Team Practice Session

185
Actor's Nightmare (aka Playbook)
Alliteration
Alphabet Scene
Arms
At The Movies
Body Leads

Boris
Categories
Chance of a Lifetime
Conducted Scenes
Counting Words
The Die Game
Dr. Know-It-All

Dubbing/Double Talk
Emotional Boundaries
Entrances and Exits
Experts
Fortune Cookie
Freeze Tag
Freeze Tag (Large Group Version)
Gibberish
Good Thing/Bad Thing
Half-Life
Hat Game
Hitchhiker
Human Prop
Infomercial
Last Letter/First Letter
Media Challenges
Modern Fairy Tale
One Word Scene
Options
Party Quirks/Endowments

Props
The Purloined Letter
Remote Control
Scene Without "_____"
Scenes from a Hat
Sentence Scenes
Should Have Said
Sit, Stand, Lean
Slide Show
Sound Effects
Space Jump
Statues/Moving People
Styles
Superheroes
Superhero Eulogy
Tag Team
Temperamental Director
Town Meeting
Two Heads
Typewriter Scene (aka Typist/Narrator)

Single Group Performance

185
Actor's Nightmare (aka Playbook)
Alliteration **
Alphabet Scene
Arms
At The Movies
Body Leads
Boris **
Categories
Chance of a Lifetime
Conducted Scenes
Counting Words
The Die Game
Dr. Know-It-All
Dubbing/Double Talk
Emotional Boundaries
Entrances and Exits **
Experts
Fortune Cookie
Freeze Tag
Freeze Tag (Large Group Version)
Gibberish
Good Thing/Bad Thing
Half-Life
Hat Game
Human Prop

Infomercial **
Last Letter/First Letter
Media Challenges
Modern Fairy Tale **
One Word Scene **
Options
Party Quirks/Endowments
Props
The Purloined Letter
Remote Control
Scene Without "_____"
Scenes from a Hat
Sentence Scenes
Should Have Said
Sit, Stand, Lean
Slide Show
Sound Effects
Space Jump
Statues/Moving People
Styles
Superheroes
Superhero Eulogy **
Tag Team
Temperamental Director
Town Meeting **
Two Heads
Typewriter Scene (aka Typist/Narrator)

Indices

Inter-Group Competition
(Competitive Round)

Alliteration **
Arms
At The Movies
Body Leads
Boris **
Categories
Counting Words
Dubbing/Double Talk
Emotional Boundaries
Entrances and Exits
Experts
Fortune Cookie
Gibberish
Good Thing/Bad Thing
Half-Life
Hitchhiker
Human Prop
Infomercial **
Last Letter/First Letter
Media Challenges
Modern Fairy Tale **

One Word Scene **
Options
Party Quirks/Endowments
The Purloined Letter
Remote Control
Scene Without "_____"
Should Have Said
Sit, Stand, Lean
Slide Show
Sound Effects
Space Jump
Statues/Moving People
Styles
Superheroes
Superhero Eulogy **
Tag Team
Temperamental Director
Town Meeting **
Two Heads
Typewriter Scene (aka Typist/Narrator)

Inter-Group Competition
(Non-Competitive Cross-Team Round)

185
Actor's Nightmare (aka Playbook)
Alphabet Scene
Arms
At The Movies
Body Leads
Chance of a Lifetime
Conducted Scenes
The Die Game
Dr. Know-It-All
Dubbing/Double Talk
Emotional Boundaries
Entrances and Exits
Experts
Freeze Tag
Freeze Tag (Large Group Version)
Half-Life
Hat Game
Hitchhiker
Human Prop
Last Letter/First Letter

Media Challenges
Modern Fairy Tale **
Options
Party Quirks/Endowments
Props
The Purloined Letter
Remote Control
Scene Without "_____"
Scenes from a Hat
Should Have Said
Sit, Stand, Lean
Slide Show
Sound Effects
Space Jump
Statues/Moving People
Styles
Superheroes
Temperamental Director
Two Heads
Typewriter Scene (aka Typist/Narrator)

Inter-Group Competition
(Tie-Breaker Round)

185
Alliteration
Alphabet Scene
Categories

The Die Game
Hat Game
Props
Scenes from a Hat

** advanced groups only

CPSIA information can be obtained at www.ICGtesting.com
Printed in the USA
LVOW07s2313031215

465283LV00014B/233/P

MAY 1 6 2016

9 780692 518144